PROGRAMMING YOUR APPLE II™ COMPUTER

PROGRAMING YOUR APPLE II™ COMPUTER

BY PAUL BRYAN

TAB BOOKS Inc.
BLUE RIDGE SUMMIT, PA. 17214

FIRST EDITION

FOURTH PRINTING

Printed in the United States of America

Library of Congress Cataloging in Publication Data

Bryan, Paul.
Programming your APPLE II computer.

Includes index.
1. Apple II (Computer)—Programming. I. Title.
QA76.8.A662B78 001.64'2 81-18221
ISBN 0-8306-0081-7 AACR2
ISBN 0-8306-1394-3 (pbk.)

Contents

Introduction

This book is about an incredible success story called the Apple Computer. It is not necessary to own one in order to derive value from this book. In fact, the book may entice you to make the giant move into the marketplace. It will certainly give you enough information about the Apple for you to make an informed decision.

If you do own an Apple, and you were one of the early buyers, it is possible that your system is still running under Integer BASIC. Since Apple spends very little time or money supporting this system anymore, most of the information and software on the market is aimed at the APPLESOFT user. This book is no exception. Though most of the information applies to any Apple computer, there are sections where only the APPLESOFT operations are discussed. The Integer user has three choices.

1. Ignore those parts of the book.
2. Purchase an APPLESOFT Card at $200. (This is the cheapest way if you do not have a disk drive.)
3. If you have a disk and DOS 3.3, you can buy a Language Card and load Applesoft off of the disk, onto the card. (Price $225)

Apple used to sell APPLESOFT on tape or disk. This would load directly into RAM, but the option is no longer available.

If you are one of the 100,000 people to buy an Apple in the last year or so, don't worry. Your machine already has APPLESOFT in ROM.

PROGRAMMING YOUR APPLE II™ COMPUTER

Chapter 1

Getting to Know Your Apple

This book shows you how to set up your APPLE and then tells you how to use it. It is organized with a logical arrangement of topics so that it can be read straight through, if desired. Wherever possible, major topics are self-contained. That is, it's not necessary to read an entire chapter to extract one idea. However, since Chapter 1 discusses the special features of the computer, you should read and understand this material fully before going on to isolated topics.

Whether you are experienced at programming or a beginner, the new features of the APPLE II computer will make programming more fun and convenient. If you are a beginner at programming, keep in mind that the only way to learn is to do. It is a good idea to practice as you read through this book.

If you are using a cassette or diskette, watch for special information that applies to you. You may lose your program if you don't read these sections carefully. Also watch for notes on special features that are unique to APPLESOFT and that may cause problems.

SETTING IT UP

To set up your APPLE II computer, you will need to supply the following:

1. Either a cassette recorder or the APPLE II disk drive with a controller card. (Both would be useful).

2. Either a color TV monitor and a cable with the proper plugs at each end, or an ordinary home color TV and an rf modulator with connecting cable.

NOTE: The computer may only be connected to a standard TV receiver through an rf modulator that has been certified by the FCC.

You will also need the following items, which are supplied with the computer:

1. The cord which plugs into the outlet on the wall.

2. Two black boxes with buttons and knobs, connected with a cord. These are game controllers.

3. A cable to connect the computer to the tape recorder. It has two plugs on each end.

4. Cassette tapes or disks, which contain programs for the computer.

To plug in the game controllers, place the plug into the GAME I/O socket. This socket is found in the right rear corner of the APPLE board. The plug's white dot should be toward the front of the computer and all of the pins must be in the socket.

Complete instructions for installing the disk drive (if you have one) are included in the package. To connect the cassette recorder, see the section in this book on using a tape cassette.

The modulator comes with instructions telling how to hook it up. To hook up the monitor, simply connect the cable from the jack marked VIDEO OUT to the input of the monitor. If you are using an ordinary TV, install an rf modulator. To open the top of the APPLE, pull straight up on the back of the lid. Then you can install the modulator according to the directions included with it.

THE DISPLAY

To set the TV color, use the demo called STANDARD COLOR NAMES. This demo is supplied free of charge on tape to purchasers of the 16 or 32k Apple, and disk when you buy a disk drive. Type the number of the COLOR NAMES DEMO, 1, and press RETURN. A number of bars of light will appear. Under each of these bars you will see a four letter abbreviation of a color name. The full names are:

0 BLACK
1 MAGNETA
2 DARK BLUE
3 PURPLE
4 DARK GREEN
5 GREY
6 MEDIUM BLUE
7 LIGHT BLUE
8 BROWN
9 ORANGE

10 GREY
11 PINK
12 GREEN
13 YELLOW
14 AQUA
15 WHITE

Next, turn off any automatic color switch. Turn the volume control all the way down. Turn the Picture (or Contrast) control to its "fuzziest" position, and then turn the Brightness control down until the background just goes completely dark. Turn the Color control to the middle of its range. Then turn up the Picture control to sharpen things up. Now adjust the Color knob. The colors should be intense but not spilling into one another. Finally, turn the hue knob until all the colors agree with their names. Especially pay attention to the purple, pink, and yellow. The three blues should be distinct. Magenta is a slightly bluish red. The purple should be rather light.

When you have set the colors so that they are appealing to you, press the RETURN key. Now try DEMO 2, and then the other demonstrations.

Notice that up to 960 characters can appear on the display at any one time and the computer's text capacity is 24 lines containing 40 characters each.

While playing around with the keyboard, it is likely that you will generate an ERROR. Notice that after an error occurs, BASIC

Fig. 1-1. The Apple System.

returns to command level as indicated by the] prompt character and a flashing cursor. The program will remain intact, but cannot be continued and all GOSUB and FOR loop counters are set to 0. The ONERR GOTO statement can be used with an error-handling routine to avoid this interruption. For a complete description and listing of the error codes, see Appendix A.

COLD START AND RESET

There are a few things you should check each time you plan to use the computer.

If the computer is turned off:

- Turn on the TV or monitor.
- Turn the computer on by pushing the switch located on the back of the computer into the upward position.
- When the POWER light at the bottom of the keyboard comes on and APPLE II appears on the display, the computer is ready to operate.

If the computer is turned on and the display is blank.

- Press the key marked RESET in the upper right-hand corner of the keyboard.
- If you have the APPLESOFT II Firmware Card, make sure that the switch on the back of the card is in the up position.
- If the display still remains blank, turn the computer off, then a few seconds later, turn it on again.

When the title APPLE II appears at the top of the screen, the prompt symbol (]) should also appear to the far left of the display. These signal that the computer is ready for use.

USING THE APPLE II KEYBOARD

Most keys, when pressed, cause the character or characters represented on the particular keys to be displayed. There are, of course, exceptions. As you learn about the various keys, it will become apparent why a particular key acts as it does.

A Preview of the Keys

There are no lower case letters. You can only get capital letters, since this is all you need for programming your APPLE, however a lower case kit is available for word processing. In addition to the absence of lower case letters, there is another difference between the APPLE keyboard and the keyboard of a standard typewriter. Instead of simply holding down a key so that it will repeat, it is also necessary to hold down the REPT key.

RESET: When this key is pressed, all processing stops. When the key is released, the computer starts a reset cycle. Sometimes you may accidentally press this key instead of the RETURN key; the screen will light up. To recover, simple type CTRL B, or in DOS type 3OOG.

SHIFT: The two shift keys allow for the use of more characters without adding more keys. If you press a key while holding a SHIFT key down also, the upper symbol on the key will appear. If there is only one symbol on a key, using the SHIFT key will have no apparent effect, with one exception. When the M key is shifted, it gives a right hand square bracket (]).

ESC: The escape key is always used with another key. The ESC key is pressed and released, then the other key is pressed. One use of this key is to clear the screen. To do this, press the ESC key and then the at sign @. The at sign is typed by pressing the key marked P while holding down the SHIFT key so you are actually holding down 2 keys and typing a third. For other escape codes, see Appendix B.

CTRL: While the SHIFT key allows some keys to perform a second function, the CTRL (Control) key is used to perform a third function. The key does not cause a new character to appear; rather, it causes the computer to perform certain actions. For example, when the CTRL key is held down and the G key is pressed, the computer beeps.

REPT: Holding down this key while you press any other key makes that key's character appear repeatedly on the screen. First press and hold the key for the character and then hold down the REPT key.

RETURN: This key causes the computer's blinking cursor to go back to the left margin, but there is also a special message to the computer which will be discussed later.

The ← and → Keys: These keys move the cursor to the left and right and will be discussed in more detail later.

NUMBERS

When a number is printed, the following rules are used to determine the exact format:

1. If the number is negative, a minus sign (–) is printed.

2. If the absolute value of the number is an integer in the range 0 to 999999999, it is printed as an integer.

3. If the absolute value of the number is greater than or equal to .01 and less than 999999999. 2, the number is printed in fixed point notation, with no exponent.

4. If the number does not fall under categories 2 or 3, scientific notation is used.

Scientific notation is used to print real precision numbers, and is formatted SX.XXXXXXXXESTT, where each X is an integer 0 to 9. The leading S is the sign of the number, nothing for a positive number and a minus sign for a negative number. One nonzero digit is printed before the decimal point. This is followed by the decimal point and then the other eight digits of the mantissa. An E is then printed (for Exponent), followed by the sign (S) of the exponent; then the two digits (TT) of the exponent itself. Leading zeroes are never printed; i.e., the digit before the decimal is never zero. Also, trailing zeroes are never printed.

If there is only one digit to print after all trailing zeroes are suppressed, no decimal point is printed. The exponent sign will be plus for positive numbers and minus for negative ones. Two digits of the exponent are always printed; that is, zeroes are not suppressed in the exponent field. The value of any number expressed in the form of scientific notation as described above is the number to the left of the E times 10 raised to the power of the number to the right of the E.

The following examples illustrate the various formats used for numbers:

NUMBER	OUTPUT FORMAT
+1	1
−1	−1
6523	6523
−23.460	−23.46
45.72E5	4572000
1*10↑20	1E+20
(−12.34567896*10)↑10	−1.2345679E+12
1000000000	1E+09
999999999	999999999

Significant Digits

A number typed on the keyboard, or a numeric constant used in an APPLESOFT program, may have as many digits as desired, up to the maximum length of 38 digits. However, only the first 10 digits (including the decimal) are usually significant, and the tenth digit is rounded off. For example, if you type PRINT 1.23456787654321 APPLESOFT responds with 1.23456788.

Rounding

Rounding is performed as follows. The first excess digit is checked. If its value is 5 or above, the digit immediately preceding it is incremented (rounded-up) by one. When a number is converted to an integer, it is rounded down. For example:

```
A%=–.01
PRINT A%
–1
```

The graphics mode automatically rounds coordinate values down to the nearest integer whose value is less than or equal to the given value.

Calculating

The Apple can be used as a simple-minded desk calculator. The Apple can do five different elementary arithmetic operations:

1. Addition. Indicated by the usual plus sign.
2. Subtraction. Uses the conventional minus sign.
3. Multiplication. Since the X or . can be confused with other things, the Apple uses * for multiplication.
4. Division. Indicated by the usual slash.
5. Exponentation. The upward pointing arrow, typed by shifting the N key, is used. For example, 4^5 would be 4↑5.

Arithmetic Hierarchy

In a mathematical expression (which is a sequence of numbers separated by numeric symbols), there is a prescribed order of execution. The order of execution, called the hierarchy, is the same as the order commonly used in standard arithmetic. It is:

1. ( )
2. NOT – (for inverted values)
3. ∧
4. * /
5. + –
6. > < = > = < = < >
7. AND
8. OR

The order of execution is from 1 to 8. When an expression contains two or more symbols at the same level in the hierarchy, the order or execution is from left to right. For example, here is the step-by-step evaluation of the following expression: 2*3 ∧ 3+4* ((5– 3)/2+1)

1. The expression in the most deeply nested parentheses, (5–3), is evaluated. 2*3 3+4*(2/2+1)

2. The expression in the remaining parentheses is simplified, and since division is above addition in the hierarchy, it is performed first. 2*3 3+4*(1+1)

3. These parentheses are then totally eliminated. 2*3 3+4*2

4. Now exponentation is performed 2*27+4*2

5. The two multiplication operations can then be evaluated. 54+8

6. So if the original expression is keyed in, the result will appear as: 62.

Variables

Often it is convenient to assign values to letters and then use these letters in expressions. In programs a letter can have its value constantly updated—hence, the term variable. In some cases a letter (variable) is used as an intermediate storage device. For instance, to keep the running total of a group of numbers being added together. Other times, a variable in a particular formula may have several different values inserted into the formula to determine what effect these values have on the result. A letter can also be used for convenience; just as π is used to designate the value 3.14159265 . . ., an equally cumbersome number that you are using over and over can be designated by a letter.

A variable name must begin with an alphabetic character and may be followed by an alphanumeric character. An alphanumeric character is any letter from A through Z, or any digit from 0 through 9. A variable name can be up to 238 characters long, but APPLESOFT uses only the first two characters to distinguish one name from another. In a variable name, any alphanumeric characters after the first two are ignored unless they contain a reserved word. (For a list of these reserved words, see Appendix C.)

Another type of variable is the array variable. Arrays enable you to select any element in a table of numbers, and the programming power they give you more than compensates for the bit of thinking and experimenting you must do to become familiar with them.

Any array is a table of numbers. The name of this table, called the array name, is any legal variable name: A, for example. The array name A is distinct and separate from the simple variable A. To create an array, you must first tell the computer the maximum number of elements you want the array to accommodate. To do this you use a DIM statement. The elements in an array are numbered from 0 so to DIMension an array called A that will have a maximum of 16 elements, type DIM A(15). More information on arrays and the DIM statements will be given in Chapter 3.

Arrow Keys

The left arrow key is rather like the backspace key on a typewriter so we will call it the backspace key. A few experiments will make this clear. Type PRINT "COMPUTER" and press the RETURN key. The computer will reply 0 because of the missing quote. Now, without pressing RETURN, type PRINT "COM-FUTER". To change COMPUTER to COMPUTER, we can use the left arrow key. Each time you press the key, the cursor moves back one space to the left. Backspace the cursor to the F. Type a P. If you type RETURN now, COMP would appear. To correct this, either type the remaining letters, or use the right arrow key. Pressing this key has the same effect as is the characters had been retyped, so this is called the retype key. For more information on the use of these keys, see Appendix B.

FUNCTIONS

A function is something that takes one or more numbers and then performs some operation on them to yield a single value. The following mathematical functions can be executed:

ABS (aexpr)—determines the absolute value of the expression

EXP (aexpr)—raises the constant e (the natural log), to the power of the computed expression

INT (aexpr)—gives the expression an integer value less than or equal to the value of the expression

LOG (aexpr)—determines the logarithm of a positively valued expression to the base e.

RND (aexpr)—gives a random number between 0 and 1; the expression is a dummy argument

SGN (aexpr—returns a 1 if the expression is greater than zero; returns a 0 if the expression equals 0; or returns a −1 if the expression is less than 0.

SQR (aexpr)—computes the positive square root

The following trigonometric functions can be executed:

SIN (aexpr)—determines the sine of an expression

COS (aexpr)—determines the cosine of an expression

TAN (aexpr)—determines the tangent of an expression

ATN (aexpr)—determines the arctangent of an expression

The angle is assumed to always be in radians.

LOGICAL EVALUATIONS

In logical evaluation, expressions can be compared by using relational operators and/or logical operators. For a list of the relational operators and their in use in IF . . . THEN statements, see Chapter 3. The logical operators are as follows; AND, OR, and NOT.

AND compares two expressions. If both expressions are true, the result is true. If one or both of the expressions are false, the result is false.

OR compares two expressions. If one or both of the expressions is true, the result is true. If neither expression is true, the result is false.

NOT changes the logical value of an expression. If the expression if true, NOT changes it to false, and vice versa.

Here is an example of the AND operator. First, let's assign values to the variables A, B, C, and D. Let A=0, B=2, C=4, and D=4. Consider the following expression:

A<B AND C=D

Since both relational expressions, A<B and C=D, are true, the result is true.

Chapter 2
The System

MEMORY

Before reading any further, it may be useful to include some information about Apple's memory. The memory is used in many different ways;

1. To store the diskette version of the Applesoft programming language. Applesoft BASIC is available in two versions; firmware Applesoft and diskette Applesoft. Firmware Applesoft comes with Applesoft in ROM (permanent, Read-Only Memory). The Applesoft ROM chips may be installed in sockets D0 through F0 on the Apple's main printed circuit board, or they may be on a plug-in Applesoft II Firmware Card. Firmware Applesoft is instantly available when you turn your Apple on when you type the disk command FP. This saves some time over loading the language from diskette every time. Aside from this convenience, having Applesoft in ROM frees about 10K of Apple's memory for the use of programs.

2. To store the instructions that make up your program. This is the text you see when you type LIST.

3. To store your program's variables, strings, and intermediate and final results. You assign these in your program.

4. To store various information which the Apple itself needs, about the system, your program, and where different things are stored in memory. This includes the stack and pointers the interpreter uses.

5. To create the text and low-resolution graphics which normally show on your TV screen. This is the video memory-mapped area.

6. To create the high-resolution graphics that can be shown on your TV screen. The high-res pages which are interpreted as user defined graphics.

Each of these activities, in general, occupies a different portion of the Apple's memory. Information is placed in various memory "pigeonholes", called memory addresses. These addresses let the Apple find that location, and the item of information stored there, again. These items of information, which you rarely see in their raw, machine-language form, are called bytes of information. Each byte of information occupies one memory location. A block of 1024 memory locations is called 1K of memory.

The portion of Apple's memory that is used by a particular activity can be described in terms of the memory locations used, usually specified as a range of memory addresses. If a certain range of memory locations is being used to store your program, for instance, those same memory locations must not be used to create a high-resolution graphics display, or your program will be lost.

In Applesoft BASIC, memory addresses and other numbers are expressed in the usual decimal form. The computer itself uses numbers in a different form called binary. To aid advanced programmers, memory addresses are sometimes given both in the normal decimal and in special binary groupings called hexadecimal form. Hexadecimal numbers are usually preceded by a dollar sign ($) and may be safely ignored by the BASIC programmer.

FIRMWARE

The firmware APPLESOFT card simply plugs into a socket inside the APPLE II. Care must be exercised, however, so follow these instructions exactly:

1. Turn the APPLE off. This is very important to prevent damage to the computer.

2. Remove the cover from the APPLE II. This is done by pulling up on the cover at the rear edge (the edge farthest from the keyboard) until the two corner fasteners pop apart. Do not continue to lift the rear edge, but slide the cover backward until it comes free.

3. Inside the APPLE II, across the rear of the circuit board, there is a row of eight long, narrow sockets called slots. The leftmost one (looking at the computer from the keyboard end) is slot #0; the rightmost one is slot #7. Hold the APPLESOFT card so that its switch is toward the back of the computer. Insert the connector portion of the card into the leftmost slot, slot #0. The fingers will enter the slot with some friction, and will then seat firmly. The

APPLESOFT card must be placed in slot #0.

4. The switch on the back of the APPLESOFT card should protrude part way through the slot on the back of the APPLE II.

5. Replace the APPLE's cover. First slide the front edge into place, then press down on the two rear corners until they pop into place.

6. Now turn on the APPLE II.

When the APPLESOFT card's switch is in the downward position, the APPLE II will begin operating in Integer BASIC when you use RESET CTRL B (this book's way of saying: press the key marked RESET, then hold down the key marked CTRL while typing B). You will see the prompt character>, which indicates Integer BASIC.

With the switch in the upward position, reset ctrl B will bring up APPLESOFT BASIC, instead of Integer BASIC. The prompt character] tells you you're in APPLESOFT. When using the Disk Operating System, the computer will automatically choose Integer BASIC or APPLESOFT, as required. It does not matter in which position the switch is set.

You can also change from Integer BASIC to APPLESOFT, or vice versa, without operating the switch on the firmware card. To put the computer into APPLESOFT, use this sequence:

RESET, C080 RETURN, CTRL B, RETURN

and to put the computer into Integer BASIC, use this sequence;

RESET, C081, RETURN, CTRL B, RETURN

Note: Sometime you may accidentally hit RESET and find yourself in the Monitor, as shown by the prompt character, *. You may be able to return to APPLESOFT BASIC, with APPLESOFT and your program intact, by typing CTRL C, RETURN, or 3DOG, RETURN, if you are in DOS. Applesoft is also on a file in DOS 3.3, but does not work exactly the same as does the firmware version of Applesoft that resides in ROM either on the Apple's main printed circuit board or on a plug-in Applesoft II Firmware Card. Most of this book describes the firmware version of Applesoft. The following comments point out how diskette Applesoft differs from firmware Applesoft.

Firmware Applesoft does not occupy any space in the user memory, and therefore may be used with Apples of almost any size memory. Diskette Applesoft occupies approximately 10K bytes of memory, the Apple uses another 2K bytes for text screens and other system needs, and the Disk Operating System (DOS) occupies another 10. 5K bytes. Thus, diskette Applesoft cannot be used in Apples with less than 24K bytes of memory. With diskette Applesoft loaded into the Apple, the lowest memory location available to the user is 12291.

DISKETTE

The Apple Disk II Floppy Disk Subsystem increases the capability of your Apple Computer System through the use of 5¼″ floppy disks for data storage. Expanded memory capacity, greater data retrieval speed, and random access to your stored data are made available through the Disk II Subsystem.

The Hardware

The Apple Disk II Floppy Disk Subsystem optimizes efficiency by offering one of the highest storage capacities available with any personal computer on today's market. Other benefits include:

1. Offers an economical advantage over other disk drives, by providing one of the lowest storage costs per character of any personal computer disk drive.
2. Increases productivity by allowing you to access data much more quickly than is possible with cassette tape.
3. Makes possible a wide range of computer applications by allowing software to access data.
4. Provides for greater system expansion than is possible with any other personal computer system, because it supports up to three interface cards and six disk drives.

The Disk II drive, unlike the Apple II, is a mechanical device with motors and moving parts. Understanding the principle behind the Apple Disk II drive is as simple as understanding the way a phonograph turntable works. Disk II has been designed in the same manner, although it is enclosed in a special cabinet. The record, or diskette, is flexible and fits on a spindle inside the drive. The drive turns the diskette at 300 revolutions per minute.

Within the drive, a special record/playback head replaces the phonograph needle, and it reads the diskette the way a tape head reads an audio cassette. The head is mounted on a positioner, the counterpart of the phonograph arm, and it moves the head laterally across the floppy diskette to any area requested by the computer program. This capability is called random access. It allows you to retrieve information from the diskette much more quickly than is possible with cassette tape.

Apple's Disk II may be purchased with or without a controller; however, the first one you buy must have the controller in order to interface the Disk II system to your Apple. Because each controller supports two disk drives, you'll be able to attach a second drive to it when you wish to expand your system. The Apple will support a recommended maximum of three interface cards and six disk drives.

In addition to the advantages offered by a disk storage system, you'll also receive a special disk operating system program (DOS) when you purchase a Disk II with controller. It automatically keeps track of your files, saves and retrieves information on a diskette, and performs a variety of other functions.

To use the Apple Disk II Floppy Disk Subsystem, you will need the Apple II or Apple II Plus, with a minimum of 16K, but 32K is recommended.

The disks are softsectored, which means that the disk only has one hole in it for reference, but the timing is good enough that hard sectored disks may be use. Data is only recorded on one side of the disk (single sided) and there are 35 concentric circle tracks on each disk.

The disk must be formatted with the address marks the computer will look for, and a minimum disk I/O system. DOS contains a routine to do this. Once formatted the disk still has room for 137 K of memory if you are using Pascal, and 124K if you are using DOS. If you control the I/O with software from memory, it is possible to obtain 140K bytes of storage from a single disk.

The data is arranged in sectors, each one being 1/16th of a track for Pascal and DOS 3.3. Earlier DOSes had 13 sectors, but DOS 3.3 includes a utility for converting those disks to 16 sector.

Three factors are involved in determining how fast a sector can be accessed.

1. The time it takes to move the head from one track to another.

2. The time it takes for disk rotation to bring the sector under the head.

3. The time it takes for the head to read the information.

A stepper motor moves the head from track to track and in the Apple takes about 25 milliseconds. If you want to move across several tracks, the computer can feed impulses to the stepper fast enough that it doesn't slow down, thus decreasing the total time. Maximum time to move from track 1 to track 35 is 600 milliseconds instead of the 850 you would expect.

When the head arrives at the proper sector if, by chance, the very next sector it encounters is the one you want, the time delay is zero for rotation delay. If it just went by, the maximum is just under

200 milliseconds. Neither case is very likely, so the average rotational delay is about 100 milliseconds.

Finally, a complete sector is read into a memory buffer, one bit at a time, as the sector passes under the head. This buffer must then be passed to main memory in time to read the next sector. If the next sector doesn't need to be read the operation is done. This head load time takes about 50 milliseconds. This means the maximum delay to read all the track 35 when the head is at track 1 is 1.6 seconds.

The controller card can fit into any of the eight expansion slots, and each controller can handle two disk drives. The power is supplied by the Apple main board, so no external power connections are needed; a very nice feature if there are a limited number of outlets near your desk. The drawback is that this lowers the recommended number of drives to 6, but that is still two more than most microcomputers allow.

The disk fits horizontally into the 3.25 by 5.75 by 8.0 inch drive, and each unit weighs 3 pounds.

The Software

With each Disk II, Applesoft II BASIC is provided on the Integer BASIC System Master Diskette, in a file called APPLESOFT.

To use diskette Applesoft, the disk must be booted and at least one disk drive must contain a diskette which has the file APPLESOFT on it (such as the System Master Diskette). Do not use the command RUN APPLESOFT. This command does not properly initialize the language. Applesoft will look as though it is running correctly, but you will be in trouble as soon as you press the RESET key or type a DOS command. Instead, use the DOS command FP (for Floating Point BASIC). When you issue the DOS command FP your computer will attempt to load the APPLESOFT language program from the diskette in the default (last used) disk drive. If the program APPLESOFT is not on that diskette, the message LANGUAGE NOT AVAILABLE is given. In that case, you have two choices. You may place in that drive a diskette with the APPLESOFT program on it, and type FP again, or, if you know that a different drive contains a diskette with APPLESOFT on it, you may issue the FP command with slot and drive parameters. For example, to load Applesoft from the diskette in drive 2 connected to a disk controller card in slot 6, you would type FP, S6, D2.

When you LOAD or RUN a diskette program written in

Applesoft, DOS automatically switches to the correct language. If this necessitates a change to Applesoft, DOS will attempt to find the APPLESOFT program on the diskette in the disk drive specified by the LOAD or RUN command, or on the diskette in the default disk drive if none is specified. You may, of course, use the FP command to change languages yourself, as described above.

A disk drive is much quicker and easier to use than a cassette recorder. However, diskettes and disk drives are delicate creatures, and some care must be taken to protect them. Make sure to read your DOS manual carefully.

CASSETTE

Use the following procedure to load a program from your cassette unit:

1. Start up BASIC by typing; RESET, ctrl B. You will know when you are in BASIC when you see the prompt character displayed on the TV screen, followed by the blinking, square cursor.

2. Place the tape in your cassette recorder and rewind the tape to the beginning.

3. Type LOAD.

4. Press the recorder's play lever to start the tape playing.

5. Press the key marked RETURN on the APPLE II keyboard. When you do this the blinking cursor will disappear. After 5 to 20 seconds the APPLE II will beep, to signal that the tape's information has started to go into the computer. After about 1-½ minutes (time varies with the length of the program), there will be another beep and the prompt character followed by a cursor will reappear.

6. Stop the tape recorder and rewind the tape. The program is now in the computer.

7. Type RUN and press the key marked RETURN.

Sometimes you may accidentally hit the RESET key and find yourself in the Monitor program, as shown by the prompt character;*. You may be able to return to Applesoft, with your program and Applesoft itself intact, by typing ctrl C, or in DOS type 3D0G, RETURN. If this does not work, you will have to reload. Typing ctrl B from the Monitor program will transfer you to BASIC. This will erase the program.

Use the supplied cable to connect the Apple to your cassette recorder. Connect one black plug to the MIC or MICROPHONE jack on the recorder, and the other black plug to the jack on the back of the computer marked CASSETTE OUT. Connect the grey plug on the recorder end of the cable to the recorder's EAR or EAR-

PHONE or MON or MONITOR jack on the recorder. Connect the grey plug on the computer end of the cable to the jack marked CASSETTE IN. OUT means "out of the computer" and IN means "into the computer." All that remains is to plug the cassette recorder's power cord into a wall outlet, and it will be ready for use.

Now you are ready to set the volume control on the tape recorder. When you play a tape recorder, it is usually with the intent of making sounds that you can hear. If it is too soft, you miss some of the words or music. If it is too loud, it is annoying. When you play the tape recorder into the Apple, it is with the intent of putting the tape's information into the computer. If the volume setting is too soft, the Apple will miss some of the information, and it will complain by giving an error message. If the volume setting is too loud, the Apple will also complain.

To find the right volume setting, you will use a trial-and-error method. You will play tape softly to the computer and see if the information got in OK. If it doesn't work, you will try the tape again, a little louder this time. Eventually the volume will be just right for the Apple, and it will say so with a beep. To clear the screen for action, type ESC@.

Experiment with the tape marked COLOR DEMOSOFT. For each position of the volume control you are going to do the following:

1. Rewind the tape to the beginning.
2. Start the tape playing.
3. Type LOAD and press RETURN.

When you do this, the cursor will disappear. It may take up to 15 seconds before something happens. There are these possibilities:

1. The message ?SYNTAX ERROR appears.
2. Nothing at all happens.
3. The message ERR or ERRERR appears (with or without a beep).
4. The computer goes beep and nothing appears.

In case 1, do not reset the volume control, but go back to step 1 where you rewind the tape. In cases 2 and 3, make sure you waited for 15 seconds before giving up. If there is no prompt character or cursor, and the Apple does not respond to its keyboard, press RESET, set the volume control a bit higher and go back to step 1. Once in a while the LOAD command may not work properly, and the cursor will appear on the screen immediately without waiting for the tape to LOAD. If this happens just turn your Apple off and then on again with the power switch on the rear of the computer, and then try LOADing the tape again.

In case 4, you are on the right track. When you hear the beep, wait another fifteen seconds. Either you will get an error message (case 3), or the prompt character and the blinking cursor will reappear. If they do reappear, stop and rewind the tape. Mark the position of the recorder's volume control, so that you can use this setting each time you LOAD a tape in the future. Then type RUN and press RETURN.

THE APPLE GRAPHICS TABLET

The Apple Graphics Tablet turns your Apple II Personal Computer System into an artist's canvas or illustrator's drawing board by offering a medium for creating and displaying pictorial information electronically. Block diagrams, architectural renderings, logic diagrams, schematics, mechanical shapes and fine art are just a few of the applications of the Graphics Tablet. Its advanced features, combined with surprising simplicity of operation, make it an ideal tool for transforming the creative idea into visual reality.

Benefits from the Apple Graphics Tablet are many but a few are listed below:

1. Lets you free your imagination to create detailed illustrations and other artwork, because results are displayed in Apple's high resolution graphics mode.

2. Can be quickly understood and operated by anyone, from a small child to a professional artist, because the easy-to-use command menu eliminates the need for any prior knowledge of computer operations.

3. Allows you to modify the system to fit your particular graphics needs, because you can change, delete, or add to existing software.

4. Permits you to save your creations on a diskette and later recall them for review or change, through its convenient image storage and editing features.

5. Protects your initial investment by providing for the expansion and future growth of your present software.

6. Offers a low-profile desktop package that fits easily into even the smallest workspace, because the power supply and control electronics reside within your Apple.

The Graphics Tablet and its pen connect to the Tablet Interface Card, which plugs into one of the peripheral connector slots in the Apple computer. After installation, insert the Apple Graphics Tablet Software diskette into your Apple disk drive, turn on the power and, within seconds, you're ready to start creating.

The command boxes across the top front of the Tablet offer the 22 separate functions available, and make it possible for you to switch modes simply by pressing the Tablet's pen to the desired command box.

Suppose you want to attempt a landscape layout. Begin by pressing the DRAW command box and then the PEN COLOR command box. The color options menu will appear on your screen.

Move the pen lightly across the Tablet. An indicator will drift across your screen, signaling that the pen is in contact with the Tablet. Move the pen until the indicator rests on the color block you want, then pressdown on the Tablet's surface. The color menu will disappear. The blank screen is ready for your first stroke in the chosen color. Changing colors simply requires pressing the PEN COLOR command box and repeating the selection process.

As you progress with the landscape layout, you might make an error here and there. No problem. To erase, simply select the background color and draw over the mistake; then choose the appropriate color and redraw.

Maximum drawing space on the Tablet is 11 by 10 inches. If you wish to draw in a smaller area, press the VIEWPORT command box with the pen. Place dots in the diagonal corners of the desired drawing area; the Tablet will automatically draw the borders. You will then be able to draw only in the specified area.

Suppose you want to include an intricate flower in the landscape layout, but feel uncertain about using the tiny drawing strokes it will require. The Tablet software was designed with that problem in mind. Set a VIEWPORT surrounding the area in which the flower will be drawn; then simply press the REDUCER command to shrink the entire Tablet working area into the VIEWPORT on the screen. This converts large pen motions on the Tablet into small motions on the screen, thus allowing you to draw intricate, detailed designs.

To achieve the opposite result—a large pen motion on the screen from a small motion on the Tablet—press the WINDOW command box. Select the portion of the Tablet to be enlarged, and that surface will be expanded to fill the screen.

When you have completed the landscape layout, or if you want to stop drawing for awhile, save the creation for future review or revision by pressing the SAVE command box. The picture will disappear from the screen and your Apple will ask you for the name of the drawing. Type in the name you choose, press the RETURN key, and the drawing will be safely stored on a diskette.

Because the Graphics Tablet employs your Apple's problem solving capability, it does more than allow you to create drawings. Suppose you want to include a swimming pool in the landscape layout, First, draw the pool into the landscape. Then, to determine how many square feet of land you've used, convert the screen units into feet. To do this, simply press the CALIBRATE command box and wait for BEGINNING POINT? to appear. Select any point on the screen and press down on the Tablet with your pen. ENDING POINT? will then be displayed. Choose a destination point and again press down with the pen. Your Apple will automatically convert the distance between those two points into screen units and ask you to assign your value—for example, 10 screen units equals two feet. Then, using the AREA command, move the pen over the perimeter of the pool. Your Apple will convert the units into square feet automatically.

The Graphics Tablet can also be programmed to be a powerful tool for special applications. Suppose, for example, that you're conducting a telephone survey on laundry detergent. Instead of marking the responses on separate sheets and totaling them when the survey is complete, you can draw the form on your Tablet and write a program which will total the responses as you enter them with the pen. Your program could even request that the Apple break down the responses into different categories.

To use the Apple Graphics Tablet, you will need the following system:

1. Apple II with Applesoft Firmware Card, or Apple II Plus, with 48K of memory; or

2. Apple II or Apple II Plus, with the Apple Language System.

3. A composite video color monitor or television (black and white if color is not required).

4. An Apple Disk II disk drive with controller.

Technical specifications include:
Power Requirements (supplied from Apple power supply):

230mA + 5VDC
40mA + 12VDC
20mA – 5VDC
40mA – 12VDC

Software/Firmware:

Control program in Applesoft BASIC.

Quick-draw routine in Assembly Language.
Interface Firmware in ROM.

Digitizing Area:
28cm × 38cm (11 in × 11 in).

Overall Size:
39.5 cm × 39.5 cm × 2.5 cm (15.5 in × 15.5 in × 1 in).

Controller Card Size:
17.8 cm × 7.0 cm × 1.3 cm (7 in × 2.75 in × .5 in).

Pen Size:
15.2 cm (6 in) with 1.8 m (6 ft) cable.

Data Rate:
Up to 120 coordinate pairs per second.

Coordinate System:
Absolute cartesian with selectable origin and scale.

Output Forms:
Eight-bit binary coordinate pairs.

Interface Levels:
TTL—provided by Apple interface.

Operating Modes (Selectable from Tablet Menu):

RESET
Sets Tablet to default modes.

CLEAR
Clears Apple screen or VIEWPORT, whichever is smaller.

WINDOW
Selects active portion of Tablet surface.

BKGND COLOR
Sets entire screen to chosen color.

DELTA
Sets the number of dots to move before drawing a line.
Also turns audio feedback ON/OFF.

SOFT RESET
Clears the viewport.

VIEWPORT
Sets a sub-area of the screen as the active area.

CALIBRATE
Sets screen scale.

REDUCER
Maps the entire tablet surface into the current viewport.

PEN COLOR
Sets drawing color to one of the six Hi-Res colors.

DRAW
Draws lines.

LINES
Draws a line between two specified points.
DOTS
Draws a single dot each time the pen is placed on the active tablet area.
FRAME
Draws an open rectangle given diagonal corners.
BOX
Draws a solid rectangle using the current pencolor, given diagonal corners.
CATALOG
Displays names of files currently stored on a diskette.
SAVE
Saves the current picture to diskette.
LOAD
Loads a previously generated picture file.
SEPARATE
Removes all colors from the screen except the selected color.
SLIDE
Repositions the image on the screen using both horizontal and vertical wraparound.
DISTANCE
Calculates the scale value of the length of a drawn line.
AREA
Calculates the scaled area of a drawn enclosed figure.

THE SILENTYPE™ THERMAL PRINTER

The Apple Silentype is a quiet, versatile, and compact thermal graphics printer. It offers increased flexibility over other printers, at a fraction of the cost, because the Silentype receives both its power and intelligence from the Apple computer. To the extent you can program the Apple, you can program the Silentype whether machine language, BASIC, or Apple Pascal is being used. The Silentype can be used effectively without doing any programming at all. With a few simple keystrokes, you can change margins and line spacing, specify printing intensity, and print finely detailed charts and graphs.

Listed below are some of the benefits from The Apple Silentype:

1. Offers you higher reliability than other microprocessor-based printers, since it contains fewer components.

2. Offers you more printing flexibility, because it has the capability of printing high resolution graphics.

3. May be used in any office or home environment without a muffler, because it's quiet.

4. Can be transported easily along with the Apple, because it takes up little space and weighs just six pounds.

5. Saves you time and money, because it requires no preventive maintenance, adjustments, or lubrication.

Connecting the Apple Silentype to the Apple Computer System takes just minutes. Begin by making sure your system is off. Plug the printer cable into the Silentype interface card (supplied with the Silentype package) and remove the Apple's cover. Then plug the interface card into one of its expansion slots (usually slot #1), and replace the cover.

The Silentype prints upper and lower case text at up to 40 characters per second, 80 characters per line; high resolution graphics are printed at 60 dots per inch. The Silentype prints clear, readable copy on white paper. There's no hard-to-read, scratch-susceptible, aluminized paper required.

The Silentype paper path is short and straight, so you don't need to worry about paper jams. Paper is available in 80 ft. rolls and, because the Silentype has no tractors loading it into the printer takes just a minute. To alert you that reloading is necessary, a colored stripe along one edge signals the last few feet of the roll. While the printer cannot be damaged by running without paper, changing the roll when the stripe appears will ensure that you don't run out of paper in the middle of printing a file. Because the Silentype is a thermal printer, there are no ribbons or messy ribbon changes.

Technical specifications for the Apple Silentype Thermal Printer are:

Text Mode:
Print Rate—Up to 40 characters/second, bidirectional
Line Length—80 characters
Horizontal Spacing—10 characters/inch, nominal
Vertical Spacing—6 lines/inch, nominal
Line Feed Time—65 milliseconds, nominal
Character Format—upper and lower case, 5×7

Graphics Mode:
Print Rate—240 columns of 7 dots each per second
Line Length—480 dots
Horizontal Resolution—60 dots/inch, nominal
Vertical Resolution—60 dots/inch, nominal
Line Feed Time—55 milliseconds, nominal

Interface:
Power Supply—From Apple computer via 9-conductor data/power interface cable (supplied)
Interface—Custom synchronous serial
Interface Cable—9-conductor, 1.2 meters (3½ feet) nominal length

Paper:
Width—21.6 cm (8½ in) nominal
Length—24.4 m (80 ft) nominal
Technology—Thermal, low temperature; black image

THE DAISY WHEEL PRINTER

The Qume Sprint 5™ is a popular, fully-formed character, impact printer that produces documents of better than typewriter quality, at an average speed of 45 characters per second. Field-proven and highly reliable, it works with the Apple II, Apple II Plus computer system, in applications ranging from word processing to business forecasting.

The printer plugs into a connector on the High-Speed Serial Interface Card (A2B0005), which is then installed in any unused expansion slot in the Apple. It handles all kinds of documents, from form letters printed on letterhead, to financial statements up to 198 characters per line in length. A daisy wheel printer is the professional printer for professional-looking documents. Some of the benefits are listed below:

1. Improves the quality and impact of your letters and documents, because its fully-formed, highly readable characters give all your printed communications a thoroughly professional look.

2. Increases office productivity, through letter-perfect, 45 character per second printing.

3. Allows you to match type styles with your needs, because it connector on the High-Speed Serial Interface Card for the Apple II or Apple II Plus.

4. Increases printing reliability, thanks to its field-proven, highly dependable design and components.

5. Interfaces quickly with your system by plugging into a provides a variety of available type fonts on easily interchanged printwheels.

The Technical Specifications for the Qume Sprint 5™ include:

Parameter Description

Print Speed: 45 characters/second (average)

Interface: Asynchronous Serial (RS-232C or 20 milliamp dc current loop)

Forms: 15″ max. width, single sheet or continuous forms

Fonts: 96-character daisy printwheels in various styles/alphabets

Character Spacing: 10, 12, and 15 characters/inch or proportional spacing

Horizontal Format:

10 pitch	132 columns
12 pitch	158 columns
15 pitch	198 columns

Vertical Format: 6 lines/inch (normal)

Vertical Slew Rate: 5 inches/second

Plotting Resolution: Two modes—5760 or 2880 points/inch^2

Paper Feed: Pressure platen (standard); forms tractor (optional)

Ribbon: Cartridge type; carbon or fabric ribbon

Printwheel: Easily changeable; large variety of typestyles

Operator Controls: Horizontal/Vertical Forms Positioning
Forms Thickness
Manual Ribbon Advance
Communications
Form Feed
Printer Control Functions

Temperature:
Operating 10 to 40 degrees C. (50-105°F.)
Storage −40 to +76 degrees C (−40 to +170° F.)

Relative Humidity:
Operating 10% to 90% (no condensation)
Storage 2% to 98% (no condensation)

Size:
Width 59.7 cm (23.5 in)
Height 19.4 cm (7.6 in)
Depth 47.8 cm (18.8 in)

Weight:

Power Requirements: 115 volts @ 3.0 amps (A2M0045)
230 volts @ 1.5 amps (A2M0046)

Chapter 3

Applesoft BASIC

The programming language APPLESOFT II BASIC is an extension of BASIC that allows full use of APPLE's unique features. These features include direct analog inputs and color graphics. In this chapter, the APPLESOFT statements are individually discussed. Before discussing each statement, a quick introduction to writing and running a program will be presented.

PROGRAM WRITING

A program is a set of instructions organized to accomplish certain tasks. It is organized by lines (statements) with each statement preceded by a unique line number. The computer stores and executes statements in order of increasing line number. However, you can type program lines in any order because lines are automatically sorted as they are entered. Line numbers 0 through 63999 are allowed.

Program lines can be a maximum of 239 characters in length. In general, any spacing between characters that you use is totally arbitrary. The computer inserts appropriate spacing into each line that is entered into memory to make the line easily readable upon review.

PROGRAM EXECUTION

A PRINT statement typed without a line number will be executed as soon as the RETURN key is pressed. However, line numbers are used in a program and RUN must be typed in order for it to be executed. The first kind of command explained is called an immediate-execution command. The second command, used to build programs, is called a deferred-execution command.

If the program is working properly, it will perform the required tasks and then halt. You can tell it where to halt a program with a STOP or END command. If you use the STOP command, the program is stopped, control of the computer is returned to the user, and a message is displayed which tells the line number of the statement that contained the STOP. The END command does not cause the line number message to be printed.

APPLESOFT STATEMENTS

The rest of this chapter is devoted to discussing each Applesoft statement. For this purpose, "aexpr" means arithmetic expression.

The LET statement assigns values to variables. These values can be other variables, constants, or expressions. An equals sign separates the variable (on the left) from its assigned value (on the right). The LET is optional.

Example:LET T=2
and
T=2
are equivalent statements.

The PRINT statement can cause various outputs on the video:

- Text can be displayed in any form you want.
- The values of variables, expressions, and constants can be printed.
- Print lines can be sent to separate outputs.

Any text that is to be printed must be enclosed by quotation marks; e.g., "ABCDE". The information within the quotation marks is often referred to as a quote field. Several variables, expressions, and constants can be included in the same PRINT statement as long as they are separated by commas or semicolons. If a comma is used, the computer will space over to the next tab field before printing the value after the comma. Including a semicolon in a PRINT statement will cause the next value to be printed immediately following the previous value.

Examples:
```
PRINT 1,2,3
1  2  3
PRINT 1;2;3
123
```

Text can also appear in a PRINT statement with variables, expressions, and constants. Aside from the quotation marks, no additional punctuation is necessary when separating text from other information. If neither the comma nor the semicolon is used, the semicolon is assumed. The following information about PRINT statements is important to know. The examples given first show what is typed into the computer and then what would be printed.

Variables must have assigned values before being used in a PRINT statement. Example: 10 X=3.

Quote fields are printed exactly as seen. Spaces are not ignored in quote fields as they are in other places. The semicolon between the quote field and the variable, X, in the example below is not needed since a semicolon would have been assumed anyway. The variable, X must have an assigned value or an error causes when the program is run.

Example: 20 PRINT "X IS EQUAL TO";X
X IS EQUAL TO 3

Simply typing PRINT after the line number causes the printer to skip a line before doing any more printouts. Additional printouts can then begin on the following line. Example: 30 PRINT.

A variable, a quote field, and an expression are all designated in each of the PRINT statements in the following examples. Ending the first of two PRINT statements with a semicolon causes both printouts to appear on the same line.

Example: 40 PRINT X" SQUARED ="X∧2;
50 PRINT Y "SQUARED = "Y∧2

3 SQUARED = 9 4 SQUARED = 16

Without any punctuation at the end of the first line, the printout would be:

3 SQUARED = 9
4 SQUARED = 16

The maximum printout per line using the PRINT statement is 240 characters. After this point, the computer will start to beep and gives a backward slash which lets you start over again.

The INPUT statement allows variables to be assigned values from the keyboard during program execution. When the INPUT statement is executed, a '?' appears on the display. A value can then be input for each of the variables designated in the INPUT statement. Example: 10 INPUT A.

Another INPUT statement takes the form of INPUT [string;] var [, var]. The string is then printed exactly as specified. The computer waits for the user to type a number which is assigned to the variable. Multiple entries to INPUT may be separated by commas or RETURNs. Example: 20 INPUT "TYPE AGE.";B

The IF statement is a conditional operation based on the "truth" of an expression. First, the expression is logically evaluated. If it is evaluated as "true", the program then performs the specified task. But if the expression is evaluated as "false", the program continues execution in its normal sequence with the statement following IF. The expression can take the form of an assertion and the word THEN. An assertion consists of two expressions separated by one of the following symbols:

SYMBOL	MEANING
=	Equal to
>	Greater than
<	Less than
< > or > <	Not equal to
< =	Less than or equal to
> =	Greater than or equal to

Example: 22 IF Y < X ∧2 THEN GOTO 333

Avoid unnecessary punctuation. For example, a comma inserted before the THEN would cause an error to occur.

The GOTO statement is used to alter the normal sequence of program execution. The program continues execution at the line number specified in the GOTO statement. Line numbers in GOTO statements must be constants. Furthermore, the line number specified must be in memory when the program is run or else an error will occur.

The REM (Remark) statement is merely a note to the programmer and is not executed by the program. However, the statement does appear on a program listing. Any series of characters can follow REM, the only restriction being the maximum line length. Example: 23 REM SAVE CURRENT POSITION

The FOR and NEXT statements allow for the controlled repetition of a group of statements within a program. The FOR and NEXT statements form a loop with the statements between them in a program. The FOR statement defines the number of times the loop is to be performed.

Example:
```
10 FOR I=1 TO 5
50 PRINT "HELLO"
100 NEXT I
110 END
```

This FOR . . . NEXT loop would be executed five times: when I= 1,2,3,4, and 5. Each time the NEXT statement is executed, the value of I is incremented by one. If I is less than or equal to 5, the loop is executed again. But when the value of I passes the final value, that is, when I=6, the statement following the NEXT statement (in this case, line 110) is assessed.

The advantages of using FOR . . . NEXT rather than IF can be shown in the following simple example where the numbers 1 through 100 are to be displayed in succession:

Using IF	Using FOR . . . NEXT
10 N=1	10 FOR N= 1 TO 100
20 IF N > 100 THEN 60	20 PRINT N
30 PRINT N	30 NEXT N
40 N=N+1	40 END
50 GOTO 20	
60 END	

In the example the program is easier to key in, takes up considerably less computer memory, and executes much faster if the FOR . . . NEXT loop is used.

The loop can be used to assigned values to arrays and can be nested; that is, they can be located inside one another, however, one loop cannot overlap another. Entering a FOR . . . NEXT loop at any place other than the FOR statement (with statements like GOTO or IF), can cause unpredictable results and should, therefore, be avoided. It's not necessary that the variable in the FOR . . . NEXT loop be incremented by 1 each time the loop is executed. By adding STEP to the FOR statement, the variable will be incremented by the number following STEP.

```
Example: 10 FOR I=0 TO 12 STEP 3
           .
           .
           .
         50 NEXT I
```

The loop in the example will be executed five times: when I=0, 3, 6, 9, and 12. As soon as the incremented value passes the final value, the loop is exited. If the first number is greater than the second number the loops can be incremented by negative values. The step size need not be an integer value; e.g., STEP 2.5 is allowed, and the initial variable value, the final variable value, and the step size can all be expressions.

```
Example: 10 FOR I=A/6 TO A/2 STEP 0.1*A
```

The WAIT statement introduces a timed delay between two program statements. Only reset can interrupt a WAIT. The WAIT statement takes the form:

WAIT aexpr1, aexpr2 [, aexpr3]

The aexpr1 part of the command is the address of a memory location; it must be in the range –65535 through 65535 to avoid the ?ILLEGAL QUANTITY ERROR message. The aexpr2 and aexpr3 parts must be in the range 0 through 255, decimal. The object of WAIT is to test the contents of location aexpr1 to see when any one of certain bits is high. Each of the eight bits in the binary equivalent of aexpr2 indicates whether you are interested in the corresponding bit at location aexpr1; 1 means you're interested, 0 means ignore that bit. Each of the eight bits in the binary equivalent of aexpr3 indicates which state you are waiting for the corresponding bit in location aexpr1 to be in: 1 means the bit must be low, zero means the bit must be high. If any of the bits in which you have indicated interest (by a 1 in the corresponding bit of aexpr2) matches the state you specified for that bit (by the corresponding bit of aexpr3) the WAIT is over. WAIT aexpr1, 255, 0 means to pause until at least one of the 8 bits at location aexpr1 is high.

The READ and DATA statements combine to assign values to variables. The READ statement determines the variable (for instance, 10 READ Y), while the DATA statement determines the value to be assigned to the variable (for instance, 90 DATA 12). More than one variable can be specified in a DATA statement. The computer uses an internal mechanism, called a pointer, to locate the data element that is to be read. The leftmost element of the lowest-numbered DATA statement is read first. After this element is read, the data pointer repositions itself one element to the right, and continues to do so each time another data element is read. After the last element in a DATA statement is read, the data pointer locates the next higher numbered DATA statement and repositions itself at the first element in that statement. But if there are no higher-numbered DATA statements, the data pointer remains at the end of the previous DATA statement; and any effort to read additional data will result in an error message. The location of the DATA statement in a program is immaterial unless there is more than one DATA statement; if so, just be sure they are in the order you want.

Example: 10 READ A, B, C

40 READ A1, B1

70 READ P

200 DATA 4, 5, 6, 7, 31, 2, 69, 0

Several READ statements can apply to the same DATA statement. The data pointer just moves to the right each time another data element is read. The first variable is assigned the first data value, the second variable is assigned the second value, and so on. The DATA statement is accessed only by a READ statement; otherwise, the program ignores it.

Data elements can be read more than once if the RESTORE statement is used. There are two variations of the RESTORE statement; the first takes the form of the following example:

80 RESTORE

If this type of RESTORE statement is encountered during program execution, the data pointer reverts to the first data element in the lowest-numbered DATA statement. The second type of RESTORE statement is shown by the following example:

90 RESTORE 150

This statement causes the pointer to revert to the first data element in the DATA statement specified (in this case, line 150).

The TAB command must be used with the PRINT statement. With this command, outputs can be located at a specified character position. The form used for this statement is:

TAB (aexpr)

TAB moves the cursor to the position that is aexpr printing positions from the left margin of the text window if aexpr is greater than the value of the current cursor position relative to the left margin. TAB is ignored if the character position is already past the specified TAB.

The aexpr must be in the range 0 through 255, or the message ?ILLEGAL QUANTITY ERROR is presented. TAB is stored as a BASIC reserved word only if the next non-space character after aexpr is a left parenthesis.

The GOSUB statement transfers program execution to the line number specified by GOSUB. Eventually, a RETURN statement is accessed, and the program execution is returned to the statement following the previous GOSUB statement. The GOSUB and RETURN statements eliminate the need to repeat frequently used groups of statements in a program.

Example:
```
 10 PRINT "THIS IS AN EXAMPLE"
 20 GOSUB 100
 30 PRINT "OF USING A SUBROUTINE"
 40 GOSUB 100
 50 PRINT "TO DELAY BETWEEN"
 60 GOSUB 100
 70 PRINT "LINES OF A PRINTOUT"
 80 END
100 FOR I=1 TO 200
105 NEXT 1
110 REM SUBROUTINE LOOPS TO CREATE
      DELAY
115 RETURN
```

The order of execution by line number in the example is:

10-20
100-115
30-40
100-115
50-60
100-115
70-80

Before the subroutine (lines 100-115) there is an END statement. A statement like this is necessary to ensure that a subroutine is not inadvertently run. If it is, an error will occur.

The DEF FN (Define Function) statement can define a function in one line. If an algebraic expression has to be evaluated several times in a program, it may be convenient to define the expression as a function. A maximum of 26 defined functions, FNA through FNZ, are possible in a program. Besides a function name (a letter) the function also needs a simple variable. If the variable is also included in the expression, the function can easily be evaluated for different values of the variable:

Example:
```
10 DEF FNB (X)=X*2/X
20 PRINT FNB4, FNB5, FNB6
30 END
```

In the DEF FN statement, the variable must be separated by parentheses. But in statements where the function is called, parentheses are optional.

An array is often a convenient tool for labeling large groups of data within a program. An array is specified by:

1. Name—any letter from A through Z, followed by its
2. Size—either one or two numbers enclosed within parentheses.

APPLESOFT must be told how much space to allocate for the array; this is done with a DIM statement, which is discussed next. A one-dimensional array can have several rows but only one column. A two-dimensional array is divided into rows and columns. Note that the first row or column is number 0. This means that each number you use in the DIM statement is one less than the necessary size. To input several data elements into array form, a program should perform a looping operation. The IF and GOTO statements can accomplish this looping, but it is generally easier to use the FOR . . . NEXT statements.

Example:

```
100 REM DIMENSION ARRAY CALLED 'DAYS', TO
HOLD 7 NUMBERS
110 DIM DAYS (6)
120 REM FILL THE ARRAY
130 FOR NUM=0 TO 6
140 DAYS (NUM) = NUM + 1
150 NEXT NUM
160 REM PRINT THE ARRAY ELEMENTS
170 FOR I = 0 TO 6
180 PRINT "DAYS (";I;") = ";DAYS (I)
190 NEXT I
```

This example demonstrates the use of variables and prints out a display of each array element.

The DIM (Dimension) statement causes the computer to reserve memory for the specified simple and array variables. The actual array sizes can be less than or equal to the sizes specified. The elements in an array are numbered from 0, so the DIM statement for say, 12 elements, would be written this way: DIM C(11). The statement creates 12 new variables: (C(0), C(1), . . . C(11). They can be used just as any other variable. The subscript (the number in parentheses) can be a variable or an arithmetic expression. For an example program, see the preceeding explanation of arrays. Remember that one-dimensional and two-dimensional arrays cannot have the same name.

This function returns the ASCII code for the first character of a string expression. It takes the form ASC (sexpr). ASCII codes in the range 96 through 255 will generate characters on the APPLE which repeat those in the range 0 through 95. If a literal string is the argument, it must be enclosed in quotation marks, and quotation marks may not be included within the string. If the string is null, the message ?ILLEGAL QUANTITY ERROR is given. An attempt to use the ASC function on ctrl@characters results in the ?SYNTAX ERROR message.

CALL causes execution of a machine language subroutine at the memory location whose decimal address is specified by aexpr, which must be in the range −32768 through 32767 or the message ?ILLEGAL QUANTITY ERROR is displayed. In practice, it is usually limited to the range of addresses for which valid memory devices exist, from 0 through the maximum value for HIMEM. (See HIMEM) Equivalent positive and negative addresses may be used interchangeably.

The following CALLs affect the text window, text, and the keyboard:

CALL −936

Clears the characters inside the test window, and moves the cursor to the window's top leftmost printing position. This is the same as esc@RETURN and the command HOME.

CALL −958

Clears all characters inside of text window from current cursor position to bottom margin. Characters above the cursor, and characters to the left of the cursor in its printing line will not be affected. This is the same as esc F. If the cursor is above the text window, clears from the cursor to the right, left and bottom margins as if the top margin were above the cursor. It is not usually desirable to use this command if the cursor is below the bottom margin of the text window: usually the bottom line of the text window is cleared, along with one line of text-window width at the cursor position.

CALL −868

Clears current line from cursor to right margin. This is the same as esc E.

CALL −922

Issues a line feed. This is the same as ctrl J.

CALL −912

Scrolls text up one line; i.e., moves each line of text within the defined window up one position. Old top line is lost; old second line becomes line one; bottom line is now blank. Characters outside defined window are not affected.

CHR$ returns the ASCII character whose value corresponds to the value of the argument, which must be between 0 and 255. For example, CHR$(65) returns the letter A.

CLEAR has no parameters. It zeroes all variables, arrays, and strings and resets pointers and stacks.

FLASH is used to set video output modes. It has no parameters, and does not affect the display of characters as you type it into the computer nor characters already on the screen. FLASH sets the video mode to "flashing", so the output from the computer is alternately shown on the screen in white on black and then reversed to black on white. (See also INVERSE and NORMAL)

FRE(n) returns the amount of memory (in bytes) still available to the user. You may sometimes wind up with more memory than you expected, since APPLESOFT stores duplicate strings only once. If the number of free memory bytes exceeds 32767, FRE returns a negative number. Adding 65536 to this number gives you the actual number of free bytes of memory. This free space is below the string storage space and above the numeric array and string pointer array space. What you put inside the parentheses is unimportant, as long as it can be evaluated by APPLESOFT. FRE (0) is normally used.

GET fetches a single character from the keyboard without showing it on the TV screen and without requiring that the RETURN key be pressed. For example, GET ANS$ would cause the typed character to be stored in the variable ANS$. If no key is pressed, the variable is the null string.

HIMEM sets the address of the highest memory location available to a BASIC program, including variables. It is used to protect the area of memory above it for data, graphics or machine language routines. The format is HIMEM: aexpr and the aexpr must be in the range −32768 through 32767, inclusive, to avoid the ?ILLEGAL QUANTITY ERROR message. However, programs may not execute reliably unless there is appropriate memory hardware at the locations specified by all addresses up to and including aexpr. In general, the maximum value of aexpr is determined by the amount of memory in the computer. For instance, on an APPLE II with 16K of memory, aexpr would be 16384 or less. If the APPLE II has 32K of memory, aexpr could be as high as 32767; and if the APPLE II has 48K of memory. aexpr could be as high as 49152 (which is represented by −16384). Normally, APPLESOFT automatically sets HIMEM: to the highest memory address available on the user's computer, when APPLESOFT is first entered. The current value of HIMEM: is stored in memory locations 116 and 115 (decimal). To see the current value of HIMEM:, type PRINT PEEK(116)*256 + PEEK(115). If HIMEM: sets a highest memory address which is lower than that set by LOMEM:, or which does not leave enough memory available for the program to run, the ?OUT OF MEMORY ERROR is given. The arithmetic expression may be in the range 0 increasing to 32767, or in the equivalent range −32768 increasing to −1. Equivalent positive and negative values may be used interchangeably. HIMEM: is not reset by CLEAR, RUN, NEW, DEL, changing or adding a program line, or reset. HIMEM: is reset by RESET, ctrl B, RETURN, which also erases any stored program.

HOME has no parameters moves cursor to upper left screen position within the scrolling window, and clears all text within the window. This command is identical to CALL −936 and to esc @, RETURN.

HTAB assumes the line in which the cursor is located has 255 positions, 1 through 255. Regardless of the text window width you may have set, positions 1 through 40 are on the current line, positions 41 through 80 are on the next line down, and so on. HTAB moves the cursor to the position that is aexpr positions from the left edge of the current screen line. HTAB's moves are relative to the left margin of the text window, but independent of the width. HTAB can move the cursor outside the text window, but only long enough to PRINT one character. To place the cursor in the leftmost position of the current line, use HTAB 1. Note: HTAB 0 moves the cursor to position 256.

INVERSE has similar characteristics of the FLASH command. It sets the video mode so that the computer's output prints as black letters on a white background.

IN# selects the input slot. It is used to specify which peripheral will be providing input for subsequent INPUT statements. Peripherals may be in slots 1 through 7. IN# 0 indicates that subsequent input will be from the keyboard instead of the peripheral. Slot 0 is not addressable from APPLESOFT for use with peripheral device. If no peripheral is in the indicated slot, the system will hang. To recover, use RESET, ctrl C, RETURN. If the expression is less than 0 or greater than 255, the message ?ILLEGAL QUANTITY ERROR is displayed. Note: if the expression is in the range 8 through 255, APPLESOFT is altered in unpredictable ways. For similar transfer of output, see PR#.

LEFT$ returns the specified number of leftmost characters

from the string. For example, LEFT$ ("APPLESOFT", 5) will return APPLE, the 5 leftmost characters.

LEN returns the number of characters in a string, between 0 and 255. For example, LEN ("AN APPLE A DAY") will return 14.

LOMEM sets the address of the lowest memory location available to a BASIC program. This is usually the address of the starting memory location for the first BASIC variable. Normally, APPLESOFT automatically sets LOMEM: to the end of the current program, before executing the program. This command allows protection of variables from high-resolution graphics in computers with large amounts of memory. If LOMEM: is set lower than the address of the highest memory location occupied by the current operating system the ?OUT OF MEMORY ERROR message is displayed. LOMEM: is reset by NEW, DEL, and by adding or changing a program line. LOMEM: is reset by RESET, ctrl B, which also deletes any stored program. It is not reset by RUN, by the RESET, ctrl C, RETURN sequence, or by RESET, 3D 0G, RETURN. The current value of LOMEM: is stored in memory locations 106 and 105 (decimal). Once set, unless it is first reset by one of the above commands, LOMEM: can be set to a new value only if the new value is higher (in memory) than the old value. An attempt to set a lower LOMEM: than the value still in effect gives the ?OUT OF MEMORY ERROR message. Changing LOMEM: during the course of a program may cause certain stacks or portions of the program to be unavailable, so that the program will probably not continue to execute properly. Equivalent positive and negative addresses may be used interchangeably.

MID$ returns a specified substring. For example, MID$ ("AN APPLE A DAY",4) will return the fourth through the last characters of the string: APPLE A DAY. MID$ ("AN APPLE A DAY", 4, 5) returns a string starting the fourth character and continuing for five characters: APPLE.

NEW has no parameters. It deletes current program and all variables.

NOTRACE turns off the TRACE debug mode. See TRACE.

ON . . . GOSUB executes a GOSUB to the line number indicated by the value of the arithmetic expression following ON. For example, ON ID GOSUB 100, 200, 23, 4005, 500 will cause GOSUB 100 to be executed if ID is 1. If ID is 2, GOSUB 200 is executed, and so on. If the value of the expression is 0 or is greater than the number of listed alternative line numbers, then program execution proceeds to the next statement.

ON . . . GOTO is identical to ON . . . GOSUB but in the example ON ID GOTO 100, 200, 23, 4005, 500, it executes a GOTO branching to the line number indicated by the value of the arithmetic expression following ON.

When an error occurs, ONERRGOTO may be used to avoid having an error message printed and execution halted. The command sets a flag that causes an unconditional jump (if an error occurs later in the program) to the program line indicated. The ONERRGOTO statement must be executed before the occurrence of an error to avoid program interruption.

When an error occurs in a program, the code for the type of error is stored in decimal location 222. To see which error was encountered, PRINT PEEK (222).

Code	Error Message
0	NEXT without FOR
16	Syntax
22	RETURN without GOSUB
42	Out of DATA
53	Illegal Quantity
69	Overflow
77	Out of Memory
90	Undefined Statement
107	Bad Subscript
120	Redimensional Array
133	Division by Zero
163	Type Mismatch
176	String Too Long
191	Formula Too Complex
224	Undefined Function
254	Bad Response to INPUT Statement
255	Ctrl C Interrupt Attempted

Note: Care must be taken when handling errors that occur within FOR . . . NEXT loops or between GOSUB and RETURN, as the pointer and RETURN stacks can be disturbed. The error-handling routine must restart the loop; returning to the FOR or GOSUB statement, not the NEXT or RETURN statement. After error handling, a return to a NEXT or a RETURN will cause the appropriate message: ?NEXT WITHOUT FOR ERROR or ?RETURN WITHOUT GOSUB ERROR

Note:

1. When ONERRGOTO is used with RESUME to handle errors in a GET statement, the program will hang if there are two

consecutive GET errors without an intervening successful GET. To escape, use RESET, ctrl C, RETURN. If GOTO ends the error-handling routine, everything works fine (but see next note).

2. When used in TRACE mode or in a program containing a PRINT statement, ONERR causes a jump to the Monitor after 43 errors are encountered. Where these errors are generated by an INPUT statement, everything works fine if RESUME is used; but if GOTO ends the error-handling routine, the 87th INPUT error causes a jump to the Monitor. Again, RESET, ctrl C, RETURN will get you back to APPLESOFT.

PDL returns the current value, a number from 0 through 255, of the indicated game control paddle. If two game controls are read in consecutive PDL instructions, the reading from the second game control may be affected by the reading from the first. To obtain more accurate readings, allow several program lines between PDL instructions, or place a short delay loop between PDL instructions.

PEEK returns the contents, in decimal, of the byte at the specified decimal address. For example, PEEK (37) might return 13. The following demonstrate the use of PEEK.

X=PEEK(−16384) reads the keyboard. If X >127 then a key has been pressed, and X is ASCII value of key pressed with bit 7 set. This is useful in long programs, in which the computer checks to see if the user wants to interrupt with new data without stopping program execution.

CH=PEEK(36) reads the current horizontal position of the cursor and sets variable CH equal to it. CH will be in the range from 0 through 39 and is the cursor's position relative to the text window's left-hand margin, as set by POKE 32,L. Thus, if the left margin was set by POKE 32, 5 then the leftmost character in the window is at the 6th printing-position from the left edge of the screen and at the 1st printing position from the left margin of the text window. (It sounds confusing at first, because the leftmost position is position zero, not 1.) This is identical to the POS(X) function.

CV=PEEK(37) reads the current vertical position of the cursor and sets CV equal to it. CV is the absolute vertical position of the cursor and is not referenced to the top or bottom margins of the text window. Thus CV=0 is top line on screen and CV=23 is bottom.

X=PEEK(−16336) toggles speaker once: produces a "click" from speaker.

X=PEEK(−16352) toggles cassette-output once: produces a "click" on a cassette recording.

X=PEEK(−16287) reads pushbutton switch on game control #0. If X >127 then this button is being pressed.

X=PEEK(−16286) same as above but pushbutton on game control #1.

X=PEEK(−16285) game control #2 pushbutton.

X=PEEK(218) + PEEK(219) * 256 this statement sets X equal to the line number of the statement where an error occurred if an ONERRGOTO statement has been executed.

IF PEEK(216) >127 THEN GOTO 2000 If bit 7 at memory location 222 (ERRFLG) has been set true, then an ONERRGOTO statement has been encountered.

POKE stores the binary equivalent of the second argument into the memory location whose decimal address is given by the first argument previously specified. The first four example POKE commands are used to set the size of the "window" in which text is shown and scrolled on your TV screen. These set, respectively, the left margin, line width, top margin and bottom margin of the window. Setting the text window does not clear the remainder of the screen, and does not move the cursor into the text window (use HOME or HTAB and VTAB). The VTAB command ignores the text window entirely: text printed above the window appears normally, while text printed below the window appears all on one line. HTAB can also move the cursor outside the window, but only long enough to print one character there. A change in line width goes into effect immediately, but a change in the left margin is not detected until the cursor tires to return to the left margin.

POKE 32, L sets left margin of TV display to value specified by L, in the range from 0 through 39, where 0 is leftmost position. This change is not effected until the cursor attempts to return to the left margin. The width of the window is not changed by this command: this means that the right margin will be moved by the same amount you move the left margin. To preserve your program and APPLESOFT, first reduce the window width appropriately; then change the left margin.

POKE 33, W sets the width (number of characters per line) of TV display to the value specified by W, in the range from 1 through 40. Do *not* set W to zero. POKE 33, 0 bombs APPLESOFT. If W is less than 33, the PRINT command's third tab-field may print characters outside the window.

POKE 34, T sets top margin of TV display to value specified by T, in the range from 0 through 23 where 0 is the top line on the screen. POKE 34,4 will not allow text to be printed in the first four lines of the screen. Do not set the top margin of the window (T) lower than the bottom margin.

POKE 35, B sets bottom margin of TV display to value specified by B, in the range from 0 through 24 where 24 is the bottom line on the screen. Do not set the bottom margin of the window (B) higher than the top margin.

POKE – 16368,0 resets keyboard strobe so that next character may be read in. This should be done immediately after reading the keyboard.

POKE 36, CH moves the cursor to a position that is CH+1 printing-positions from the left margin of the text window. For example, POKE 36,0 will cause next character to be printed at the left margin of the window. If the left margin of the window was set at 6 (POKE 32,6) and you wanted to provide a character three positions from left edge of the screen, then the window's left margin must be changed prior to PRINTing. CH must be less than or equal to the window width as set by POKE 22,W and must be greater than or equal to zero. Like HTAB, this command can move the cursor beyond the right margin of the text window, but only long enough to print one character.

POKE 37, CV moves the cursor to the absolute vertical position specified by CV. 0 is the topmost line and 23 is the bottom line.

POKE – 16296,1 set game control "annunciator" output #0 to TTL open-collector high. This is the "off" condition.

POKE – 16295,0 set game control output #0 to TTL low. This is the "on" condition: maximum current 1.6 milliamperes.

POKE – 16294,1 set game control output #1 to TTL high.

POKE – 16293,0 set game control output #1 to TTL low.

POKE – 16292,1 set game control output #2 to TTL high.

POKE – 16291,0 set game control output #2 to TTL low.

POKE – 16290,1 set game control output #3 to TTL high.

POKE – 16289,0 set game control output #3 to TTL low.

POKE 216,0 clears ERRFLG so that normal error messages will occur.

POKE 768, 104 : POKE 769, 168 : POKE 770, 104 : POKE 771, 166 : POKE 772, 223 : POKE 773, 154 : POKE 774, 72 : POKE 775, 152 : POKE 776, 72 : POKE 777, 96 establishes a machine-language subroutine at location 768, which can be used in an error-handling routine. Clears up some ONERRGOTO problems with PRINT and ?OUT OF MEMORY ERROR messages. Use the command CALL 768 in the error-handling routine. For other uses of POKE, see Chapter 6.

POP has no parameters or options associated with it. A POP has the effect of a RETURN without actually returning. the next RETURN encountered, instead of branching to one statement beyond the most recently executed GOSUB, will branch to one statement beyond the second most recently executed GOSUB. It is called a POP since it pops one address off the top of the stack of RETURN addresses. If POP is executed before a GOSUB has been encountered, then the message ?RETURN WITHOUT GOSUB ERROR is displayed because there are no return addresses on the stack.

POS (n) returns the current horizontal position of the cursor on the screen, relative to the left hand margin of the text window. At the left margin, 0 is returned. Although what you put inside the parentheses is unimportant, it is still interpreted and must not be illegal. Anything which can be interpreted as a number, a string, or a variable may be used.

PR# transfers output to the specified slot, 1 through 7. PR# 0 returns output to the TV screen.

RIGHT$ returns the specified number of rightmost characters from the string. In the example RIGHT$ ("SCRAPPLE", 5), APPLE (the 5 rightmost characters) will be returned.

SPC must be used in a PRINT statement. Introduces the specified number of spaces between the last item PRINTed and the next item PRINTed if semi-colons precede and follow the SPC command. Note that while HTAB moves the cursor to an absolute screen position relative to the left margin of the text window, SPC (aexpr) moves the cursor a given number of spaces away from the previously printed item. This new position may be anywhere in the text window, depending on the location of the previously printed item. The aexpr must be in the range 0 to 255, inclusive, or the message ?ILLEGAL QUANTITY ERROR appears. Spacing beyond the rightmost limit of the text window causes spacing or printing to resume at the left edge of the next lower line in the text window. When printing in tab fields, spacing may be within a tab field or across into another tab field, or it may occupy a tab field of its own.

SPEED sets speed at which characters are to be sent to the screen or other input/output devices. The slowest speed is 0; the fastest speed is 255. Out of range values will cause the message ?ILLEGAL QUANTITY ERROR to be displayed.

STRS returns a string that represents the value of the argument. For example, STR$(12.45) returns the string "12.45".

USR passes its argument to a machine-language subroutine.

The argument is evaluated and put into the floating-point accumulator (locations $9D through $A3), and a JSR to location $0A is performed. Locations $0A through $0C must contain a JMP to the beginning location of the machine-language subroutine. The return value for the function is placed in the floating-point accumulator. To return to Applesoft, the subroutine must do an RTS. Here is a trivial program using the USR function, just to show you the format:

```
] RESET
* 0A:4C 00 03 RETURN
* 0300:60 RETURN
* ctrl C RETURN
] PRINT USR (8)*3
24
```

At location $0A, we put a JMP (code 4C) to location $300 (low-order byte first, then high-order byte). At location $300, we put an RTS (code 60). Back in APPLESOFT, when USR (8) was encountered the argument 8 was placed in the accumulator, the Monitor did a JSR to location $0A where it found a JMP to $300. In $300 it found an RTS which sent it back to Applesoft. The value returned was just the original value in the accumulator, which Applesoft then multiplied by 3 to get 24.

VAL attempts to interpret a string as a real or an integer, returning the value of that number. The first character of the string must be a possible item in a number (leading spaces are acceptable), or 0 is returned. Each character thereafter is likewise examined, until the first definitely non-numeric character is encountered (intervening spaces, decimal points, + and – signs, and E are all possible numeric characters in the correct context). The first non-numeric character and all subsequent characters are ignored, and the string to that point is evaluated as a real or an integer. If a string concatenation consisting of more than 255 characters is the argument of VAL, the message ?STRING TOO LONG ERROR is given. If the absolute value of the number returned is greater than 1E38, or if the number contains more than 38 digits (including trailing zeroes), the message ?OVERFLOW ERROR is presented.

VTAB moves the cursor to the line on the screen specified by the argument. The top line is line 1; the bottom line is line 24. VTAB will move the cursor up or down but not left or right. Arguments outside the range 1 to 24 cause the message ?ILLEGAL QUANTITY ERROR to appear. VTAB uses absolute moves, relative only to the top and bottom of the screen. It ignores the text window.

In the Apple RND(n) returns a random value. If n is zero, the number returned will be zero. If n is a negative integer a new random table is seeded, and the position in that table indicated by the absolute value of n is returned. A positive number returns that position from the table. Result always falls between 0 and 1.

The IF statement has no ELSE in the Apple. In Integer BASIC the first item after the THEN is conditional. Any items following it are executed whether the condition was met or not. In Applesoft the entire IF . . . THEN line is executed only if the condition is met.

Chapter 4

Flowcharting Techniques

If you are a beginning programmer, you may be interested in knowing some of the techniques available that allow you to more easily advance a programming task from a conceptual stage to a finalized stage.

Flowcharts, which pictorialize the solution to a programming task, are valuable programming tools. They are often drawn long before the actual program statements are written.

While flowcharting your program, you might change or simplify your approach, or see a flaw in your logic. After several attempts, you should have a workable flowchart and, once you do, your programming task is greatly reduced.

Any flowchart that you draw is useful; but a few basic flowing conventions are described in this chapter. Terminal (that is, starting or ending) activities are represented by ovals. Arrows, indicate the order of program flow between operations. Most calculator operations are represented by rectangles. A diamond represents a decision point. If the diamond information is computed if it is computed as 'NO', the logical flow continues in another direction.

To illustrate, in the following example we have labeled each flowcharting operation with the corresponding program line number. As you can see, once the flowchart is finalized, the program can be written relatively easily.

```
10 REM—THIS PROGRAM AVERAGES UP TO 20 POSI-
   TIVE NUMBERS
20 REM—IF YOU HAVE FEWER THAN 20 NUMBERS
   TO ENTER.
```

```
30 REM—ENTER A NEGATIVE NUMBER TO END THE
   INPUTTING.
40 A=0
50 FOR I=1 TO 20
60 INPUT B
70 IF B <0 THEN 110
80 A=A+B
90 NEXT I
110 I=I-1
120 PRINT "THE AVERAGE OF THE "I" NUMBERS IS
   "A/I
130 END
```

As mentioned previously, flowcharts use boxes and lines, following a few simple rules, to represent a program design. Only a few shapes of boxes and only a few ways of drawing the connecting lines are used. These restrictions, allowing only a few flowcharting structures, are intended to make the resulting flowcharts easy to understand by displaying the relationship of parts very clearly. After a correct flowchart has been drawn, translation to a program (writing statements corresponding to the boxes) is relatively simple.

FLOWCHARTING SYMBOLS

Five different shapes of boxes are usually required for most flowcharts.

Rectangle

A rectangle indicates any processing operation except input/output or a decision.

Diamond

A diamond indicates a decision. The lines leaving the box are labeled with the results that cause each path to be followed.

Parallelogram

A parallelogram indicates an input or output operation.

Oval

An oval indicates the beginning or ending point of a program or program segment.

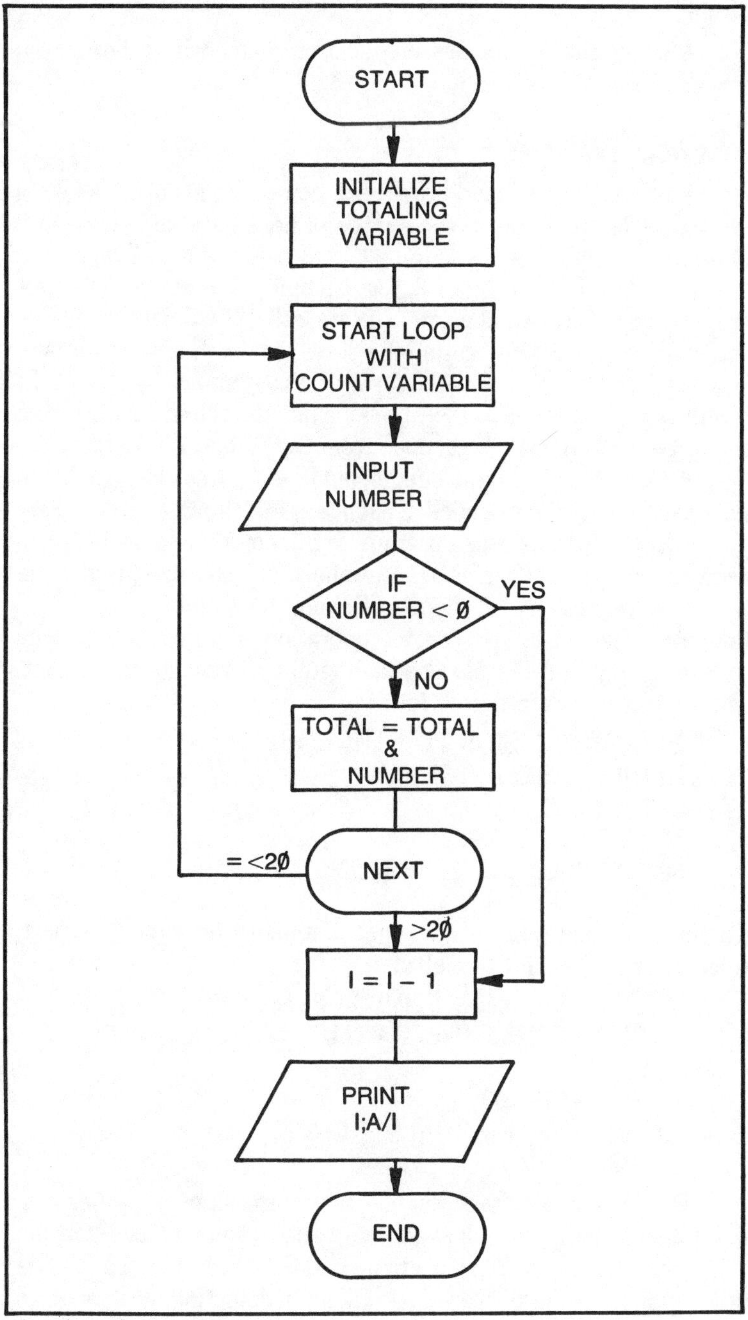
START
INITIALIZE TOTALING VARIABLE
START LOOP WITH COUNT VARIABLE
INPUT NUMBER
IF NUMBER < Ø
YES
NO
TOTAL = TOTAL & NUMBER
= <2Ø
NEXT
>2Ø
I = I – 1
PRINT I;A/I
END

Fig. 4-1.

Circle

A small circle indicates a collection point, where lines from other boxes join.

PRACTICAL EXAMPLES

To better understand how these boxes are used, let's take a few examples to see how the shapes of boxes are combined with lines to design the processing that is to be done by a program.

The flowchart in Fig. 4-2, for example, is a very simple program that reads data and prints it. Notice that the flowchart begins and ends with ovals, indicating the start and finish of the program. The sequence of execution (the flow) is always shown by arrows. In this flowchart it is immediately obvious that the actions in the boxes are to be carried out in sequence from top to bottom. Usually the flow of control will not be so simple, but it will always be possible to tell exactly what the intended sequence is by following the arrows.

The purpose of the program represented by this program design is to convert Celsius to Fahrenheit. The parallelogram in the flowchart represents an input of Celsius temperature. The rectangle represents the processing operation of converting Celsius to Fahrenheit, and the next parallelogram represents the output. The corresponding program follows.

```
10 REM *CELSIUS TO FAHRENHEIT
20 DISP "CELSIUS TEMP"
30 INPUT C
40 LET F=1.8*C+32
50 PRINT C; "C EQUALS "; F; "F"
60 END
```

The program may be easily changed, but using the same flowchart, to convert Fahrenheit to Celsius:

```
10 REM *FAHRENHEIT TO CELSIUS
20 DISP "FAHRENHEIT TEMP";
30 INPUT F
40 C=5/9*(F-32)
50 PRINT F; "F EQUALS "; C;"C"
60 END
```

The fundamental function of a flowchart, as of any other program design tool, is to show in exact and unambiguous detail the sequence in which actions are to be carried out and the conditions under which alternatives are to be taken. In depicting these matters in flowcharts, three control structures are normally used.

Sequence

When an arrow leads from one box to the next, that means simply that the two are to be executed in sequence in the order shown.

Selection

The choice indicated by a decision box always has just two outcomes, depending on whether the condition is true or false.

Iteration

Processing actions are executed repeatedly until a stated condition terminates the repetition. The number of repeats may in some cases be zero.

The basic structures stated above may be combined. For example, a path coming out of a decision box may lead to another decision or perhaps an iteration. Furthermore, it will commonly happen that the actions specified in a loop will include decisions. This is perfectly acceptable so long as only the three basic structures are used.

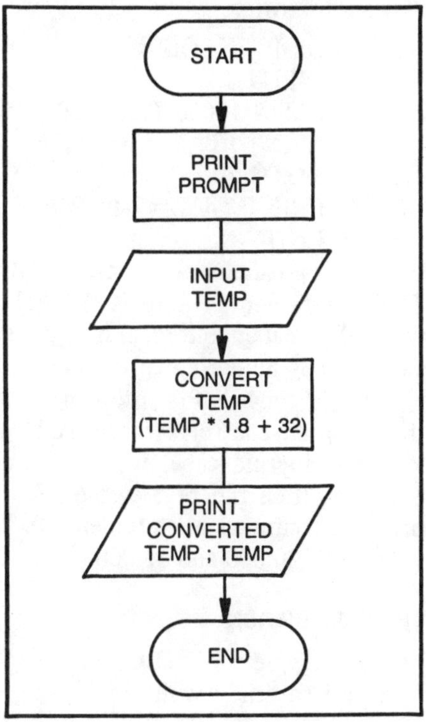

Fig. 4-2.

THE IF STATEMENT

Often there are times when you want to make a decision. In the averaging program discussed previously we wanted the program to branch to either the end of the program, or to the inquiry for more information. The branch was dependent on the outcome of a specified condition, using the IF . . . THEN statement.

IF numeric expression THEN statement

The IF . . . THEN statement makes a decision based upon the outcome of the numeric expression. If the expression is true, the THEN part of the statement is executed. If the outcome is false, execution continues with the statement following the IF . . . THEN statement.

For example, suppose an accountant wishes to write a program that will calculate and print the amount of tax to be paid by a number of persons. For those with incomes of $10,000 per year or less, the amount of tax is 17.5%. For those with incomes of over $10,000, the tax is 20%. A flowchart for the program might look like the one in Fig. 4-3. The diamond in the flowchart would be represented by an IF . . . THEN statement in a program. A sample program may look like the following:

```
10 DISP "INCOME"
20 INPUT I
30 IF I > 10000 THEN 60
40 PRINT "TAX ="; I* .175
50 GOTO 70
60 PRINT "TAX="; I* .2
70 END
```

As you can see, we used a relational operation in the IF . . . THEN statement. The IF . . . THEN statement is most often used with relational operators, although the decision can be based on the value of any numeric expression.

If the condition is true—the income greater than $10,000—then program control is transferred to statement 60. If the condition is false—in this case, if the income is less than or equal to $10,000—then the rest of the IF statement is ignored and the program continues at statement 40. To test this program, use the values of $20,000 and $9,000.

THE ELSE OPTION

The Apple does not have the ELSE option, however its action is useful to study while discussing flowcharts. In the previous

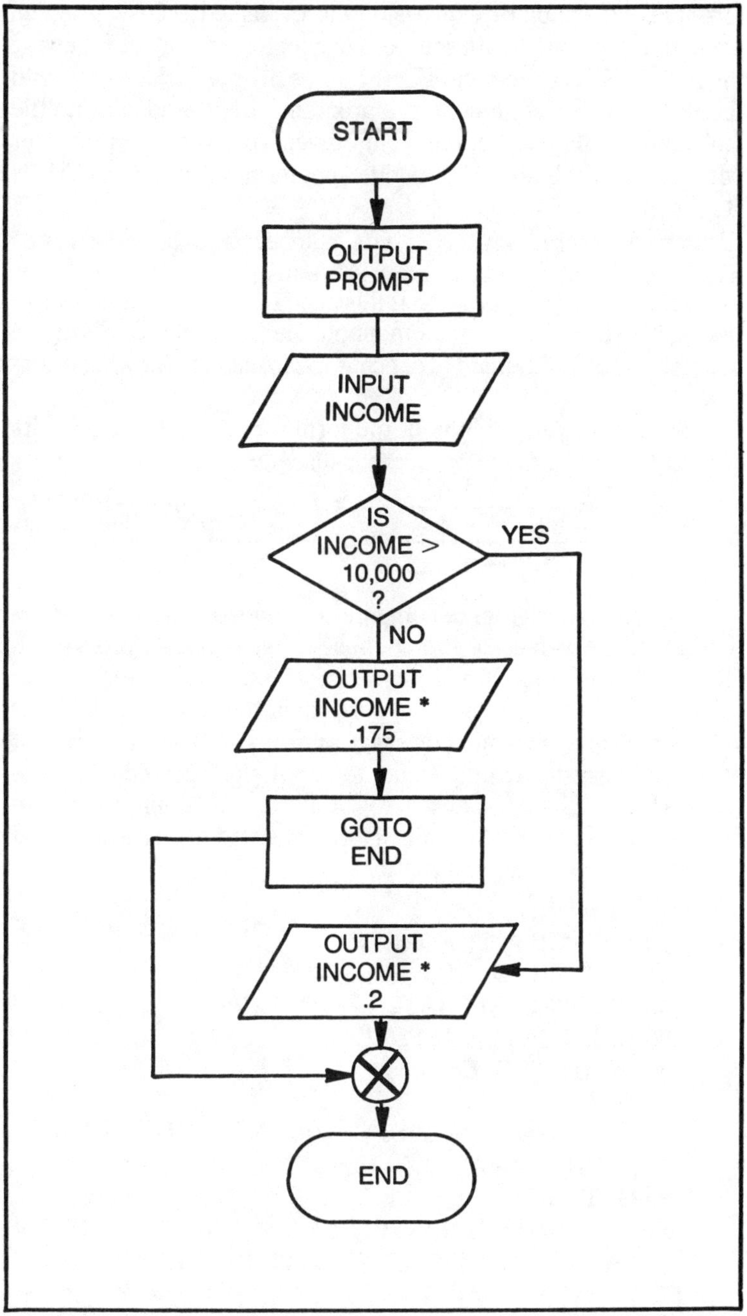

START
OUTPUT
PROMPT
INPUT
INCOME
IS
INCOME >
10,000
?
YES
NO
OUTPUT
INCOME *
.175
GOTO
END
OUTPUT
INCOME *
.2
END

Fig. 4-3.

example, if the numeric expression was evaluated as false, program execution continued with the next sequential statement following the IF . . . THEN statement. But if you specify the ELSE option with the IF . . . THEN statement, the program will instead perform the indicated ELSE instructions. This gives you tremendous power with conditional branching; six different forms of the IF . . . THEN statement are available.

IF numeric expression THE state number or executable instr. ELSE statement number or executable instr.

If the numeric expression is false and ELSE is specified execution is transferred to the statement number following ELSE or the indicated ELSE statement is executed. Look at the following example.

A quadratic equation is of the form $0=ax^2+bx+c$. If $a \neq 0$, its two roots may be found by the formulas

$$r_1 = \frac{-b+\sqrt{b^2 - 4\,ac}}{2a} \text{ and } r_2 = \frac{-b-\sqrt{b^2 - 4ac}}{2a}$$

To write a program to compute the roots of a quadratic equation given the values of the coefficients a, b, and c, proceed as follows: If a is zero, display an error message and reenter new values. If $b^2 - 4\,ac$ is less than zero, then the square root of that value would give a warning message or an error. So make sure that $b^2 - 4ac$ is greater than or equal to zero before you compute the roots. The flowchart is shown in Fig. 4-4. In this solution we use two forms of the IF . . . THEN . . . ELSE statement. Study it carefully and then load the program and run it.

```
10 REM *ROOTS*
20 DISP "IF A QUADRATIC"
30 DISP "EQUATION IS OF THE"
40 DISP "FORM 0=A*X  2+B*X+C
50 DISP "ENTER A, B, C"
60 INPUT A, B, C
70 D=B*B-4*A*C
80 IF A=0 THEN DISP "A=0; NOT QUADRATIC.
   REENTER VALUES" ELSE 100
90 GOTO 60
100 IF D >=0 THEN 120 ELSE DISP "COMPLEX ROOTS:
   CANNOT COMPUTE. REENTER VALUES."
110 GOTO 60
120 R1=(-B+SQR(D))/(2*A)
```

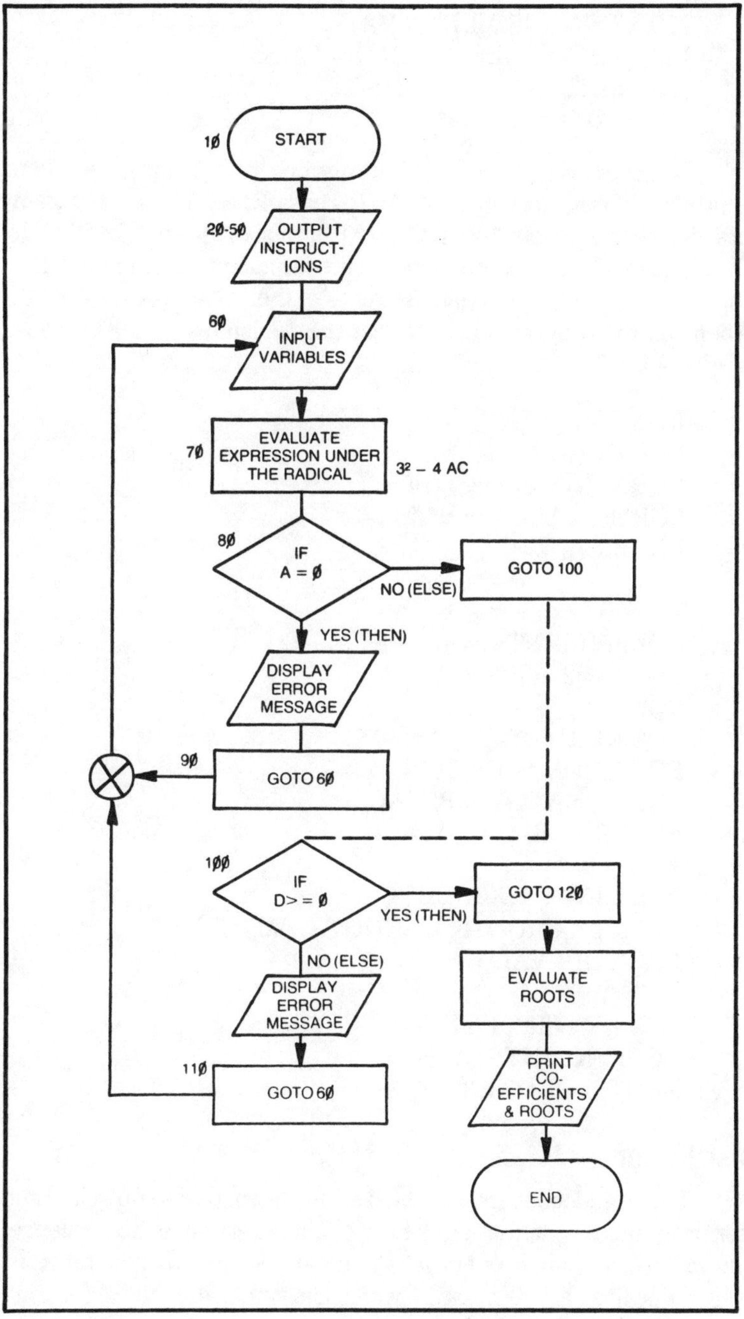

1Ø
START
2Ø-5Ø
OUTPUT INSTRUCT-IONS
6Ø
INPUT VARIABLES
7Ø
EVALUATE EXPRESSION UNDER THE RADICAL
3² – 4 AC
8Ø
IF A = Ø
NO (ELSE)
GOTO 100
YES (THEN)
DISPLAY ERROR MESSAGE
9Ø
GOTO 6Ø
1ØØ
IF D> = Ø
YES (THEN)
GOTO 12Ø
NO (ELSE)
DISPLAY ERROR MESSAGE
EVALUATE ROOTS
11Ø
GOTO 6Ø
PRINT CO-EFFICIENTS & ROOTS
END

Fig. 4-4.

```
130 R2=(-B-SQR(D))/(2*A)
140 PRINT "COEFFICIENTS=";A;B;C
150 PRINT "ROOTS=";R1;R2
160 END
```

To summarize, if A=0, the program displays message, then continues to next statement. If A=0, reads ELSE 100 and program branches to statement 100. If D >=0, branches to statement 120. If D <0, displays ELSE message then continues to statement 110.

Run the program to find the roots of the equation $x^2+x-6=0$. Then run the program again to test the decision with $x+1=0$ and $x^2+2x-1=0$

```
RUN
IF A QUADRATIC EQ
EQUATION IS OF THE
FORM 0=A*X∧2+B*X+C
ENTER A, B, C
?
1,1, -6   (x² + x - 6)
COEFFICIENTS = 1 1 -6
ROOTS=2 -3
RUN
IF A QUADRATIC
EQUATION IS OF THE
FORM 0=A*X∧2+B*X+C
ENTER A, B, C
?
1, 2, 2 (X² + 2 X + 2)
COMPLEX ROOTS: CANNOT COMPUTE
REENTER VALUES
?
3, 2, -1   (3X² + 2X -1)
COEFFICIENTS=3 2 -
ROOTS= .333333333333 -1
```

PSEUDOCODE

The pseudocode may be used as an alternative to flowcharting for program design; that is, the logic that determines the sequence in which processing operations are carried out. In general, this technique uses a code notation which has similarities to BASIC, but is not quite the same.

In pseudocode, we are restricted to just three logic control elements; sequence, selection, and iteration. In pseudocode, the selection element is IF . . . THEN . . . ELSE and the iteration element is PERFORM . . . UNTIL. However, the overall structure of the pseudocode need not show all the details of processing, just as a flowchart need not show them.

Sequence requires no special notation. It is simply a convention that unless specified otherwise, operations are carried out from top to bottom in the order written.

Chapter 5
Graphics

In the past, computer graphics terminals have cost around $5,000 for a single unit and therefore, have been out of reach for most home computer users. The Apple II emerged with a cost-effective remedy—providing reasonably high graphics resolution and true graphics capability at a price affordable by many home users of microcomputers.

HIGH-RES GRAPHICS

Apple's software—known as APPLESOFT—has five special commands which allow you to manipulate shapes in high-resolution graphics:

1. DRAW
2. XDRAW
3. ROT
4. SCALE
5. SHLOAD

Before these commands can be used, a shape must be defined by a shape definition. This consists of a sequence of plotting vectors that are stored in a series of bytes in Apple's memory. One or more such shape definitions, with their index, make up a shape table that can be created from the keyboard and saved on disk or cassette tape for future use.

Each byte in a shape definition is divided into three sections, and each section can specify a plotting vector that tells whether or not to plot a point, and also a direction to move either up, down, left, or right. DRAW and XDRAW step through each btye in the shape definition section by section, from the definition's first byte through its last byte. The shape definition is complete when a byte containing all zeros is reached. Figure 5-1 shows how the three sections A, B, and C are arranged within one of the bytes that make up a shape definition.

Each bit pair DD specifies a direction to move, and each bit P specifies whether or not to plot a point before moving, as shown below:

If DD = 00 move up
= 01 move right
= 10 move down
= 11 move left
If P = 0 don't plot
= 1 do plot

Notice that the last section in Fig. 5-1, which is C and contains the two most significant bits, does not have a P field (by default, P= 0), so section C can only specify a move without plotting. Each byte can represent up to three plotting vectors, one in section A, one in section B, and a third (a move only) in section C.

DRAW and XDRAW process the sections from right to left (least significant bit to most significant bit, thusly, section A, then B, and then C). At any section in the byte, if all the remaining sections of the byte contain only zeros, then those sections are ignored. Thus, the byte cannot end with a move in section C of 00 (a move up; without plotting) because that section which contains all zeros will be ignored. Similarly, if section C is 00 (ignored), then section B cannot be a move of 000 as that will also be ignored. A move of 000 in section A will end your shape definition unless there is a 1-bit somewhere in section B or C.

Let's say that you want to draw a shape such as the one illustrated in Fig. 5-2. First, draw it on a piece of graph paper, one dot placed in the middle of each square as shown in Fig. 5-3. Then decide where to start drawing the shape. As illustrated, this one was started in the center. Draw a path through each point in the shape, using 90 degree angles on the turns.

Next, redraw the shape as a series of plotting vectors, each one moving one place up, down, right, or left, and distinguish the

Section:	C		B			A		
Bit Number:	7	6	5	4	3	2	1	Ø
Specifies:	D	D	P	D	D	P	D	D

Fig. 5-1. Byte Definition.

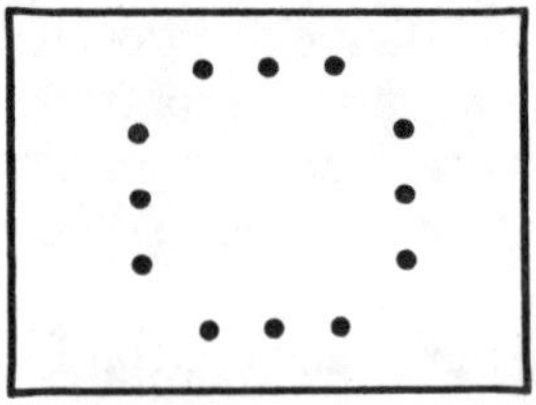

Fig. 5-2. Plot the Shape and Vectors.

vectors that plot a point before moving (a dot marks vectors that plot points). See Fig. 5-4.

Now "unwrap" the vectors and write them in a straight line as shown in Fig. 5-5, then draw a table like the one shown in Fig. 5-6.

For each vector in the line, determine the bit code and place it in the next available section in the table. If the code will not fit (for example, the vector in section C can't plot a point), or is a 00 (or 000) at the end of a byte, then skip that section and go on to the next. When the vectors are all coded, check your work to make sure of its accuracy.

Make table like the one shown in Fig. 5-7 and recopy the vector codes from the table in Fig. 5-6. Recode the vector information into a series of hexadecimal bytes, using the hexadecimal codes from Fig. 5-8.

The series of hexadecimal bytes that are in Fig. 5-7 is the shape definition. There is still a little more information you need to provide before you have a complete shape table. The form of the shape table, complete with its index, is shown in Fig. 5-9.

For this example, the index is easy as there is only one shape definition. The shape table's starting location, whose address is S, must contain the number of shape definitions (between 0 and 255) in hexadecimal. In this case, that number is just one. For simplicity, the shape definition is placed immediately below the index. That means, in this case, the shape definition will start in byte S+4: the address of shape definition #1, relative to S, is 4 (00 04, in hexadecimal). Therefore, index byte S+2 must contain the value 04 and index byte S+3 must contain the value 00. The completed shape table for this example is shown in Fig. 5-10.

Fig. 5-3. Plot the Shape and Vectors.

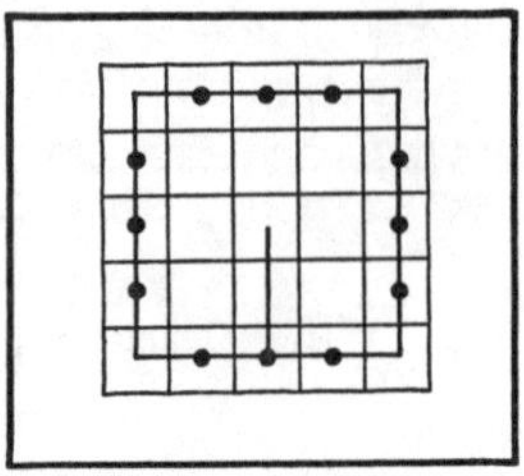

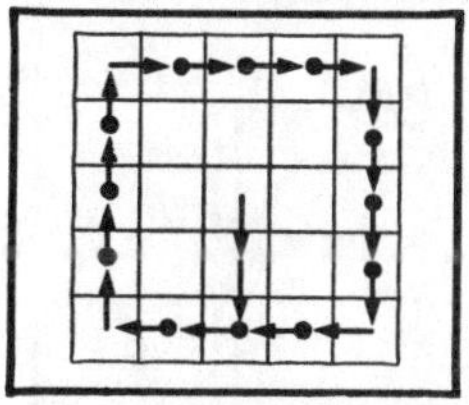

Fig. 5-4. Plot the Shape and Vectors.

The shape table is now ready to be typed into APPLE's memory. First, choose a starting address and for this example, the hexadecimal address 1DFC is used. Press the RESET key to enter the Monitor program, and type the Starting address for the shape table:

1DFC

if you press the RETURN key now, APPLE will show you the address and the contents of that address. This is how an address is examined to see if the information is correct. If instead you type a colon (:) followed by a two-digit hexadecimal number, that number will be stored at the specified address when you press the RETURN key. Try this:

1DFC RETURN

What does APPLE say the contents of location 1DFC are?
Now try this:

1DFC:01 RETURN
1DFC RETURN
1DFC–01

The APPLE now says that the value 01 (hexadecimal) is stored in the location whose address is 1DFC. To store more two-digit hexadecimal numbers in successive bytes in memory, just open the first address:

1DFC:

and then type the numbers, separated by spaces:

1DFC:01 00 04 00 12 3F 20 64 2D 15 36 1E 07 00 RETURN

You have just typed in your first complete shape table. To check the information in the shape table, examine each byte separately or simply press the RETURN key repeatedly until all the bytes of interest have been displayed:

1DFC RETURN
1DFC– 01

Fig. 5-5. List and Encode Vectors.

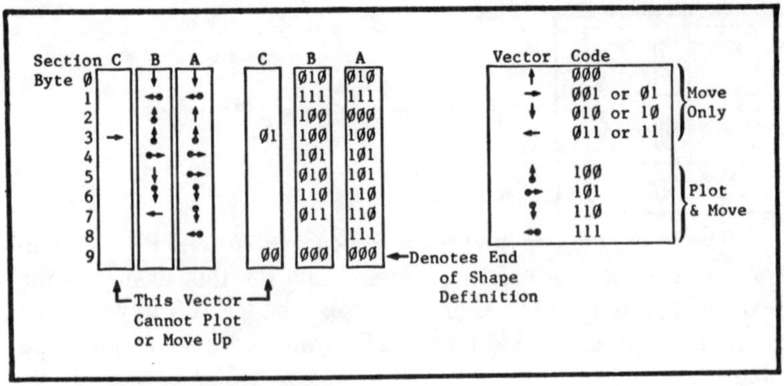

Fig. 5-6. List and Encode Vectors.

RETURN
00 04 00
RETURN
1E00– 12 3F 20 64 2D 15 36 1E
RETURN
1E08– 07 00 DF 1E 23 00 00 FF

If the shape table looks correct, all that remains is to store the starting address of the shape table where APPLESOFT can find it (this is done automatically when you use SHLOAD to get a table from cassette tape). APPLESOFT looks for the four hex digits of the table's starting address in hex locations E8 (lower two digits) and E9 (upper two digits). For this table's starting address of 1D FC, this would be used:

E8:FC 1D RETURN

Byte	C	C	B	B	B	A	A	A		Bytes Recoded in Hex	
0	0	0	0	1	0	0	1	0	=	1	2
1	0	0	1	1	1	1	1	1	=	3	F
2	0	0	1	0	0	0	0	0	=	2	0
3	0	1	1	0	0	1	0	0	=	6	4
4	0	0	1	0	1	1	0	1	=	2	D
5	0	0	0	1	0	1	0	1	=	1	5
6	0	0	1	1	0	1	1	0	=	3	6
7	0	0	0	1	1	1	1	0	=	1	E
8	0	0	0	0	0	1	1	1	=	0	7
9	0	0	0	0	0	0	0	0	=	0	0
	Digit 1				Digit 2					Denotes End of Shape Definition	

Fig. 5-7. Conversion Charts.

CODES

BINARY		HEX
0000	=	0
0001	=	1
0010	=	2
0011	=	3
0100	=	4
0101	=	5
0110	=	6
0111	=	7
1000	=	8
1001	=	9
1010	=	A
1011	=	B
1100	=	C
1101	=	D
1110	=	E
1111	=	F

Fig. 5-8. Conversion Charts.

To protect the shape table from being accidentally erased by your APPLESOFT program, it might also be a good idea to set HIMEM: (in hex locations 73 and 74) to the table's starting address:

73:FC 1D

This, too, is done automatically when you use SHLOAD to get the table from cassette tape.

SAVING TO TAPE

To save the shape table just made on tape for future use, you need to know the following three things:

1. Starting address of the table (1DFC, in the example)
2. Last address of the table (1E09, in the example)
3. Difference between 2. and 1. (000D, in the example)

Item 3, the difference between the last address and the first address of the table, must be stored in hex locations 0 (lower two digits) and 1 (upper two digits):

0:0D 00 RETURN

Now you can "Write" (store on cassette) first the table length that is stored in locations 0 to 1, and then the shape table itself that is stored in locations Starting Address through Last Address:

0.1W 1DFC.1E09W

Don't press the RETURN key until a cassette has been put in the

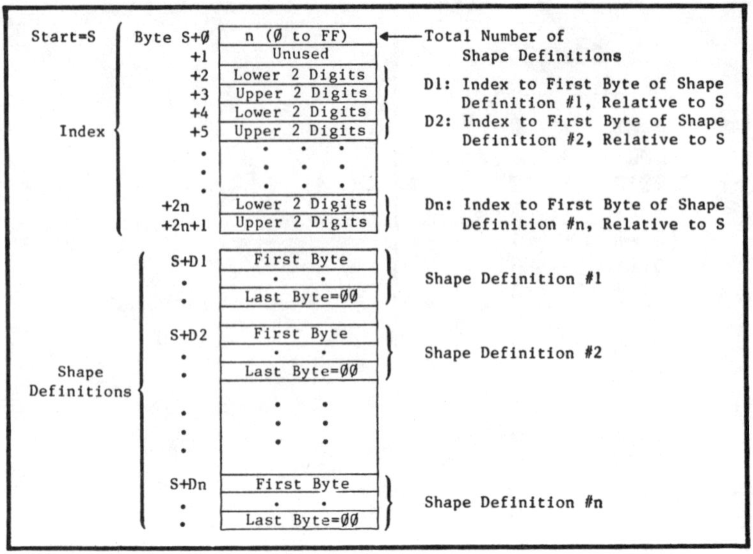

Fig. 5-9. Shape Table Structure.

tape recorder, rewind it, and start it recording (press PLAY and RECORD simultaneously). Now press the computer's RETURN key. To use the tape, rewind it, start it playing (press PLAY), and (in APPLESOFT, now) type

SHLOAD return

You should hear one "beep" when the table's length has been read successfully. and another "beep" when the table itself has been read.

You are now ready to write an APPLESOFT program using the shape-table commands DRAW, XDRAW, ROT and SCALE. The following is a sample APPLESOFT program that will print the defined shape, rotate it 16 degrees, and then repeat, each repetition larger than the one before.

```
10  HGR
20  HCOLOR = 3
30  FOR R = 1 TO 50
40  ROT = R
50  SCALE = R
60  DRAW 1 AT 139, 79
70  NEXT R
```

To see a single "square", add a line:

```
65 END
```

To pause and then erase each square after it is drawn add these lines:

63 FOR I=0 TO 1000: NEXT I
65 XDRAW 1 AT 139, 79

DRAW

The DRAW command takes two forms:

DRAW aexpr1 AT aexpr2, aexpr3 DRAW aexpr1

DRAW with the first option draws a shape in high-resolution graphics starting at the point whose x-coordinate is aexpr2 and whose y-coordinate is aexpr3. The shape drawn is aexpr1 in the shape table. Aexpr1 must be in the range 0 through n, where n is the number (from 0 through 255) of shape definitions given in byte 0 of the shape table. Aexpr2 must be in the range 0 through 279 and aexpr3 in the range 0 through 191. If any of these ranges is exceeded, the message

?ILLEGAL QUANTITY ERROR

will be displayed.

The color, rotation and scale of the shape to be drawn must have been specified before DRAW is executed.

The second option is similar to the first, but draws the specified shape starting at the last point plotted by the most recently executed HPLOT, DRAW, or XDRAW command.

XDRAW

The XDRAW command takes the form:

XDRAW aexpr1 [AT aexpr2, aexpr3]

```
      Start           Byte Ø  |Ø1|<--Number of Shapes
(Store address             1  |ØØ|
 in E8 and E9)             2  |Ø4| }  Index to Shape Definition #1,
                           3  |ØØ| }             Relative to Start
                           4  |12| }<--First Byte
                           5  |3F| }
                           6  |2Ø| }
                           7  |64| }
                           8  |2D| }  Shape Definition #1
                           9  |15| }
                           A  |36| }
                           B  |1E| }
                           C  |Ø7| }
                           D  |ØØ| }<--Last Byte
```

Fig. 5-10. Shape Table Structure.

This command is the same as DRAW, except that the color used to draw the shape is the complement of the color already existing at each point plotted. These pairs of colors are complements:

Black and White
Blue and Green

The purpose of XDRAW is to provide an easy way to erase. If you DRAW a shape, and then XDRAW it again, you'll erase the shape without erasing the background.

ROT

The ROT command takes the form:

ROT = aexpr

It sets angular rotation for shape to be drawn by DRAW or XDRAW. The amount of rotation is specified by aexpr, which must be between 0 to 255.

ROT=0 will cause the shape to be DRAWn oriented just as it was defined, ROT=16 will cause the shape to be DRAWn rotated 90 degrees clockwise, ROT=32 will cause the shape to be DRAWn rotated 180 degrees clockwise, etc. The process repeats starting at ROT=64. For SCALE=1, only 4 rotation values are recognized (0, 16, 32, 48); for SCALE=2, 8 rotations are recognized, etc. Unrecognized rotation values will cause the shape to be DRAWn with the orientation of the next smaller (usually) recognized rotation.

ROT is stored as a reserved word only if the next non-space character is the replacement sign (=).

SHLOAD

The SHLOAD command loads a shape table from cassette tape. Shape table is loaded just below HIMEM: and HIMEM: is set to just below the shape table to protect it. The shape table's starting address is given to APPLESOFT's shape-drawing routines automatically. If a second shape table is loaded, replacing the first table, HIMEM: should be reset prior to loading to avoid wasting memory. Shape table tapes are prepared using the instructions at the beginning of this chapter.

On 16K systems, HGR clears the top 8K of memory, from location 8192 to location 16383. To force SHLOAD to put the shape table below page 1 of high-resolution graphics, set HIMEM:8192 before executing SHLOAD. On 24K systems, do not use HGR2 (which clears memory from location 16384 to location 24575), or else set HIMEM: 16384 before SHLOAD and do not use HGR. If you have more than 24K and are sure there is enough safe memory above location 24575 to hold your shape table, there is nothing to worry about.

Only reset can interrupt SHLOAD. If the reserved word SHLOAD begins a variable name, the reserved-word command may be executed before any ?SYNTAX ERROR is given For example, the statement

SHLOADER = 59

hangs the system, while APPLESOFT waits indefinitely for a program from the cassette recorder. Use RESET, ctrl C to regain control of the computer.

A SAMPLE GAME

There are also ways of setting up a shape table from BASIC, and a way to draw high-res shapes without using the shape table at all. Both of these will be used in a sample game, showing the simple use of one high-res page.

Figure 5-11 shows the flowchart for a simple game where a spider tries to shoot down flies before they can destroy her web. The left and right arrows control the spider, and the space bar fires a stream of webbing at the flies. If a fly hits the spider directly, or destroys the web on both sides of the spider, you lose. No score is kept, and the game continues until the spider loses. Features that can be added will be discussed at the end of the chapter.

Figure 5-12 is the listing, and each segment will be discussed as we go along. I suggest that you delete the REM lines before you actually run the program. This will help speed it up. Notice that several other things have been done to speed up the program. The instructions and data have been placed at the end of the program. They are only used during set up of the game, and the speed at which they execute is not critical. During the game they are out of the way, and branching doesn't have to search through them to find the lines it wants, thus speeding things up. Use this same idea in your BASIC programs.

After the instructions are printed, line 840 waits until any key is hit to return to the main program. Notice that no references are made to the REM lines, so that they may safely be deleted without worrying about errors.

Line 50 reads the data for the shape table and POKES it into location 31000. The computer will look for this address in location E8 and E9 hex, but instead of using the monitor to store it there, we

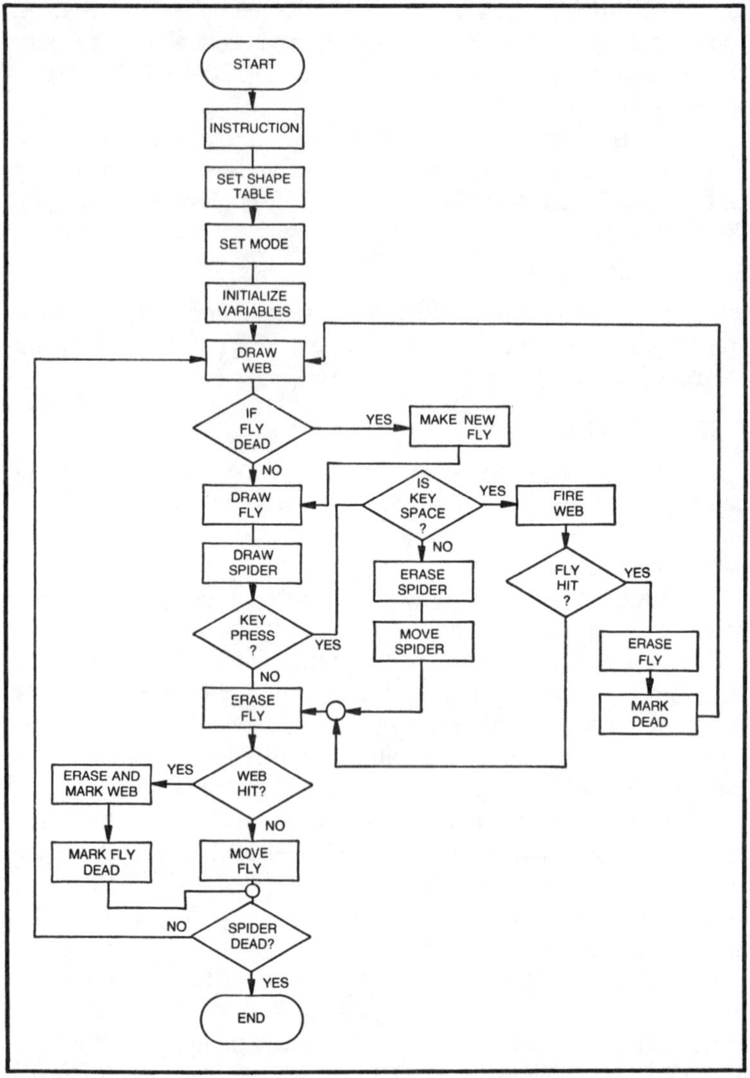

Fig. 5-11.

use the POKE statement. E8 hex is 14*16+8 or 232. The least significant byte goes here, and the most significant byte goes in the next location. But what to POKE there? There is an easy way and a hard way to figure out. I'll show the hard way first, so you will understand the concept, and then show the easy way.

31000 is equivalent to 7918 hex. You determine this by dividing by 4096 (the value on the fourth position in hex), dividing the remainder by 256 (value of the third position), that remainder by 16 (the second position), and that remainder is the ones digit just as in decimal. Remember that if a number is in the 10 to 15 range, it is represented by the letters A through F. For a number under 65535 you will never have a digit higher than 15 (F).

7918 breaks into two bytes; 79, which is the most significant, and 18 which is least. These are the numbers you would enter if you used the monitor, but BASIC works with decimal only, so you must convert each byte back to decimal separately. 18 is 24 decimal, and that is the value poked into 232, and 79 is 121, the value put into 233.

The easy way is to simply divide 31000 by 256 to get the decimal value of the most significant byte. The remainder is the least significant byte. Check these values against line 70, and also

```
   5 GOTO810
  45 REM SET UP SHAPE TABLE
  50 FOR I=1TO75: READ SH:POKE 30999+I, SH:NEXT I
  55 REM SET UP GRAPHICS MODE AND CLEAR
  60 POKE-16304, 0:POKE-16302, 0:POKE .16300, 0:POKE-16297, 0:HGR:HCOLOR=1
  65 REM DIRECT COMPUTER TO SHAPE TABLE BY POKING 31000 TO E8, E9
  70 POKE233, 121:POKE232, 24
  75 REM A,B=SPIDER X(), Y()=FILES C()=WEB INTACT C,D=WEB
  80 D=190:A=140:B=180:DIM C(20), X(4). Y(4)
  85 FORI=0TO279 STEP14:IF C(I/ 14)=0 THEN DRAW 1 AT I, D:NEXT I
  86 REM THIS IF STATEMENT WORKS IN BOTH BASICS
  90 FORI=1TO4:IF X(I)<>0 THEN 95
  91 X(I)=INT(5+270*RND(-1)):Y(I)=1
  95 DRAW 2 AT X(I), Y(I):NEXT I
 100 DRAW 3 AT A,B
 105 GET A$:REM SEE IF A KEY HAS BEEN PRESSED
 110 IF A$<> "THEN 500: REM A KEY WAS PRESSED
 120 FORI=1TO4:XDRAW 2 AT X(I), Y(I): IF Y(I)<195 THEN 125
 121 C(INT(X(I)/14))=1:X(I)=0:GOTO 135
 125 Y(I)=Y(I)+1:X(I)=X(I)-2+(INT(3*RND(-1))):IF X(I)> 274 THEN X(I)=274
 130 IFX(I)<5 THEN X(I)=5
 135 NEXT I:REM THIS LOOP ERASES FLIES AND UPDATES POSITIONS
 140 FOR I=0TOA/14:IF C(I)=1 THEN L=1:REM WEB GONE TO THE LEFT
 145 NEXT I:FORI=INT(A/14)TO20:IF C(I)=1 THEN R=1:REM WEB GONE TO THE RIGHT
 150 NEXT I:IF NOT(L AND K) THEN 155
 151 XDRAW 3 AT A,B:END:REM IF FLY HITS SECTION THAT SPIDER IS ON L AND K=1
 155 L=0:R=0:GOTO85:REM BEGIN MAIN LOOP AGAIN
 500 IF A$=" " THEN 700:REM WEB FIRED
 510 XDRAW 3 AT A,B:IF A$=CHR$(8) THEN A=A-1:REM LEFT ARROW
 515 IF A$=CHR$(21) THEN A=A+1:REM RIGHT ARROW
 520 IF A< 7 THEN A=7
 521 IF A> 270 THEN A=271
 525 GOTO120:REM BACK TO MAIN LOOP
 700 FORI=1TO4:IF A=X(I) THEN 710
 705 HPLOT A,B - 1 TO A,0:HCOLOR=0:HPLOT A,B-1 TO A, 0:HCOLOR=1: NEXT I:GOTO120
 710 HPLOT A,B - 1 TO X(I), Y(I):XDRAW 2 AT X(I), Y(I):HCOLOR=0
 715 HPLOT A,B - 1 TO X(I), Y(I):HCOLOR= 1 : X (I) = 0:GOTO85
 800 REM INSTRUCTIONS
 810 HOME: PRINT"MOVE THE SPIDER WITH LEFT AND RIGHT ARROWS"
 820 PRINT"FIRE WEB WITH SPACE BAR. FLIES DESTROY WEB."
 830 PRINT"SPIDER BETWEEN TWO PIECES OF DESTROYED WEB LOOSES"
 840 PRINT"PRESS ANY KEY TO PLAY"
 850 GET A$:IF A$="" THEN 850
 855 GOTO50
1000 DATA3.0.8.0.19.0.29.0.21.46.46.53.45.45.37.45.44.100.5.252.191.77.45.12.173.30,
        255. 31. 63. 31. 7. 224. 23. 150. 23. 150
1010 DATA41.82.44.224.99.5.32.63.72.49.102.46.32.36.44.54.54.14.36.36.12,22.182,178.
        33. 13. 56. 56. 104. 1. 56. 56. 103. 8. 32. 24. 23. 6. 0
```

Fig. 5-12.

↑ ØØ
→ Ø1
↓ 1Ø
← 11

DEC		HEX		PLOT
21	=	15	=	ØØØ1Ø1Ø1
46	=	2E	=	ØØ1Ø111Ø
46	=	2E	=	ØØ1Ø111Ø
53	=	35	=	ØØ11Ø1Ø1
45	=	2D	=	ØØ1Ø11Ø1
45	=	2D	=	ØØ1Ø11Ø1
37	=	25	=	ØØ1ØØ1Ø1
45	=	2D	=	ØØ1Ø11Ø1
44	=	2C	=	ØØ1Ø11ØØ
1ØØ	=	64	=	Ø11ØØ1ØØ
5	=	05	=	ØØØØØ1Ø1

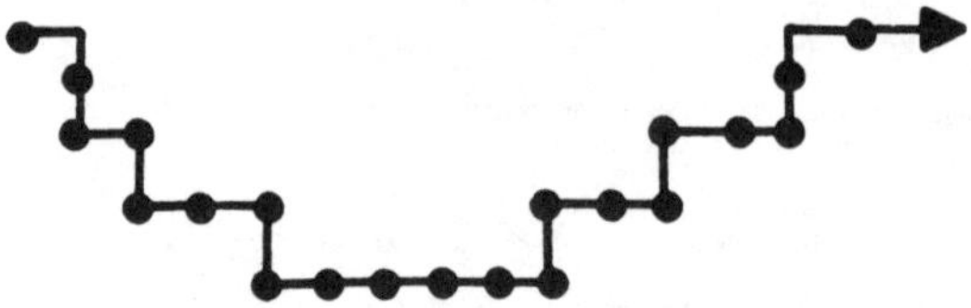

Fig. 5-13. Defining Shapes.

note that to get the first byte of the shape table into the proper location the offset in line 50 is 30999. This is because the loop starts at 1, and 30999 plus one is 31000.

The high-res figures for the web, flies, and spider are shown in Figs. 5-13 and 5-14. On the spider, in particular, care was taken that there were not three consecutive "move up with no plot" commands. The finished table is in Fig. 5-15. Refer to the earlier part of this chapter if you need a refresher on how this was done. Also, remember that these hex values had to be converted to decimal to work with the POKE statement.

Several other things concerning the high-res characters are worth noting here. First, the starting location of the spider is important because it will be used as a reference to where the stream of web material will shoot out at the flies. It must be one of the two front dots to keep programming to a minimum. Second, on the spider and the fly it doesn't matter which way the final vector moves after plotting, but on the web it does, as option two of the draw statement may be used.

Any time you have a character that might be strung together you should make sure the final move puts the pointer in the proper place to start drawing the next character. The program, in its present form, doesn't use this technique to draw, but if you were to add a feature in which the spider could repair its web, then a

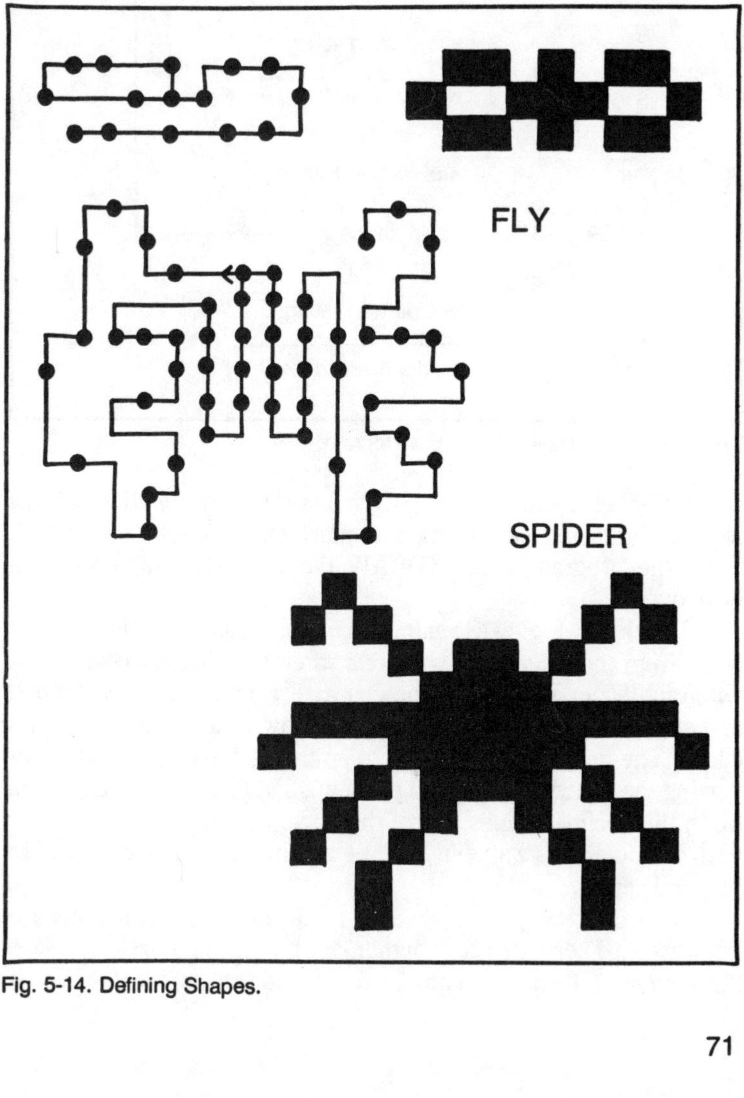

Fig. 5-14. Defining Shapes.

Address	Value	Description
31000	3	number of shapes
	0	unused
31002	8	shape 1 displacement
	0	
31004	19	shape 2 displacement
	0	
31006	29	shape 3 displacement
	0	
31008	21	begin shape 1
	46	
	46	
	. . .	see data in listing
	5	
31019	252	begin shape 2
	191	
	77	
	. . .	see data in listing
	63	
31029	31	begin shape 3
	7	
	224	
	. . .	see data in listing
	6	
31074	0	marks end of table

Fig. 5-15. Shape Table for Sample Program.

complete web could be drawn much faster by putting DRAW 1 in a loop, and allowing each segment to start where the last one left off. Then the program could XDRAW the portions that have been destroyed.

Looking at Fig. 5-13 again, you can see that I combine several steps from the original instructions when creating my characters. On graph paper I block out the character, then redraw with dots, make my connection lines, and write down the vectors and plot codes. The graph blocks help to keep things lined up neatly. Converting the binary to hex is no problem, and then all I have to do is fill in the decimal values. All of the documentation is together for each character this way. If a mistake was made, it is much easier to find and repair.

Line 60 sets up the display mode using several software "switches". These are areas of memory that when addressed cause the computer to output data to the screen in different ways. It doesn't matter if you read or write to them, or what value you use if you write, the mere fact that they are addressed does the job. Figure 5-16 shows the possibilities.

Each address is given in hex and in decimal, and there are two addresses in a box. The two addresses are mutually exclusive. For instance, –16304 and –16303 cannot both be set. The last one addressed sets the mode. In addition, the state of the first set of addresses changes the meaning of several of the other pairs. For instance, if switch –16303 is set (the all text mode) then switch –16301 is meaningless. Similarly, setting switch –16297 would be a mistake in the all text mode, as no text can be displayed in the high-res mode unless –16304 is set.

Line 60 in the program sets the all high-res graphics mode, using the first page of high-res memory. This is the last 8K of a 16K machine. The second high-res page is the first 8K of the next 16K block of memory, so unless you have a minimum of 24K, you only have one page of high-res graphics. This program only uses the first page, so that 16K owners can run it.

Machine language users can create smooth, fast graphics by drawing on one page while viewing the other. Once a character is set up on page one, the actual bytes can be block moved to the second page of memory, with the location slightly altered, and then the switch made to display the second page. The old character is then erased from page one, the new one block moved to its new location on page one, and the switch set back to page one. If you get courageous you might want to try this, either writing your own move routine, or jumping to the one in the monitor.

LOCATION		
HEX	DECIMAL	DESCRIPTION
CØ5Ø CØ51	–163Ø4 –163Ø3	A GRAPHIX MODE A TEXT MODE
CØ52 CØ53	–163Ø2 –163Ø1	ALL TEXT OR GRAPHICS MIXED TEXT & GRAPHICS
CØ54 CØ55	–163ØØ –16299	PRIMARY PAGE SECONDARY PAGE
CØ56 CØ57	–16298 –16297	LO-RES HIGH-RES

Fig. 5-16. Video Switches. It is only necessary to address the switch to set it.

The rest of this program is pretty routine, drawing the characters, inputting any moves, blanking the characters with XDRAW, updating the location and redrawing them. Follow the flowchart and the REM statements.

I mentioned that there was another way to draw high-res figures, and it is used in lines 700 and 710. HPLOT will draw a line between two points, using what ever color mode is set. The syntax is HPLOT (co-ordinate pair one) TO (co-ordinate pair two). This will plot both points named, and draw a line between them. Additional pairs of co-ordinates can be tacked on to this statement, separated by the word TO, and the second point will be joined to the third, the third to the fourth, and so on. The only way to blank out this character is to either clear the high-res page with HGR or to set the color to zero (black) and redraw it, and then reset the color to its original value. This is the method used to draw the jet of webbing that the spider shoots. You may wish to alter the program so that two streams are shot, one from each side of the head, to make the game easier.

Other variations to the game might include:

1. Limiting the length of the stream of webbing.

2. Using the ROT command to make the flies aim the direction they are traveling.

3. Allowing the spider to turn and shoot. (Check to see if the fly is hit by calculating the slope of the line between spider and fly and seeing if it matches the slope of the angle the spider is rotated to.)

4. Use the SCALE command to make the flies larger as they approach the spider.

5. As the spider survives, increase the amount of webbing it can crawl on by making higher levels.

And, of course, anything else you can think of. This simple program could become a full fledged arcade game, with sound, score, and color!

Chapter 6
The Built-in Monitor

In Chapter 5 use of the monitor was briefly discussed as a tool for entering a shape table into memory and saving it to tape. This is one very minor job that the monitor can do, but it is capable of much more. Before the power of this piece of software can be understood, however, we must dig deep down into the inside of the Apple II.

WHAT *IS* A COMPUTER?

In simplest terms a computer is a device that receives information, manipulates it, and sends it back out. If it doesn't do all three of these operations, it just isn't a computer. A radio sends and receives, but doesn't manipulate the data, so it isn't a computer. A light bulb receives electricity, sends out light, but instead of manipulating the data, it merely converts it to another form (heat and light), so it isn't a computer either. But by our definition the machine that senses if a prize was put into the Cracker Jack™ box, and knocks it off the line if not, is a computer, and so is a pocket calculator!

Exactly right. The first computers, big though they were, did little more than the $9.95 calculator does today. So what made those first giant machines, and today's microcomputers so special? Mostly the ability to store the input, and later interpret it as series of instructions.

ENIAC, the first working computer in the U.S., had a series of cables, like an old telephone switchboard, that could be plugged into the proper holes to tell the computer what to do with the data that was input on a strip of paper. The paper had little holes punched into it to represent the data. See Fig. 6-1.

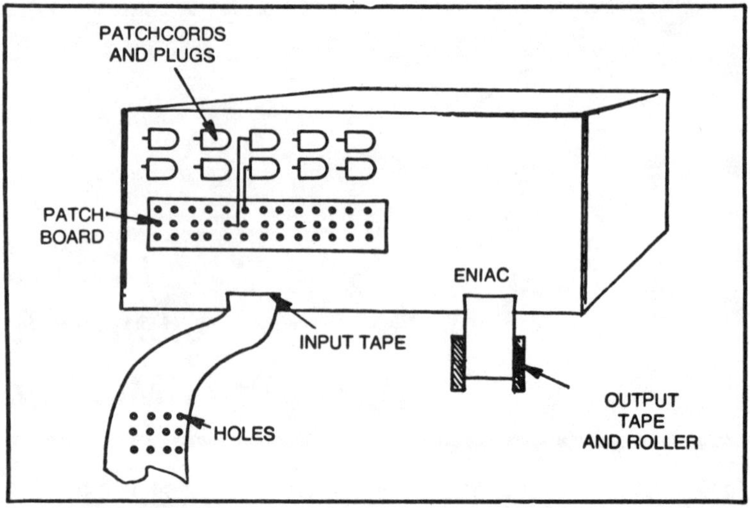

Fig. 6-1. This representation of the ENIAC (it looked much different) shows the input tape (which is taken up in back), the output tape (fed from a blank roll), and the patchboard. Actual machine took up several rooms and had 55,000 vacuum tubes.

The description, so far, tells what a computer *does*. It doesn't tell what it is made of. What secret alchemy allows it to perform these tasks?

The input section and the output section are pretty obvious. Input can be as simple as a set of switches and output could be a series of light bulbs. These are the first two important parts. How data is represented and manipulated is a little more complicated.

One of the sections must do the various arithmetic routines. Just like a human, it can only really add two numbers together at a time. When you add a column of numbers you are using a routine that allows you to come up with the right answers. The computer must also use a routine to arrive at its answers. These two parts are called the Arithmetic Logic Unit (ALU) and the Central Processing Unit (CPU) in a computer. The CPU keeps track of which step to do next, figures out what that step means, and where to send the information. The routine is called a program, and if the program says to add two numbers together the CPU must figure out that add is what is wanted, then send the first number to the ALU, tell it that it is to add, then send the second number. Finally, the CPU must go look for the next step.

Still using the column of numbers analogy, if you have to carry a number you simply write the amount at the top of the next column. If you were doing an equation that required you to add two numbers, subtract two others, and then multiply the two results together, you would simply write the results down. The computer has no way of writing down anything but the final result, so it must remember it. This memory is the last part of a computer that allows manipulation, and every computer will have all five of the parts discussed. Figure 6-2 depicts the layout.

Your Apple has no patchboard, and neither does the drawing. This is because early in the development of computers the designers figured out that the program could occupy a part of the same memory that was used to store intermediate answers and data that wasn't ready to send. (John Von Neumann usually gets the credit for this idea, but in truth he was just the one picked to write the paper for the group that developed the idea.) The importance of the stored program concept is as significant as that of the computer itself. It involves speed.

A program could be punched onto tape and read into the computer much more quickly than technicians could plug in a bunch of patch cords, and much more accurately. Size of the program was limited only by the size of the memory, and it now became feasible to write a program in several parts and load each part when it was needed. Also, it was now possible to leave off the patch board and simply mass produce memory, lowering the cost.

It was still necessary to hardwire a small amount of memory with instructions on how to read the program tape in, but this was

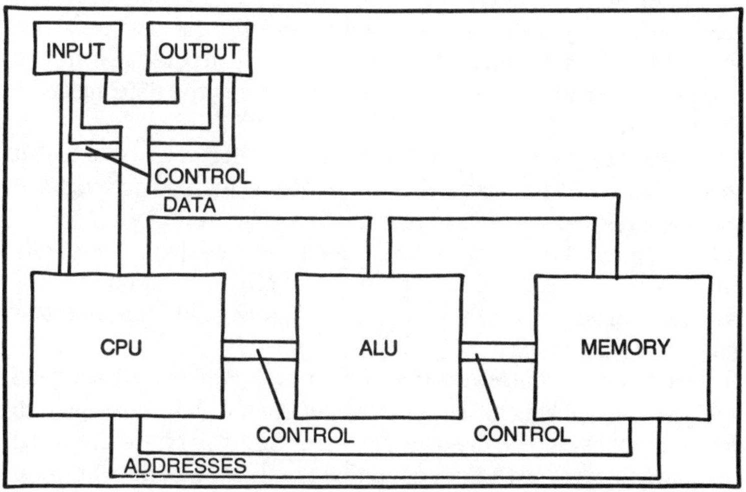

Fig. 6-2. The five parts of a computer and how they are connected.

standard in every computer and would never be changed, so it too could be mass produced. At this point, the computer had reached a structure that has not signficantly changed even in the Apple.

HOW IT WORKS

The number system we use has ten digits; zero through nine. It would be possible to represent each of these digits with a different voltage, but that would require very complex power supplies and circuitry. Computers like this exist but they are very small and have limited use. They are called analog computers.

The easiest way to represent numbers with electricity is in binary. In binary you use only two digits; zero and one. Everything works the same way, with each position representing the base raised to the power of the position, but the advantage of binary is that you can then use a wire with electricity in it to represent one and a wire with no electricity to represent zero. See Fig. 6-3.

The number of electrical lines read at the same time determines how large a number can be represented at one time. The Apple uses eight lines for data and sixteen for addresses. This means it can address 65536 different memory positions, each of which holds eight binary digits (bits). These eight bits (called a byte) can represent 256 different values. Larger numbers can be represented by the programmer if he or she strings several of these bytes together, but the computer doesn't know how to do it without being told.

In modern computers the CPU, ALU, control lines, and a few memory locations that are not addressed by the address lines (called registers) are all enclosed in a single small package called an integrated circuit (IC). The CPU in the Apple is the 6502 made by MOS Technology.

The CPU performs a different function for each code that it reads. These codes also tell it if it needs to read any data to complete the task, where to put the data when it is done, and if it needs to note anything in particular about a value that results from this action. These codes are called the computer's instruction set. Writing a program with these instructions is called machine language programming.

The first computers could only be programmed in this way, and it is a slow confusing process if you have to punch it into tape, flip switches, or even type the ones and zeros in with a typewriter. The hex code, discussed in the section on graphics, was developed to make things easier, but looking up all the codes was still a big chore, and those were exactly the kinds of things computers were made to relieve people of, so a program was developed that would read short abbreviations of the English equivalents of the instructions and convert them into the proper codes. This program was called an assembler, and the built-in monitor in your Apple contains one. It also contains a method of looking at memory locations, changing them, moving them, and looking at the value in each of the registers.

WHY WRITE IN MACHINE CODE?

With a high level language like BASIC you may well wonder why you should bother with registers and machine code and the like.

For many applications BASIC is fine, but it requires a large interpreter to decode your statements into something the machine understands, and then to execute it. Even if you have a compiler, which generates machine code and stores it for later running, you have the overhead of a compiler taking up memory space and you don't get very efficient code. Also, if you are writing a program to control a peripheral like a printer or a disk drive it would be almost impossible to do in BASIC. Finally, the speed factor comes into play again. A program in machine language will take about one quarter the amount of space needed by the equivalent BASIC program, and run about 80 times faster at a minimum.

Appendix F has a list of the instructions for the 6502 CPU. Study this and Fig. 6-4 before continuing.

THE MONITOR

All input and output of the monitor is in hex format. There are 22 command characters that it recognizes, and it names the registers as seen in Fig. 6-4.

BASE 1Ø								
...	6	5	4	3	2	1	0	POSITION
...	1Ø^{6}	1Ø^{5}	1Ø^{4}	1Ø^{3}	1Ø^{2}	1Ø^{1}	1Ø^{0}	POWER
...	1,ØØØ,ØØØ	1ØØ,ØØØ	1Ø,ØØØ	1ØØØ	1ØØ	1Ø	1	VALUE

BASE 2								
...	6	5	4	3	2	1	Ø	POSITION
...	2^{6}	2^{5}	2^{4}	2^{3}	2^{2}	2^{1}	$2^{Ø}$	POWER
...	64	32	16	8	4	2	1	VALUE

13 base 10 would be 1 ten and 3 ones, or thirteen.
1101 base 2 would be 1 eight and 1 four and no twos and 1 one, or thirteen.

Fig. 6-3.

```
*300S

0300-    A2 02          LDX    #$02
 A=0A X=02 Y=D8 P=30 S=F8
*S

0302-    B5 00          LDA    $00,X
 A=0C X=02 Y=D8 P=30 S=F8
*S

0304-    95 10          STA    $10,X
 A=0C X=02 Y=D8 P=30 S=F8
*12

0012- 0C
*S

0306-    CA             DEX
 A=0C X=01 Y=D8 P=30 S=F8
*S

0307-    8D 30 C0       STA    $C030
 A=0C X=01 Y=D8 P=30 S=F8
*S

030A-    10 F6          BPL    $0302
 A=0C X=01 Y=D8 P=30 S=F8
*S

0302-    B5 00          LDA    $00,X
 A=0B X=01 Y=D8 P=30 S=F8
*S

0304-    95 10          STA    $10,X
 A=0B X=01 Y=D8 P=30 S=F8
*
```

Fig. 6-4. Single stepping through a short program with the built-in monitor.

The monitor tells you that it is ready for input with the star (*) prompt. Your entry should end with RETURN. The values used in this discussion will probably differ from those that you get, but the idea holds.

If you type in an address, the monitor responds with the address, a dash, and the hex value of the contents of that address. The monitor then stores an internal pointer at that address. If you simply press RETURN again, anywhere from 1 to 8 more bytes will be displayed according to the following rule.

The display will contain the bytes in memory address from the one the pointer is at up to an address that ends in 7 or F. When the first byte is from an address starting with 0 or 8, the address is displayed, followed by a dash, and a maximum of 8 bytes is shown, up to the one whose address ends in 7 or F. The pointer is updated to the last address shown.

A decimal point followed by an address will print the value of all of the bytes from the pointer to the address typed, formatted by the same rule as above. The pointer is updated to the last address displayed.

If you type a colon (:) followed by a hex value less than or equal to FF it will be written to the location being pointed to. The address, colon, and up to 85 bytes to be written to consecutive memory locations can be entered at once. The bytes should be separated by a space. The pointer is updated. This is how you would enter a program for the first time, if you wrote it in machine language yourself.

By typing a beginning and ending address, separated by a period and followed by a W, you can save a block of memory to tape. Use the same technique as when saving a BASIC program. The same syntax with an R instead of a W will read the tape back into memory.

An address, a less than sign, two addresses separated by a period and an M will move the block in the specified range to a new location which starts at the first address. The destination can be inside of the range of the block, but make sure you know what you are doing if you try it. The same syntax, with a V instead of the M will verify that the two blocks are identical. If they are, the prompt will simply return with no indication. If they are not, the address in the original block where the discrepency occurs will be printed, followed by a dash, the value there, and the value in the second block in parentheses.

An address followed by a G will jump to the address and start running a machine language program. The monitor treats this like a subroutine, so if it finishes with an RTS (code 60) you will come back to the monitor when the program is done.

An address followed by an L will display a screen full of lines, each of which contains; an address, a dash, the value stored there (if it is an instruction that assumes data follows, the value of that data will also be there separated by a space), and a disassembly of the instruction. This means that the monitor prints the abbreviated English description of what the instruction means. This is exactly the opposite of what an assembler does, so it is a dis-assembly. Typing L and RETURN without an address will display from the current pointer. The pointer is updated.

The monitor can also be called a mini assembler. It is called by typing F666G. The assembler actually resides in the Integer BASIC ROM, so if you have Applesoft in ROM you will not have this feature unless you get it in another software package.

An address, a colon, and a valid instruction mneumonic will return the address, a dash, the hex values of the bytes that make up the instruction, and the mneumonic. The bytes are written to the indicated address, and the pointer is updated. Larger assemblers will allow you to assign labels to memory locations and refer to the label instead of the addresses, but this one doesn't, so it is called a mini assembler. It is still quite useful.

An address and the S command will cause a single pair of lines to appear that are identical to the lines generated in Fig. 6-4. The address, command in hex, and disassembly are on the first line, and the registers and their values in hex are on the second line. The S by itself will execute the instruction at the pointer. The instruction is actually performed, and the pointer is updated after the display.

The T command will start at the indicated location or the current pointer and step continuously until a BRK (code 00) is encountered. If there is no BRK you must hit RESET to stop it.

CONTROL COMMANDS

CTRL E will display just the registers and their contents. A colon followed by five hex values, separated by spaces, will change the values in the registers to their respective values on the line you type. You can stop short of changing all five, but if you want to change the S register you must retype the value that is presently in the four registers before it. Example:

A=FF X=FF Y=FF P=00 S=F8
*:00 00
CTRL E
A=00 X=00 Y=FF P=00 S=F8
*:00 00 FF 00 01
CTRL E
A=00 X=00 Y=FF P=00 S=01

CTRL B will put you into BASIC with all pointers reset and variable tables cleared.

CTRL C will return you to BASIC with pointers and variables intact.

CTRL P will direct the monitor output to the indicated slot for printer output. Format is (slot number) CTRL P. Slot number 0 will return it to the video.

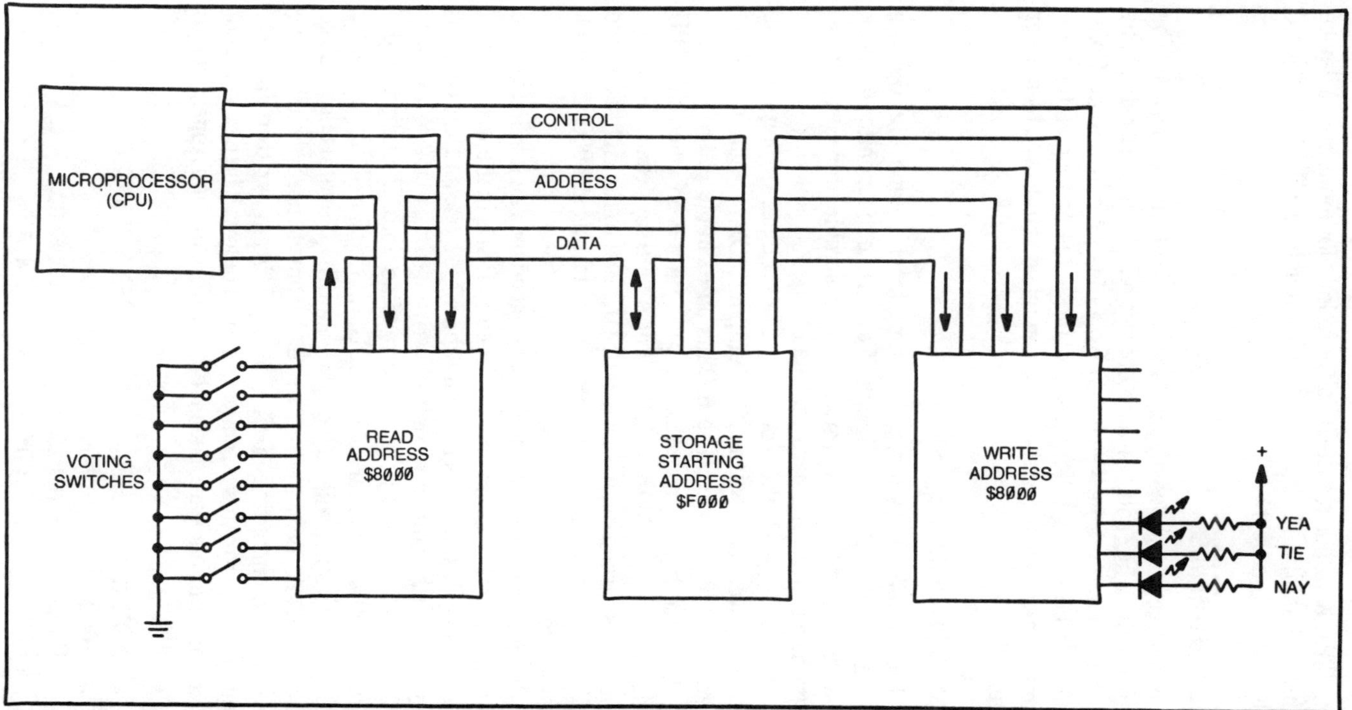

Fig. 6-5. Block diagram of a computer set up as a dedicated voting machine.

CTRL K will direct the monitor to look for input from a device in the slot indicated. Format is (slot number) CTRL K. Slot 0 returns it to the keyboard.

OTHER COMMANDS

I inverses the video display, and N will return it to normal. The monitor will do hex addition and subtraction with no carry simply by typing the numbers in, separated by a plus or minus sign. Commands can be strung together on a single line as long as they are separated by spaces, and the store command is followed by a letter command.

AN EXAMPLE PROGRAM

Figure 6-5 shows a simple voting machine and Fig. 6-6 is a flowchart for the tallying program. We will use the monitor to check our work and step through it, and the assembler for entry of the program, but first, the hardware has to be explained.

Unlike Fig. 6-2, this computer has no input or output block. Some computers achieve input and output (I/O) through a technique called memory mapping. The 6502 is an example of this.

A device has been made that gets turned on when the CPU sends out address 8000 hex. If the control line says read, the device to the left is turned on, if it says write the one to the right is turned on. The program is stored in the memory starting at F000, the block in the middle.

Each bit in the byte at 8000 is replaced by a switch in the read unit and the first three bits are replaced by LEDs in the write unit. If the switch is closed in the read unit the bit is a one and it is counted as a yes vote (the software could be written to count it as a no just as easily, and an open switch is a zero or no vote. Writing 1 to the address 8000 will turn on the nay LED, writing 2 will turn on the tie LED, and writing 4 will turn on the yea LED. Several consecutive addresses could be wired up to read from if more switches are needed. A commented listing of a program written in 6502 mneumonics to run this machine is shown below. The hex values of the instruction codes are also given. Use Fig. 6-6 and Appendix F to follow along.

```
ADDR.    HEX        MNEUMONIC
F000     A9 00      LDA #0
F002     8D 25 F0   STA $F025
F005     A2 08      LDX #8
```

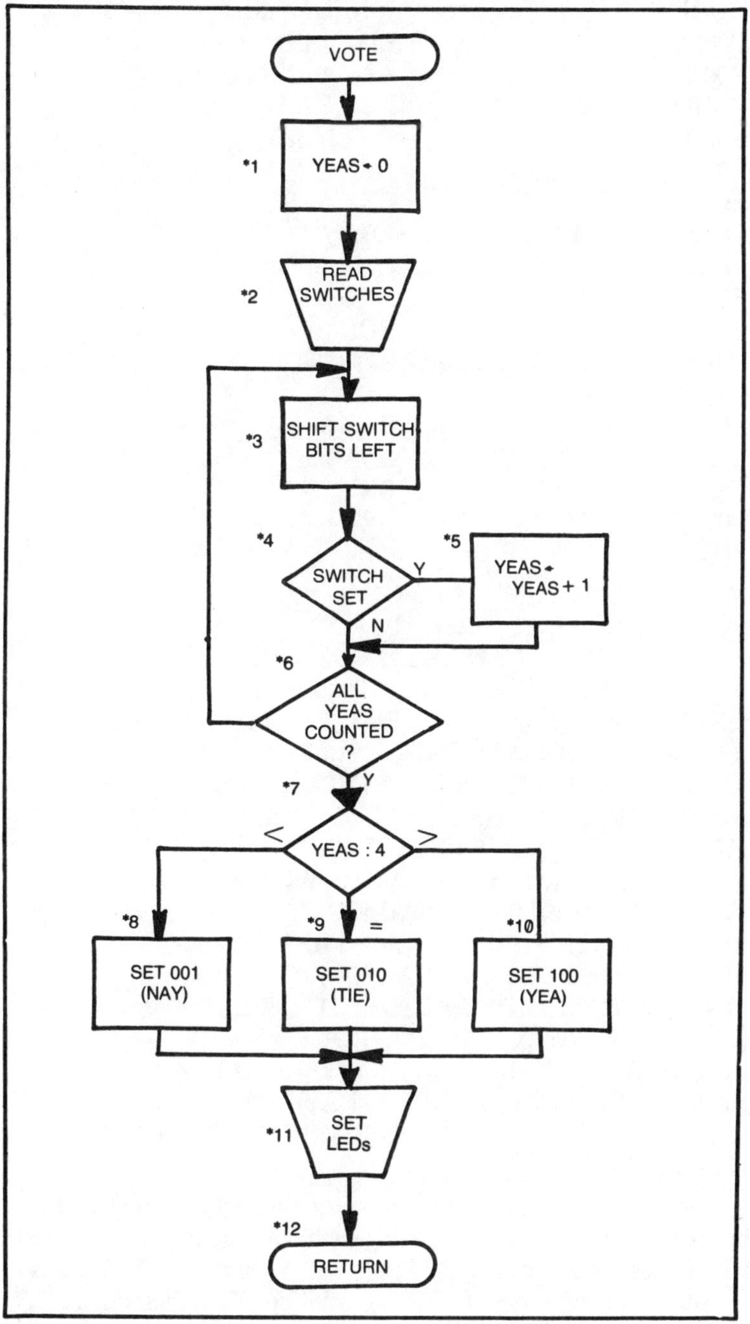

Fig. 6-6. Flowchart of program for voting machine.

ADDR.	HEX	MNEUMONIC
F007	AD 00 80	LDA $8000
F00A	0A	ASL A
F00B	90 03	BCC $+3
F00D	EE 25 F0	INC $F025
F010	CA	DEX
F011	D0 F7	BNE $–9
F013	A9 04	LDA #4
F015	CD 25 F0	CMP $F025
F018	D0 05	BNE $+5
F01A	6A	ROR A
F01B	8D 00 80	STA $8000
F01E	60	RTS
F01F	90 FA	BCS $–6
F021	A9 01	LDA #1
F023	D0 F6	BNE $–A
F025	00	BRK

```
COMMENT
;ZERO THE ACCUMULATOR
;AND STORE IT AT F025   *1
;LOAD X WITH 8. IT WILL BE COUNTER
;LOAD A WITH THE BYTE AT 8000 HEX   *2
;SHIFT LEFT INTO CARRY. FILL WITH 0   *3
;IF CARRY=0 BRANCH PAST TALLY   *4
;OTHERWISE INCREMENT THE TALLY   *5
;DECREMENT REG. X
;AND JUMP BACK 9 IF IT ISN'T 0   *6
;WHEN DONE TALLYING LOAD A WITH 4
;AND COMPARE IT WITH TALLY   *7
;IF THEY AREN'T EQUAL JUMP PAST TIE   *9
;IF THEY TIE PUT 2 INTO A   *9
;AND WRITE IT OUT TO LED   *11
;THEN RETURN TO CALLING ROUTINE   *12
;IF CARRY SET TALLY >4. A=4 (YEA) SO JUMP   *10
;OTHERWISE LOAD A WITH 1 (NAY)   *8
;WHICH SETS N SO YOU CAN JUMP TO OUTPUT   *8
;TALLY STORAGE BYTE
```

If you are going to use the monitor simply type F000: and the bytes listed under hex, separating each byte (a pair of hex digits) with a space, and pressing RETURN when you are finished. To use the mini-assembler type F666G to call it up. Then type F000:LDA #0, and press RETURN. The assembler should return the address followed by the hex code and mneumonic. Do not type in the comments.

Using the assembler, each successive mneumonic command can be entered just by typing the command. When you are finished, return to the monitor by typing $F069G and pressing RETURN.

List the program by typing F000L and check it against the listing above. Next type F000S to step through the routine and see that it is doing what it should. At F00B it should jump to F010 if the carry bit isn't set in register P. Use the guide in Appendix F to determine which is the carry bit.

At F011 the program should jump back to F00A if X is not 0. At F018 the jump should be to F01F if the N bit is set in register P. F01F should jump to F01B if the C bit is set in P. F021 should set the N bit so that F023 always jumps to F01B.

You may quit stepping at any time and examine F025 by simply typing that address and pressing RETURN. After the monitor returns the prompt you can continue stepping where you left off just by typing S and RETURN.

Try loading address 8000 with different values before stepping. These will simulate different switch settings. Examining 8000 when the program is done will show if the program works. When you are satisfied, save it to tape.

Chapter 7
Other Languages

Most home computer systems are factory programmed in BASIC, and while this is the most used computer language for home use, there are others . . . many others . . . COBOL, LISP, FORTRAN, and PL/1 just to name few. To better understand the various computer languages, and to enable you to select the one(s) best suited to your own application, let's take a look at some of the more popular languages available for the Apple II home computer.

The Apple Language system provides Apple users with the powerful Pascal language, as well as both the Integer and Applesoft BASIC interpreters. It does this by means of the language card, which provides an extra 16K of RAM memory by side-stepping the ROM firmware built into each Apple II. This technique gives Apple II owners access to all available languages, as well as to the hardware needed to run future language processors as they appear.

PASCAL

Pascal has always been a computer language with great promise and potential, and the Apple Pascal system is intended to run on the Apple II and Apple II-Plus computers. The system requires 48K bytes of installed memory, one or more Apple Disk II disk drives and the Apple Language System.

The Apple Pascal system includes a Filer for handling disk files, a powerful text Editor for writing programs, a Pascal Compiler to convert your programs into executable P-code, a 6502 Assembler to convert assembly language routines into machine language code, and a Linker to combine other routines into your program.

The Apple Pascal operating system always uses a display that is 80 characters wide. The Apple's 40 character screen normally shows only the left-most 40 characters (the left page) of the Pascal display, which is sufficient for most applications. To see the right-most 40 characters (the right page) of the display, type A while holding down the CTRL key. Press this key again to go back to the left page of the display. When the white square cursor is on the screen, you can make the Apple screen scroll right and left to follow the cursor automatically, by pressing CTRL-Z. CTRL-A (like many other commands) cancels CTRL-Z.

At most times you will see a *prompt line* which shows the command options available to you at the moment. Here are 2 examples:

COMMAND: E(DIT, R(UN, F(ILE, C(OMP, L(IN
K, X(ECUTE, A(SSEM, D(EBUG,?

In response to this prompt line, you can use the Editor, Run a program, operate the Filer, or choose any of several other options, just by typing a single letter. Typing E, for example, will invoke the Editor.

When you do invoke the Editor (or exercise almost any of the other options), you will usually be shown another prompt line that allows you to choose command options appropriate to that activity. The command tree shown in Fig. 7-1 will help you find your way around in the various levels of the operating system.

Sometimes the prompt line contains too many options to fit on the screen's two 40 character pages. If this happens, a question mark (?) may appear at the end of the prompt line. Whether or not the ? appears in the prompt line, typing ? will cause any remaining command options to be displayed.

On some occasions, you will have to type a name or other information longer than a single character. These entries are terminated by pressing the RETURN key. If you make a typing mistake before pressing the RETURN key, you can backspace over the error by pressing the backspace key (left-pointing arrow key) near the right side of the keyboard. Typing a CTRL-X will erase all the characters you have just typed. On a terminal such as the Soroc IQ 120, a RUB key may do this quick-erase. If you wish to get rid of the question altogether, just press the RETURN key.

The system Apple diskfile is needed for the first stage of a "cold boot" of the system.

The system is cold booted every time the Apple's power is turned on, or when the H(alt option is selected from the COM-

MAND prompt line. The file SYSTEM.APPLE contains the interpreter, which allows compiled P-code to be executed by Apple's 6502 processor. The interpreter is loaded into the Language Card's memory, and write-protected there. It does not have to be re-loaded until the next cold boot of the system. This file is normally found on diskette APPLE1: and also on diskette APPLE3; so either of those diskettes may be placed in the boot drive to begin a cold boot.

The following diskfiles are needed to *complete* a cold boot of the system, or to effect a warm boot of the system:

SYSTEM.PASCAL	(in the boot drive; required)
SYSTEM.MISCINFO	(in the boot drive; required)

The system is warm booted when the Apple's RESET key is pressed, when the I(nitialize option is selected from the COMMAND prompt line, or when any system error causes the system to be re-initialized (rebooted). These two files are normally found on diskette APPLE0: and also on diskette APPLE1:, so either of these diskettes may be placed in the boot drive to effect a warm boot, or to complete a cold boot. The diskette which supplies these two files becomes the system's boot diskette.

In general then, it is easiest to cold boot any system with diskette APPLE1: in the boot drive. Once this cold boot is complete, one drive users may wish to switch to APPLE0: as their system diskette, by placing APPLE0: in the boot drive and pressing the RESET key. A warm boot may be carried out if either diskette APPLE0: or diskette APPLE1: is in the boot drive.

Note: If Apple3: is used to start a cold boot, no message appears on the screen. When all action ceases, put APPLE0: or APPLE1: in the boot drive and press the RESET key to complete booting.

The Apple Pascal system makes frequent use of a "workfile". The workfile is a special default file used during the development of a program or a piece of text. You can Edit, Save and Update, Compile or Assemble, Link and Run the workfile as often as you wish, without having to specify the name of the workfile for each operation. These operations automatically assume you are referring to the workfile on the boot diskette, if there is a workfile currently stored on that diskette, and if that diskette can be found in one of the disk drives. The boot diskette is the diskette that was in the boot drive (slot 6, drive 1), the last time the system was booted.

The system always stores the workfile on the boot diskette using the filename SYSTEM.WRK. This is handy for you and the system, as it makes it easy to find the current file on which you are

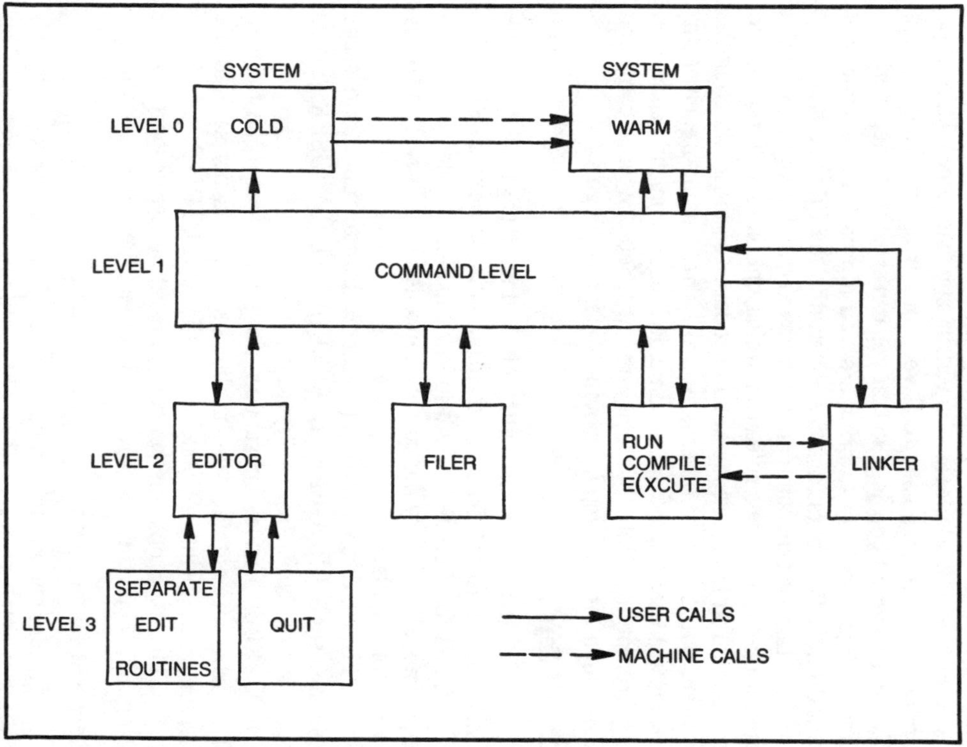

Fig. 7-1. The Command Tree. Functions at any level must terminate by stepping up to a higher level. To go between two functions on the same level requires returning to a higher level first.

working. For text, the stored workfile's full name is always SYSTEM.WRK.TEXT. For programs, the stored workfile often consists of both the text version (SYSTEM.WRK.TEXT) and the compiled or assembled version (SYSTEM.WRK.CODE) which are saved and retrieved together. Individual commands automatically use the correct version of the workfile.

It is also possible to designate any other filename as the next workfile, using the Filer's G(et command. This command removes any old files named SYSTEM.WRK from the boot diskette, but does NOT create a new file named SYSTEM.WRK. Instead, the next time any command (such as Edit, Compile, or Run) attempts to use the workfile, the file designated by G(et is used.

Only one workfile is allowed at any one time. This is no limitation, since it is easy to Save your current workfile under a filename of your choosing, so that you can create another workfile. And it is just as easy to bring a saved file back to be your new workfile. These operations are covered in the Filer section.

Certain system commands can be executed at *any* level of the operating system, regardless of which option is in force at the moment. You have already been introduced to those affecting the screen, but there are others, as well. These omni-present commands are listed below; at no time do these commands appear on any prompt line. Note that the system will detect a typed command only when the next input or output operation begins.

Control Keys

CTRL-A: Shows the other 40 character page of the Apple Pascal system's 80 character display, until the next CTRL-A.

CTRL-Z: Initiates "Auto-follow" mode; the screen scrolls right and left to follow the cursor. Cancelled by CTRL-A and many other commands.

CTRL-@: Causes current program to be interrupted and issues the message PROGRAM INTERRUPTED BY USER. Press spacebar to reinitialize the system.

CTRL-F: Causes subsequent program output to be flushed. The program continues to run, but its output is not sent to the screen or the printer. Cancelled by the next CTRL-F.

CTRL-S: Stops any on-going operating system process or program. When the next CRTL-S is typed, the process continues.

Cold and Warm Starts

Turning the Apple's power switch off and then on again does a cold boot of the system, just as if the system were being turned on for the first time. This command will stop any on-going process, at the expense of losing whatever is in the Apple's memory. When the system hangs (stops and does not respond to the keyboard, even when you press the RESET key), this command will re-start the system. After this command, you will have to repeat the entire normal startup procedure. The P-code interpreter is loaded into the Language Card and write-protected there, so the file SYSTEM.APPLE must be on the diskette in the boot drive. To accomplish a cold boot, one disk systems and multiple disk systems must both start with diskette APPLE1: in the boot drive. **Do not power down with the disks in the drive units!**

Pressing the Apple's Reset key does a warm boot of the system. This command will stop almost any on-going process, at the expense of losing whatever is in the Apple's memory. When the system hangs, this command will usually re-start the system. The P-code interpreter is not re-loaded into the Language Card by a warm boot, so the diskette file SYSTEM.APPLE need not be present. To accomplish a warm boot, either diskette APPLE1: or diskette APPLE0: must be in the boot drive.

The Command level of the Apple Pascal system is reached whenever you boot or reset the system (by any means), when the system reinitializes itself after a fatal run-time error, when you Q(uit the Editor, or the Filer, and when you finish C(ompiling, A(ssembling, L(inking, X(ecuting, or R(unning any utility or other program. You have already seen the COMMAND prompt line:

COMMAND: E(DIT, R(UN, F(ILE, C(OMP, L(IN
'K, X(ECUTE, A(SSEM, D(EBUG, ?

Use CTRL-A to see the right page of the prompt line. After typing a ? , the remaining Command options are shown:

COMMAND: U(SER RESTART, I(NITIALIZE, H(ALT

The Apple Pascal operating system is much too large a program to be kept entirely in the Apple's memory all the time. Besides, you use only a small part of the operating system at any given time. For this reason, the operating system is broken into several smaller portions, and these program portions are stored in separate diskfiles on the system diskettes, under filenames such as SYSTEM.FILER, SYSTEM.EDITOR, and SYSTEM.COMPILER. Each option from the COMMAND prompt line uses one or more of these special diskfiles.

Before you specify a particular Command option, you must first make sure that the diskfiles needed by that portion of the operating system are available. In most cases, the required diskfile is allowed to be on ANY diskette in any of your system's disk drives. The system just goes through the diskettes in every drive until it finds a file with the necessary filename.

The workfile (SYSTEM.WRK.TEXT and SYSTEM. WRK.CODE) and the Compiler's error-message file (SYSTEM.SYNTAX) will be found by the system ONLY if they are on the boot diskette.

The diskfiles SYSTEM.PASCAL and SYSTEM.LIBRARY are usually accessed by going directly to their positions on the diskette in the boot drive. During the booting process, the system notes the positions of these two files on the boot diskette. Thereafter, whenever the system needs either of those files, it assumes that the diskette in the boot drive still contains the needed files in exactly the same diskette positions occupied by those files during the last boot. If the system does not find the correct information at those diskette locations, the system may hang, and you will have to reboot. If you change the contents or the position of either of these files, you should RESET or I(nitialize the system to let it discover the change.

During program execution, the information in SYSTEM.LIBRARY is accessed by its boot-time position in the boot drive. During linking, however, the Linker searches for *SYSTEM.LIBRARY by name, and will find it in any drive.

The SYSTEM.PASCAL diskfile is needed each time the system attempts to return to the Command level following the termination of any option or program.

This file contains the Command level portion of the operating system. The system tries to re-enter the Command level after any program is terminated by Q(uitting any portion of the operating system, by reaching the END. of any option or any program that you are executing, or by any non-fatal execution error.

When the system attempts to return to Command level it first checks to be sure the diskette in the boot drive is the correct diskette. If the diskette is in the boot drive, but does not have SYSTEM.PASCAL in the expected diskette locations, the system may hang, and may not respond even to the RESET key. In this case, you will have to cold boot the system by turning the power off and then on again, with diskette APPLE1: in the boot drive.

Each return to Command level must find the boot diskette in the boot drive. If a return to Command level finds the wrong diskette in the boot drive, you will be prompted:

PUT IN APPLE1:

(if APPLE1: was your boot diskette). The boot drive will start again and again, until you press RESET or put the correct boot diskette in the boot drive.

The file SYSTEM.PASCAL in normally found on diskette APPLE0: and also on diskette APPLE1: . However, you must stick with one or the other (the one which is your boot diskette) when leaving the Command level and returning to it. To change from using one of these diskettes to the other as your boot diskette, you should place the new diskette in the boot drive and press the Apple's RESET key to re-boot. You should also re-boot the system any time you move the file SYSTEM.PASCAL on your system diskette. Re-booting lets the system discover the new boot-diskette's name, and also discover SYSTEM.PASCAL's new diskette location.

The following table summarizes the diskfiles needed by various command options:

COMMAND	FILES NEEDED	WHERE FILES MUST BE FOUND
F(ile	SYSTEM.FILER	(any disk, any drive; needed only at start)
	Files to be moved	(any disks, any drives; T(ransfer requires source file to be present; can prompt for destination file)
E(dit	SYSTEM.EDITOR	(any disk, any drive)
	Textfile to be Edited	(any disk, any drive; optional; default boot disk's SYSTEM. WRK. TEXT,)
C(ompile	SYSTEM.COMPILER	(any disk, any drive;
	Textfile to be Compiled	any drive; default is boot disk's SYSTEM.WRK.TEXT,)
	SYSTEM.LIBRARY	(boot disk, boot drive; required only if program USES Intrinsic Units)
	SYSTEM.EDITOR	(any disk, any drive; optional; to

COMMAND	FILES NEEDED	WHERE FILES MUST BE FOUND
		fix errors found by Compiler)
	SYSTEM.SYNYAX	(boot disk, optional; provides error messges on entering Editor)
A(ssemble	SYSTEM.ASSMBLER	(any disk, any drive)
	6500.OPCODES	(any disk, any drive; required)
	6500.ERRORS	(any disk, any drive; optional; provides error messages in Assembler)
	Textfile to be Assembled	(any disk, any drive; default is boot disk's SYSTEM. WRK. TEXT,)
	SYSTEM.EDITOR	(any disk, any drive; optional; to fix errors found by Assembler)
L(ink	SYSTEM.LINKER	(any disk, any drive; needed only to start)
	Host Codefile	(any disk, any drive; default is boot disk's SYSTEM, WRK. CODE,)
	Library Codefile	(any disk, any drive; default is boot disk's SYSTEM.LIBRARY)
X(ecute	Codefile to be eXecuted	(any disk, any drive; required only when loading, if no segment overlays)
	SYSTEM.LIBRARY	(boot disk, Boot drive; required if the program uses long integers, does file I/O using reals or SEEK, or USES Intrinsic Units)

COMMAND	FILES NEEDED	WHERE FILES MUST BE FOUND
	SYSTEM.CHARSET	(any disk, any drive; required if WCHAR or WSTRING called from TURTLEGRAPHICS)
R(un	Text or Codefile to be Run	(any disk, any drive; default is boot disk's SYSTEM.WRK. CODE or .TEXT)
	SYSTEM.COMPILER	(any disk, any drive; required only if file being Run is a Textfile)
	SYSTEM.EDITOR	(any disk, any drive; optional; to fix errors found by Compiler)
	SYSTEM. SYNTAX	(boot disk, optional; provides error messages on entering Editor)
	SYSTEM.LINKER	(any disk, any drive; required only if other routines need to be Linked in) (no Link needed to USE Intrinsic Units)
	SYSTEM.LIBRARY	(boot disk, required to hold needed routines if Linker called)
	SYSTEM.LIBRARY	(boot disk, boot drive; required if program uses long integers, does file I/O using reals or SEEK, or USES Intrinsic Units)
	SYSTEM.PASCAL	(boot disk, boot drive; required between Compiling, Linking, and eXecuting.

COMMAND	FILES NEEDED	WHERE FILES MUST BE FOUND
	SYSTEM.CHARSET	(any disk, any drive; required only if program uses WCHAR or WSTRING from TURTLEGRAPHICS)
U(ser restart	All files needed by last program or option	(same file locations required by last program or option)
I(nitialize	SYSTEM.PASCAL SYSTEM.MISCINFO	(any disk, boot drive; this disk becomes the new boot disk)
H(alt	SYSTEM.APPLE	(any disk, boot drive; first stage boot)
	SYSTEM.PASCAL	(any disk, boot drive; this disk
	SYSTEM.MISCINFO	becomes the new boot disk)
Return to Command Level	SYSTEM.PASCAL	(boot disk, boot drive)

The boot drive is called volume #4 by Pascal (slot 6, drive 1). The boot disk is the diskette that was in the boot drive the last time the system was booted (usually APPLE0: on one-drive systems, and APPLE1: on larger systems).

Here is where the system files needed by the Command level are normally found:

Diskette APPLE0:	Diskette APPLE1:	Diskette APPLE2:
	SYSTEM.APPLE	SYSTEM.COMPILER
SYSTEM.PASCAL	SYSTEM.PASCAL	
SYSTEM.MISCINFO	SYSTEM.MISCINFO	SYSTEM.LINKER
SYSTEM.COMPILER		SYSTEM.ASSMBLER
SYSTEM.EDITOR	SYSTEM.EDITOR	6500-OPCODES
SYSTEM.FILER	SYSTEM.FILER	6500-ERRORS
SYSTEM.LIBRARY	SYSTEM.LIBRARY	
SYSTEM.CHARSET	SYSTEM.CHARSET	
SYSTEM.SYNTAX	SYSTEM.SYNTAX	

As you can see, there is little difference between diskettes APPLE0: and APPLE1: . Diskette APPLE0: is more convenient for editing and running Pascal programs, especially on one-drive systems, because it contains the file SYSTEM.COMPILER . However,

APPLE0: cannot be used to cold-boot the system, as it is lacking the file SYSTEM.APPLE . Diskette APPLE1: contains all the files you need for editing text, and for cold-booting the system. However, APPLE1: cannot be used to R(un or C(ompile your text, as it is lacking the file SYSTEM.COMPILER . On multiple-drive systems, APPLE1: is often kept in the boot drive and APPLE2: in another drive, thus making all of the operating system available at all times. On single drive systems, cold boot with APPLE1, the warm boot with APPLE0.

Most system files must be available in one of the disk drives constantly, from the moment you select the Command option using that file until you Quit that option or until it terminates. This is true of the E(dit, C(ompile, and A(ssemble options. These programs are "overlaid", using segment procedures, so that different portions of the program are called in from disk as they are needed, to conserve memory. In such cases, if your system has only one disk drive you should use the Filer to T(ransfer all the necessary files to one diskette (usually the system diskette, APPLE0: or APPLE1:) before you select that option. Files containing non-overlayed programs are needed only at the moment the program is loaded into the Apple's memory. Once they have begun execution, the source diskette may be removed from its drive.

The F(ile Command and L(ink Command options have been purposely written without overlaying. The file SYSTEM.FILER is needed at the moment you select the F(ile option, but not subsequently. You should make sure a diskette containing SYSTEM.FILER is in one of the disk drives when you select the F(ile option, but as soon as the new Filer prompt line appears you may remove that diskette and put in any other.

Any time the Linker is invoked, SYSTEM.LINKER must be available. However, when the LINKER prompt line appears, SYSTEM.LINKER is no longer necessary and the diskette containing SYSTEM.LINKER may be removed from the system to make room for other diskettes.

The Command Line

Many of the Command options are explained only briefly below. The paragraphs on the Filer, the Editor, the Compiler, the Assembler, and the Linker discuss individual Command options in much greater detail.

F(ile: Typing F from Command level places you in a level of the system called the Filer. The Filer contains commands for saving, reading, moving and deleting the workfile and other disk files. Other commands tell you what peripheral devices and diskettes are currently available to the system, and what files are saved on each diskette. Still other commands let you check diskettes for damage of recording errors, and let you set the system's current date and the default volume name. For more documentation, see the Filer Section.

E(dit: Typing E while at the Command level invokes the Editor program. If a workfile is available, that file is automatically read into the computer for editing. Otherwise, the Editor asks you to specify a textfile or begin creating a new one. While in the Editor, you may create or alter text in the workfile or in any textfile. Various commands allow you to insert and delete information, find and replace specified character strings, change the text format, combine files, etc. On leaving the Editor, you may save your edited text in the updated workfile or in another specified file. See the Editor Section for details.

C(ompile: Typing C while at the Command level invokes the system Compiler. If a text workfile is available, that file is automatically read into the computer for compiling. Otherwise, the Compiler asks you to specify a source textfile and an object codefile. During compilation, if the Compiler detects a syntax error, it gives you the option of calling the Editor, which points out the error and lets you correct it. After a successful compilation, the resulting P-code is saved in the code workfile unless you have previously specified another object codefile. For most details, see the Pascal Compiler Section.

A(ssemble: Typing A from the Command level invokes the 6502 Assembler program. If a text workfile is available, that file is automatically read into the computer for assembling. Otherwise, the Assembler asks you to specify a source textfile and an object codefile. During assembly, if the Assembler detects a syntax error, it gives you the option of calling the Editor, which points out the error and lets you correct it. After a successful assembly, the resulting machine code is saved in the code workfile unless you have previously specified another object codefile. For more information, see the Assembler Section.

L(ink: Typing L from the Command level starts the system Linker program explicity. Unlike the automatic linking initiated by the R(un command (see description below), this option allows you to link previously compiled or assembled routines into your program, taking those routines from SYSTEM.LIBRARY or any other specified library file. For more information, see the Linker Section.

X(ecute: After typing X from the Command level, the system asks you to specify a previously compiled codefile:

EXECUTE WHAT FILE?

You should respond by typing the filename of the compiled P-coded program that you wish to be executed. It is not necessary to type the suffix. CODE. That suffix is automatically supplied by the system if you don't type it. If you wish to defeat this feature, in order to execute a program whose filename does not have a .CODE suffix, type a period (.) after the last character of the desired filename. When you have specified a codefile, that file is executed if it is available, except in the following cases:

1) If all code necessary to execute the Pascal codefile has not yet been linked in, or if the file is an unlinked assembly codefile, the message:

MUST L(INK FIRST

is displayed (see L(ink, above). You are immediately returned to the Command level, where you may carry out the necessary linking process before executing the linked file.

2) If the specified file contains anything other than the expected compiled P-code, (for example, text or linked assembly code) you will get a message similar to this:

MYDISK MYFILE.CODE NOT CODE

3) If the file SYSTEM.LIBRARY is not available in the expected diskette locations in the boot drive, or if the file is not complete, you may be shown the message:

REQUIRED INTRINSIC(S) NOT AVAILABLE

This indicates that the program you are executing uses Units or routines normally found in the file SYSTEM.LIBRARY. These include routines for long integers, random numbers, transcendental functions, game paddles, graphics, and file input and output using real numbers or SEEK.

4) If the file SYSTEM.CHARSET is not available on the boot diskette, a program using WCHAR or WSTRING from the Unit TURTLEGRAPHICS will be executed, but no characters will appear on the screen.

It is convenient to X(ecute programs which have already been compiled, but which are not currently in the workfile. Otherwise, you would have to enter the Filer, G(et the file (this identifies it as the next workfile), Q(uit the Filer, and then R(un the program.

The most common operating system functions can be selected directly from the prompt lines. Functions used more rarely are supplied as utility programs, which are available through the X(ecute command. By X(ecuting these utilities, you can format new diskettes, place compiled or assembled routines in the system library, configure your system to run with an external terminal, etc.

R(un: Typing R from the Command level initiates the R(un sequence, which combines the Command options C(ompile, L(ink, and X(ecute, as needed. If a code workfile is available, that file is automatically executed. Otherwise, the Compiler is automatically called as described above. If the compilation requires linkage to other routines, the Linker is automatically invoked and looks for the routines only in the file SYSTEM.LIBRARY on the boot diskette. After successful compilation and linking (if those were necessary), the program is executed. See the descriptions of the options C(ompile, L(ink, and X(ecute for more details. Note: Between any two portions of the R(un sequence, the system returns for an instant to the Command level. Thus the boot diskette must normally remain in the boot drive throughout the R(un sequence.

The R(un option is one part of the normal program-development process. Initially, the E(dit option is used to create the first executable portion of a new program. When this portion seems complete, it is saved in the workfile. Then, the R(un option attempts to compile the workfile and, if successful, to execute the compiled program. To expand the program or to correct compilation errors, you go back to the E(dit option. Then the workfile is U(pdated to contain this new version, and you can R(un the workfile again. And so on.

D(ebug: The D(ebug prompt does not correspond to a currently implemented command. The Compiler is called, but no debugging routines are available. Do not use this command.

U(ser Restart: Typing U from the Command level tells the system to begin executing again the last program or option which was executed. For example, if you have just Quit the Editor the U(ser restart option will reinvoke the Editor; if you have just finished executing a Pascal program, that program will be executed again.

I(nitialize: Typing I from the Command level has nearly the same effect as pressing the Apple's RESET key. The system is re-started, and everything in memory is lost, but the P-code interpreter is not re-loaded into the Language Card, so the diskette file SYSTEM.APPLE need not be present. Either diskette

APPLE1: or diskette APPLE0: must be in the boot drive. I(nitializing is a little faster than the warm boot caused by RESET and the P(refix diskette name is not forgotten as it is when RESET IS PRESSED.

H(alt: Typing H from the Command level does a cold boot of the system, just as if the system were being turned on for the first time. The P-code interpreter is loaded into the Language Card and write-protected there, so the file SYSTEM.APPLE must be on the diskette in the boot drive. To accomplish this, one disk drive systems and multiple disk drive systems must both have the diskette APPLE1: in the boot drive. After the H(alt command, you will have to repeat the entire normal startup procedure.

Many of these options use the workfile. The text portion of the workfile is SYSTEM.WRK.TEXT, created on the boot diskette by the Editor's U(pdate command. The code portion of the workfile is SYSTEM.WRK.CODE, created on the boot diskette by the R(un or C(ompile options. In addition, the Filer's G(et command can be used to designate any other text and/or code file as the workfile for the next option to use.

COMMAND LINE SUMMARY

F(ile	Invokes the Filer, which is used to save, move, and retrieve information stored on diskettes.
E(dit	Invokes the Editor, which is used to create and modify text. Reads the workfile or other specified textfile into the Apple for editing.
C(ompile	Invokes the Pascal Compiler, which converts the text of a Pascal program (found in the workfile or other specified textfile) into executable P-code.
A(ssemble	Invokes the Assembler, which converts the text of an assembly language subroutine (found in the workfile or other specified textfile) into 6502 machine language.
L(ink	Combines external P-code and machine language subroutines (found in SYSTEM. LIBRARY or other specified library code file) into a Pascal host program (found in the code workfile or other specified host codefile).

X(ecute	Loads and runs the specified Pascal program codefile.
R(un	Executes the current workfile, automatically compiling and linking (from SYSTEM.LIBRARY) first, if necessary.
D(ebug	Not implemented; do not use this option.
U(ser restart	Attempts to execute again the last program or option that was executed.
I(nitialize	Does a warm boot of the system, similar to pressing the RESET key, but faster.
H(alt	Does a cold boot of the system, like turning the Apple's power off and then on again.

The Filer

The Filer portion of the Apple Pascal operating system handles most of the tasks of transferring information from one place to another. Saving information on disk, moving and deleting disk files, sending information to the computer or to the printer—these are some of the functions of the Apple Pascal Filer. The Filer is also responsible for telling you where files have been placed on the diskettes and what devices and diskettes are available for your system's use.

Type F at the Command level to enter the Filer and the following prompt is displayed:

Filer: G(ET, S(AVE, W(HAT, N(EW, L(DIR, R (EM, C(HNG, T(RANS, D(ATE, Q(UIT

or

FILER: G, S, N, L, R, C, T, D, Q

depending on the version you have.

Typing? in response to this prompt displays more Filer commands:

FILER: B(AD-BLKS, E(XT-DIR, K(RNCH, M(AKE,
P(REFIX, V(CLS, X(AMINE, Z(ERO

or

FILER: W, B, E, K, M, P, V, X, Z

The letters and numbers enclosed in brackets which frequently appear at the end of prompt lines indicate the version number of the portion of the program with which you are working.

An individual Filer command is invoked by typing the first letter or the command option as it appears in the prompt line. For example, typing S would invoke the Save command.

In the Filer, answering a Yes/No question with any character other than Y constitutes a No answer. With most questions, pressing the RETURN key as your only response will terminate that command and return you to the outer level of the Filer.

For each command requiring a file specification, refer to the file specification diagram earlier in this chapter. In many cases, the entire file specification is not necessary, and in some cases, certain parts of the file specification are not valid. Terminate the specification by pressing the RETURN key. See the required command in the following section for more details.

Whenever a Filer command requests a file specification, you may specify as many files as desired, by separating the file specifications with commas, and terminating this file list by pressing the RETURN key. Commands operating on single filenames will keep reading filenames from the file list and operating on them until there are none left. Commands operating on two filenames (such as L(ist-directory, C(hange, and T(ransfer) will take file specifications in pairs and operate on each pair until only one or none remains. If one filename remains, the Filer will prompt for the second member of the pair. If an error is detected at any point in the list, the remainder of the list will be discarded.

The Filer

GENERAL FILE-MOVING COMMAND
T(ransfer or copy a file

GENERAL DISKFILE COMMANDS
M(ake
C(hange
R(emove
K(runch
Z(ero

WORKFILE COMMANDS
G(et
S(ave
N(ew
W(hat

INFORMATION COMMANDS
V(olumes
L(ist directory
E(xtended directory list

DISK UPKEEP COMMANDS
B(ad blocks
X(amine

MISCELLANEOUS COMMANDS
P(refix
D(ate
Q(uit

T(ransfer: Copies the specified file to the given destination. This command requires that you type two file specifications, one for the source file and one for the destination file, separated with either a comma or a RETURN. Wildcards are permitted, and size specification information is recognized for the destination file.

The source device or diskette must be available (the source diskette must be in one of the disk drives) when the Filer reads your source-file specification, but a destination diskette may be inserted later, in response to a prompting message.

Note: Do not attempt to transfer information between different diskettes having the same volume name. Instead, C(hange the name of one of the diskettes, at least for the duration of the transfer.

Suppose you wish to transfer the file FARKLE.TEXT from the diskette named MYDISK: to the diskette named BACKUP:.

Prompt: TRANSFER WHAT FILE? or TRANSFER?

Response: MYDISK:FARKLE.TEXT

When you press the RETURN key, the system checks to be sure that the specified source diskette is in one of the disk drives. If MYDISK: is not in any drive, you will see the message

MYDISK: FARKLE.TEXT
NO SUCH VOL ON-LINE (SOURCE)

If the source diskette is found in a drive, the system then checks to be sure the specified file is on that diskette. If the diskette MYDISK: is in a drive, but it has no file named FARKLE.TEXT , you will see the message

MYDISK:FARKLE.TEXT
FILE NOT FOUND (SOURCE)

In either case, you will be returned to the outer Filer level. Just insert the correct source diskette in any drive and type T again.

However, let's assume the system succeeds in finding the source diskette and file. The dialogue continues, asking you to specify the destination for the transfer:

TO WHERE?
BACKUP: NAME.TEXT

When you press the RETURN key, the system checks to be sure the destination diskette is in a disk drive. If it is, the transfer begins. If it is not, there is a pause, and then you will be prompted

PUT IN BACKUP:
TYPE (SPACE) TO CONTINUE

Put the correct destination diskette in any available drive and press the spacebar. On two-drive systems, you will normally put the source diskette in one drive and the destination diskette in the other drive. On one-drive systems, you will have to remove the source diskette from the disk drive, and then put the destination diskette in the drive.

IMPORTANT: On a single-drive system, DO NOT remove your source diskette until you are prompted to insert the destination diskette.

If the specified file is large, you may have to switch the source and destination diskettes several times, until the transfer is completed. Just follow the prompting messages.

When the transfer is complete, the Filer will give you the message

MYDISK:FARKLE.TEXT
--) BACKUP:NAME.TEXT

The Filer has made a copy of FARKLE.TEXT as found on the diskette named MYDISK: , and has stored that copy on the diskette BACKUP: under the filename NAME.TEXT .

Note: Once the Filer has been summoned, it resides entirely in the computer's memory. On a one-drive system, you can summon the Filer and then remove the system diskette from the drive in order to insert the source diskette for the Transfer. On a two-drive system, you can summon the Filer, and then remove all system diskettes from the drives in order to use both drives for source and destination diskettes during a transfer. This will save you much unnecessary switching of diskettes when copying a large file. Just remember to replace the system diskette in the boot drive before Quitting the Filer.

It is often convenient to transfer a file to another diskette without changing its filename. To make this easier, the Filer lets you use the dollar-sign character ($) as a shorthand for same name, to replace the filename in the destination file specification. In the above example, if you had wished to save the file FARKLE.TEXT on diskette BACKUP: under the same filename FARKLE.TEXT, you could have typed:

MYDISK:FARKLE.TEXT,BACKUP:$

The Editor

The Screen-Oriented Editor is specifically designed for use with video displays such as the Apple's TV or monitor. On entering any file, The Editor displays the start of the file on the second line of the screen. If the file is too long for the screen, only the first portion is displayed. This is the concept of a window. The whole file is there and is accessible by Editor commands, but only a portion of the file can be seen through the window of the screen. When any Editor command would take you to a position in the file which is not displayed, the window is moved to show that portion of the file.

The Apple Pascal Editor uses a text window that is 80 characters wide. On the Apple's TV or monitor, only the leftmost 40 characters of the window are normally displayed. To see the rightmost 40 characters of the window at any time, just press CTRL-A. Frequently, the right half of the window is just black, as there is no text to display there. Pressing CTRL-A again shifts you back to the left half of the window.

You can also make the display scroll to the right and left, by pressing CTRL-Z. In the CTRL-Z mode, the display follows the cursor everywhere it goes. As the cursor moves, the display is automatically adjusted to show the text surrounding the cursor. CTRL-Z is cancelled by CTRL-A and by many other commands.

Most programs will not require you to write beyond the leftmost 40 characters. For many other text applications, you can adjust the display's right margin to column 39 (see the E(nvironment command), so that the text will be confined to the leftmost 40 characters of the window.

The Apple Pascal Compiler

The basic purpose of the Apple Pascal Compiler is to convert the text of a Pascal program into the compressed P-code version of the program. This P-code is the machine language of the pascal Pseudo-machine, or P-machine. The P-code version of your program can then be run on virtually any computer for which the P-machine interpreter has been implemented.

The compiler control options recognized by the Apple Pascal Compiler are described in the Apple Pascal Language Reference

Manual. That manual also contains a list of the error messages reported by the Apple Pascal Compiler.

The Compiler is invoked by typing C for C(ompile or R for R(un from the outermost command level of the Apple Pascal operating system. The screen immediately shows the message COMPILING . . .

The Compiler automatically compiles the boot diskette's workfile SYSTEM.WRK.TEXT or another workfile designated by the Filer's G(et command and saves the resulting code (if compilation is successful) as SYSTEM.WRK.CODE. If there is a workfile, but you do not wish to compile that file, use the Filer's N(ew command to clear away the workfile before compiling. If no workfile is available, you are prompted for a source filename:

COMPILE WHAT TEXT?

You should respond by typing the name of the text file that you wish to have compiled.

The Assembler

You may occasionally wish to write small assembly-language routines and use them within a Pascal host program to provide low-level or time-critical facilities. The Assembler (in conjunction with the Linker) meets this need. Apple Pascal's 6502 Assembler is a version of the UCSD Adaptable Assembler, specifically implemented for the 6502 microprocessor on which the Apple Computer is based. This assembler was modeled after The Last Assembler (TLA) developed at the University of Waterloo. The basic concept behind both the TLA and the UCSD Adaptable Assemblers is the use of a central machine-independent core that is common to all versions of the assembler. This central core is augmented with machine-specific code to handle the peculiarties of each individual machine.

The Assembler is invoked by typing A for A(ssemble from the outermost Command level of the Apple Pascal operating system. The screen immediately shows the message ASSEMBLING . . .

The Assembler automatically assembles the boot diskette's workfile SYSTEM.WRK.TEXT or another workfile designated by the Filer's G(et command and saves the resulting code (if assembly is successful) as SYSTEM.WRK.CODE . If no workfile is available, you are prompted for a source filename:

ASSEMBLE WHAT TEXT?

You should respond by typing the name of the text file that you wish to have assembled.

The following assembly-language routine contains an external function and an external procedure. The function is the game paddle function, and the procedure is the routine to set or clear one of the game TTL outputs. Both are provided for you, completely assembled and ready to use, in the UNIT named APPLESTUFF

The following shows the assembly-language routine, just as you might type it into the computer, using the Editor:

```
;-------------------------------------------------------------------------
;  SAMPLE MACRO POPS 16 BIT ARGUMENT
;
     .MACRO POP
     PLA
     STA %1
     PLA
     STA %1+1
     .ENDM
     .FNC PADDLE,1 ;ONE WORD OF PARAMETERS
;-------------------------------------------------------------------------
;  SAMPLE GAME PADDLE FUNTION FOR PASCAL
; (This function provided in APPLESTUFF unit.)
;
;  FUNCTION PADDLE(SELECT: INTEGER): INTEGER:
;-------------------------------------------------------------------------
   RETURN .EQU 0  ;TEMP VAR FOR RETURN ADDR
                  ; NOTE: 0..35 HEX AVAILABLE

   POP RETURN     ;SAVE PASCAL RETURN ADDR
   PLA            ;DISCARD 4 BYTES STACK BIAS
   PLA            ;( ONLY DO FOR .FUNC)
   PLA
   PLA
   PLA            ;GET LSB SELECT PARAMETER
   AND #3         ;FORCE INTO RANGE 0..3
   TAX
   PLA            ;DISCARD MSB SELECT PARAM
   LDA 0C070      ;TRIGGER PADDLES
   LDY #0         ;INIT COUNT IN Y REG
   NOP            ;COMPENSATE FIRST COUNT
   NOP

PREAD2 LDA 0C064,X  ;TEST PADDLE
       BPL DONE     ;BRANCH IF TIMER DONE
```

```
INY                ;ELSE INC Y EVERY 12 USEC
BNE PREAD2         ;LOOP UNLESS 255 EXCEEDED
DEY                ;MAKE 0 INTO 255 (MAX COUNT)
DONE   LDA #0
PHA                ;PUSH MSB OF RETURN
                    VALUE=0
TYA
PHA                ;PUSH LSB OF RETURN VALUE
LDA RETURN+1       ;RESTORE PASCAL
                    RETURN ADDR
PHA
LDA RETURN
PHA
RTS                ;AND RETURN TO
                    PASCAL CALLER
.PROC              ;TWO WORDS OF PARAMETERS
TTLOUT,2
;------------------------------------------------------------------
;  ROUTINE TO SET OR CLEAR ONE OF THE TTL I/O
   BITS
;  (This procedure provided in APPLESTUFF unit)
;
;  PROCEDURE TTLOUT(SELECT: INTEGER: DATA:
   BOOLEAN):
;------------------------------------------------------------------
RETURN  .EQU  0         ;TEMP RETURN ADDR
        POP RETURN      ;SAVE PASCAL
                         RETURN ADDRESS
                        ;POP PARAMETERS,
                         LAST FIRST
        PLA             ;GET LSB BOOLEAN
                         DATA 1=TRUE
        LSR A           ;SAVE BOOLEAN IN
                         CARRY
        PLA             ;DISCARD MSB
                         BOOLEAN DATA
        PLA             ;GET LSB SELECT
        AND #03         ;TREAT IT MOD 4
        ROL A           ;DOUBLE, ADD DATA
                         FOR INDEX
        TAY             ;PUT I/O STROBE
                         INDEX IN Y
```

```
LDA 0C058,Y          ;ACTIVATE  I/O
                      STROBE
PLA                  ;DISCARD MSB
                      SELECT PARAM
LDA RETURN+1         ;RESTORE PASCAL
                      RETURN ADDR
PHA
LDA RETURN
PHA
RTS                  ;GO BACK TO
                      PASCAL
.END                 ;END OF ASSEMBLY
```

The preceding assembly-language routine, which we saved in the diskette file named MYDISK:ASMDEMO.TEXT , can now be assembled by the Apple Pascal 6502 Assembler. From the Command level, type the letter A for A(ssemble, and a dialog similar to the following takes place:

ASSEMBLING. . .
ASSEMBLE WHAT TEXT? MYDISK:ASMDEMO
TO WHAT CODE FILE? MYDISK:ASMDEMO
6500 ASSEMBLER 11.0 (D.4)
OUTPUT FILE FOR ASSEMBLED LISTING: (CR FOR NONE)
PRINTER:

The first response tells the Assembler to take the text version of the routine from the file MYDISK:ASMDEMO.TEXT. The second response says to save the assembled code version of the routine (when the assembly is complete) in the file MYDISK: ASMDEMO.CODE. By using the same name, we have fewer filenames to remember, and most commands will automatically choose the correct version (text or code). You could have accomplished the same thing by typing a dollar sign ($) as the second response.

If the text version of the routine had beeen available in the boot diskette's workfile SYSTEM.WRK.TEXT (or another workfile designated by the Filer's G(et command), the Assembler would automatically have assembled that file and would automatically have stored the assembled code version as SYSTEM.WRK.CODE .

The last response (PRINTER:) sends the assembled listing to the printer, and lets the usual Assembler display appear on the screen. The screen display looks something like this:

```
(110380)< 0> ..............
2 BLOCKS FOR PROCEDURE CODE 9834 WORDS LEFT
( 9827 )< 13> ..........................................................................
( 9960 )< 50> .......
CURRENT MINIMUM SPACE IS 9794 WORDS
( 9787 )< 58> ..............................
CURRENT MINIMUM SPACE IS 9794 WORDS
( 9808 )< 90>
ASSEMBLY COMPLETE:   90 LINES
  0 ERRORS FLAGGED ON THIS ASSEMBLY
```

Meanwhile, the printer has been printing the assembled listing (if we had responded CONSOLE:, the assembled listing would have replaced the Assembler's usual screen display). The assembled listing appears approximately as shown below:

```
PAGE - 0
Current memory available: 10613
  0000|
  0000|                              ;-----------------------------
  0000|                              ;
  0000|                              ;SAMPLE MACRO POPS
                                      16 BIT ARGUMENT
  0000|                              ;
  0000|                              .MACRO POP
  0000|                              PLA
  0000|                              STA %1
  0000|                              PLA
  0000|                              STA %1+1
  0000|                              .ENDM
  0000|
  0000|

2 blocks for procedure code   9834 words left
```

```
PAGE - 1   PADDLE   FILE:ASMDEMO
0000|                .FUNC   PADDLE,1 ;ONE WORD OF PARAME-
                     TERS
Current memory available: 10056

  0000|                              ;-----------------------------
  0000|                              ;
  0000|                              ;SAMPLE GAME PAD-
                                      DLE FUNCTION FOR
                                      PASCAL
  0000|                              ;(This function provided in
                                     APPLESTUFF unit.)
  0000|                              ;
  0000|                              ;FUNCTION PADDLE
                                      (SELECT: INTEGER):
                                      INTEGER;
```

```
0000|                                         ;
0000|                                         ; -------------------------------
0000|  0000                                   RETURN .EQU 0 ;TEMP
                                              VAR FOR RETURN
                                              ADDR

0000|                                   ;note;0..35 hex
0000|                                    available
0000|                  POP RETURN       ;SAVE PASCAL RETURN ADDR
0000|  68      #       PLA
0001|  85 00   #       STA RETURN
0003|  68      #       PLA
0004|  85 01   #       STA RETURN+1
0006|  68              PLA              ;DISCARD 4 BYTES
                                         STACK BIAS
0007|  68              PLA              ;( ONLY DO FOR .FUNC)
0008|  68              PLA
0009|  68              PLA
000A|  68              PLA              ;GET LSB SELECT
                                         PARAMETER
000B|  29 03           AND #3           ;FORCE INTO RANGE 0..3
000D|  AA              TAX
000E|  68              PLA              ;DISCARD MSB SELECT
                                         PARAM
000F|  AD 70C0         LDA 0C070        ;TRIGGER PADDLES
0012|  A0 00           LDY #0           ;INIT COUNT IN Y REG
0014|  EA              NOP              ;COMPENSATE FIRST COUNT
0015|  EA              NOP
0016|  BD 64C0 PREAD2  LDA 0C064,X      ;TEST PADDLE
0019|  10 **           BPL DONE         ;BRANCH IF TIMER DONE
001B|  C8              INY              ;ELSE INC Y EVEY 12 USEC
001C|  D0F8            BNE PREAD 2      ;LOOP UNLESS 255
                                         EXCEEDED
001E|  88              DEY              ;MAKE 0 INTO 255
                                         (MAX COUNT)
0019*  00
001F|  A9 00   DONE    LDA #0
0021|  48              PHA              ;PUSH MSB OF RETURN
                                         VALUE=0
0022|  98              TYA
0023|  48              PHA              ;PUSH LSB OF RETURN
                                         VALUE
0024|  A5 01           LDA RETURN+1     ;RESTORE PASCAL
                                         RETURN ADDR
0026|  48              PHA
0027|  A5 00           LDA RETURN
0029|  48              PHA
002A|  60              RTS              ;AND RETURN TO PASCAL
                                         CALLER
002B|
002B|
------------------------------------------------------------------------------
PAGE - 2    PADDLE   FILE:ASMDEMO   SYMBOLTABLE DUMP

AB - Absolute       LB - Label      UD - Undefined    MC - Macro
RF - Ref            DF - Def        PR - Proc         FC - Func
PB - Public         PV - Private    CS - Consts
```

```
DONE        LB 001F|        PADDLE    FC----|       POP   MC----|
PREAD2      LB 0016|        RETURN    AB0000|
```

```
PAGE - 3     PADDLE   FILE:ASMDEMO
Current minimum space is 9794 words
```

```
PAGE - 4     TTLOUT   FILE:ASMDEMO
0000    .PROC TTLOUT,2        ;TWO WORDS OF PARAMETERS
Current memory available:  10056

0000|      ;   ---------------------------------------------------------------
0000|      ;
0000|      ;   ROUTINE TO SET OR CLEAR ONE OF THE TTL
               I/O BITS
0000|      ;   (This procedure provided in APPLESTUFF
               Unit)
0000|      ;
0000|      ;   PROCEDURE TTLOUT (SELECT: INTEGER; DATA:
               BOOLEAN);
0000|      ;

0000|  0000       RETURN .EQU   0          ;TEMP RETURN ADDR
0000|
0000|                    POP RETURN        ;SAVE PASCAL RETURN
                                            ADDRESS
0000|  68         #      PLA
0001|  85 00      #      STA RETURN
0003|  68         #      PLA
0004|  85 01      #      STA RETURN+1
0006|                                      ;POP PARAMETERS,
                                            LAST FIRST
0006|  68                PLA               ;GET LSB BOOLEAN
                                            DATA 1=TRUE
0007|  4A                LSR A             ;SAVE BOOLEAN IN
                                            CARRY
0008|  68                PLA               ;DISCARD MSB BOOLEAN
                                            DATA
0009|  68                PLA               ;GET LSB SELECT
000A|  29 03             AND #03           ;TREAT IT MOD 4
000C|  2A                ROL A             ;DOUBLE, ADD DATA
                                            FOR INDEX
000D|  A8                TAY               ;PUT I/O STROBE
                                            INDEX IN Y
000E|  B9 58C0           LDA 0C058,Y       ;ACTIVATE I/O STROBE
0011|  68                PLA               ;DISCARD MSB SELECT
                                            PARAM
0012|  A5 01             LDA RETURN+1      ;RESTORE PASCAL RETURN
                                            ADDR
0014|  48                PHA
0015|  A5 00             LDA RETURN
0017|  48                PHA
0018|  60                RTS               ;GO BACK TO PASCAL
0019|
0019|
0019|
0019|                    .END              ;END OF ASSEMBLY
```

```
PAGE - 5     TTLOUT   FILE:ASMDEMO   SYMBOLTABLE DUMP
AB - Absolute      LB - Label        UD - Undefined     MC - Macro
RF - Ref           DF - Def          PR - Proc          FC - Func
PB - Public        PV - Private      CS - Consts

POP MC ---- | RETURN   AB 0000|  TTLOUT   PR ----|
PAGE - 6    TTLOUT   FILE:ASMDEMO
Current minimum space is 9794 words
Assembly complete:       92 lines
        0 Errors flagged on this Assembly
```

Only the assembled object code from the preceding assembly listing (the second column of information on Page - 1 and on Page - 4) is saved in the file MYDISK:ASMDEMO.CODE .

NOTES about the preceding sample assembly listing:

1) The location values in the symbol table dump refer to the locations in the listing.

2) The **'s in the listing (see Page - 1 of the listing, for example) call attention to the use of a label not yet defined. The Assembler displays one * for each hexadecimal digit to be filled in later.

3) If a * appears after the location number at the left of the listing, it indicates that a forward reference occurring earlier in the assembly has been resolved. The number to the left of the * is the location where the reference occurred while the number to the right is the new contents of that location. See Page-1 of the listing, for example.

4) The Apple Pascal 6502 Assembler uses the following non-standard notation for indirect addressing:

Apple Pascal 6502 Assembler	Standard 6502 Assembler
LDA@LOC1,Y	LDA(LOC1),Y
LDA@LOC2,X	LDA (LOC2,X)
JMP@GOVECT	JMP (GOVECT)

Calling the Assembled Routine

The following is a sample Pascal program which uses the external function and procedure assembled earlier:

```
PROGRAM CALLASM;
(*DEMONSTRATES CALLING ASSEMBLY LANGUAGE
     PROCEDURES *)
VAR I: INTEGER;
PROCEDURE TTLOUT (SELECT: INTEGER; DATA: BOO-
LEAN);
```

```
  EXTERNAL;
FUNCTION PADDLE(SELECT: INTEGER): INTEGER;
  EXTERNAL;
BEGIN
        FOR I: = 1 to 1000 DO
            BEGIN
                WRITELN(PADDLE(0):3,'   ',PADDLE(1):3);
                TTLOUT(0,ODD(I))
            END
END.
```

The Linker

The Linker is invoked automatically if needed when you type R for R(un, or is invoked explicitly by typing L for L(ink, when at the outermost Command level. The Apple Pascal Linker lets you combine code files, which may be compiled P-code or assembled machine code, into the system workfile or another specified codefile. This provides a way to incorporate certain useful routines into your programs without having to rewrite or even recompile or re-assemble these routines. For example, you might wish to use a fast assembly-language routine for some "real-time" application. This routine could be assembled separately, stored in a library, and eventually accessed via the Linker.

To link in routines (either procedures or functions), a Pascal calling program declares those routines to be EXTERNAL. This notifies the Compiler that the routines may be called but are not provided yet. The Compiler will inform the system that linking is required before execution.

The linker is also used to link in certain kinds of Pascal UNITS. A UNIT is a group of related routines which will be used together to perform a common task. Any Pascal files which reference UNITS or EXTERNAL routines, and which have not yet been linked, may be compiled and saved but will need to be linked before they can be executed.

The UNITS that are provided with the Apple Pascal language, such as TURTLEGRAPHICS AND APPLESTUFF, are special INTRINSIC UNITS, which are prelinked and are USED directly from SYSTEM.LIBRARY without linking.

Utility Programs

In the Apple Pascal operating system, the most often used program portions can be selected from the various prompt lines.

Other programs, written to accomplish less commonly needed tasks, are available through the X(ecute command, and new features can be added to the operating system at any time in this way.

Map of System.Library

```
LIBRARY MAP FOR APPLE0:SYSTEM.LIBRARY
COPYRIGHT 1979 APPLE COMPUTER INC.
Segment #30:
System version = II.1, code type is 6502
LONGINTI library unit (LINKED INTRINSIC)
TYPE DECMAX = INTEGER(36);
    STUNT = RECORD CASE INTEGER OF
        2:(W2:INTEGER(4));
        3:(W3:INTEGER(8));
        4:(W4:INTEGER(12));
        5:(W5:INTEGER(16));
        6:(W6:INTEGER(20));
        7:(W7:INTEGER(24));
        8:(W8:INTEGER(28));
        9:(W9:INTEGER(32));
        10:(W10:INTEGER(36))
        END;
PROCEDURE PREADDEC(VAR F: FIB; VAR D; STUNT;
L: INTEGER);
PROCEDURE FWRITEDEC(VAR F: FIB: D: DECMAX;
RLENG: INTEGER);
--------------------------------------------------------------------
Segment #31:
System version = II.1, code type is Undefined
PASCALIO library unit (LINKED INTRINSIC)
PROCEDURE FSEEK(VAR F: FIB; RECNUM: INTEGER);
PROCEDURE FREADREAL (VAR F: FIB; VAR X: REAL);
PROCEDURE FWRITEREAL(VAR F: FIB; X: REAL; W, D:
  INTEGER);
--------------------------------------------------------------------
Segment #29:
System version = II.1, code type is P-code (most sig. 1st)
TRANSCEN library unit (LINKED INTRINSIC)
($  )
    FUNCTION SIN(X:REAL):REAL;
    FUNCTION COS(X:REAL):REAL;
    FUCNTION EXP(X:REAL):REAL;
```

```
  FUNCTION ATAN(X:REAL):REAL;
  FUNCTION LN(X:REAL):REAL;
  FUNCTION LOG(X:REAL):REAL;
  FUNCTION SQRT(X:REAL):REAL;
--------------------------------------------------------------------
Segment #22:
System version = II.1, code type is 6502
APPLESTU library unit (LINKED INTRINSIC)
($  )
  FUNCTION PADDLE (SELECT: INTEGER): INTEGER;
  FUNCTION BUTTON(SELECT: INTEGER): BOOLEAN;
  PROCEDURE TTLOUT(SELECT: INTEGER: DATA:
  BOOLEAN);
  FUNCTION KEYPRESS: BOOLEAN;
  FUNCTION RANDOM: INTEGER;
  PROCEDURE RANDOMIZE;
  PROCEDURE NOTE(PITCH, DURATION: INTEGER);

--------------------------------------------------------------------

Segment #20:
System version = II.1, code type is 6502)
TURTLEGR library unit (LINKED INTRINSIC)
TYPE
SCREENCOLOR =(none, white, black, reverse, radar,
black1,green, violet, white1,black2,orange,blue,white2);
  PROCEDURE INITTURTLE:
  PROCEDURE TURN(ANGLE: INTEGER);
  PROCEDURE TURNTO(ANGLE: INTEGER);
  PROCEDURE MOVE(DIST: INTEGER);
  PROCEDURE MOVETO(X,Y: INTEGER);
  PROCEDURE PENCOLOR(PENMODE: SCREEN-
  COLOR);
  PROCEDURE TEXTMODE;
  PROCEDURE GRAFMODE;
  PROCEDURE FILLSCREEN(FILLCOLOR: SCREEN-
  COLOR);
  PROCEDURE VIEWPORT(LEFT, RIGHT,BOTTOM,
  TOP: INTEGER);
  FUNCTION TURTLEX: INTEGER;
  FUNCTION TURTLEY: INTEGER:
  FUNCTION TURTLEANG: INTEGER;
```

```
FUNCTION SCREENBIT(X,Y: INTEGER): BOOLEAN;
PROCEDURE DRAWBLOCK(VAR SOURCE: ROWSIZE,
XSKIP,YSKIP, WIDTH, HEIGHT,XSCREEN,YSCREEN,
MODE: INTEGER);
PROCEDURE WCHAR(CH: CHAR);
PROCEDURE WSTRING(S: STRING);
PROCEDURE CHARTYPE(MODE: INTEGER);

--------------------------------------------------------------------
Segment #21:
System version = II.1, code type is P-Code (least sig. 1st)
TURTLEGR data segment
--------------------------------------------------------------------
```

The Apple Pascal Pseudo-machine, or P-machine, a version of the UCSD Pascal P-machine, is the software-generated device which executes P-code as its machine language. Every computer operating under a form of UCSD Pascal has been programmed to look like this common P-machine, from the viewpoint of a program being executed. The P-machine supports the following:

1. Variable addressing, including strings, byte arrays, packed fields, and dynamic variables
2. Logical, integer, real, set, array, and string top-of-stack arithmetic and comparisons
3. Multi-element structure comparisons
4. Several types of branches
5. Procedure and function calls and returns, including overlayable procedures
6. Miscellaneous procedures used by systems programs

The Apple Pascal system is a version of the UCSD Pascal system, which is an interpreter-based implementation of Pascal. This means that the Compiler emits code for a Pseudo-machine or P-machine which is emulated at run time by a program written in the machine language of the host. For the Apple, this P-machine emulation program is the interpreter, written in the Apple's 6502 machine language and found in the boot diskette's file SYSTEM. APPLE.

The Apple Pascal operating system and various utilities are themselves written in Pascal and run on the same interpreter. Thus the entire system can be moved to a new host machine by rewriting the interpreter for the new host. Every host computer operating under a version of UCSD Pascal has an interpreter that makes the host computer appear, from the viewpoint of a program being executed, to be this same P-machine.

APPLE PILOT

Apple PILOT is a powerful, easy to use system designed to support program development for Computer Assisted Instruction (CAI). Based on COMMON PILOT, Apple PILOT offers color graphics, sound effects, and a character set editor, allowing lessons to be presented in words, pictures and sounds.

The benefits of the Apple PILOT are many, but the following is a summary of the most significant advantages:

1. Significantly heightens students' interest and retention through its graphics, animation and sound effects capabilities.

2. Allows educators to share material in creating new and different lessons, because libraries of pictures, sounds, character sets, and PILOT routines can be saved on diskettes.

3. Gives instructors access to large libraries of material, because programs written PILOT 73 and COMMON PILOT may be run on the Apple system.

4. Provides the capability of recording both student lessons and grades on the same diskette, because the author can programmatically create files for general purpose record keeping.

5. Places no restriction on lesson length, since a single lesson may span many files and/or diskettes.

6. Helps evaluate student performance by timing individual student responses.

7. Assists in foreign language instruction, because character sets in different languages can be developed easily.

8. Allows educators to make hardcopy files of lesson text through a built-in print routine.

Apple PILOT operates in two modes—Author and Lesson. In Author Mode, the instructor/designer creates lessons and stores them on a lesson diskette. The student then uses that diskette to take a lesson, that is, interact with the computer as specified by the teacher.

In Author mode, menus and HELP screens direct and assist in creating a lesson. The main menu provides the following options:

1. Initialize a Diskette—Automatically formats a diskette and copies from the Author diskette certain required system programs and files.

2. Create/Edit PILOT Lesson Text—PILOT is a high level language particularly suited to the needs of courseware developers. It is the heart of the system. Using simple commands, the author defines the flow and logic of a lesson and integrates any previously

defined graphics, sound effects, and special characters into that lesson. The lesson can also be tested by using the RUN option.

3. Create/Edit Graphics—The author can create high-resolution color graphics to include anywhere in the lesson(s). Simple keyboard commands draw lines, circles and rectangles; or the control paddles can be used to sketch free form designs. Text may be written anywhere on the graphic screen. These pictures are stored on diskette.

4. Create/Edit Sound Effects—Music/sounds can be dynamically created and played back using simple menus and keyboard commands. The sounds are stored on diskette for inclusion in any lesson.

5. Create/Edit Character Sets—User-defined characters are simply drawn on a grid using keyboard commands or control paddles. These special characters can be associated with any Apple keyboard printing characters.

6. Copy a Lesson Diskette—Allows the author to make multiple copies of a lesson diskette for wide distribution or concurrent use by students. In Lesson Mode, the student merely inserts a lesson diskette into a disk drive and is presented with the material as specified by the author/teacher.

To use Apple PILOT, you will need the following system which includes the Apple II or Apple II Plus, with 48K of memory; One Apple DiskII drive with controller for the Lesson Mode, or two Disk II drives, one with controller, for both Author and Lesson Modes. No more than two drives are supported. Also you will need DOS 3.3 or the Apple Language System, each with 16-sector state and boot PROMS and a video monitor or television.

Optionally, if lessons are to be printed, a compatible printer and printer controller cards are required. The Apple Computer System works with several printers and appropriate controller cards, including those specified below:

a. Apple Silentype Printer
Card: Silentype Interface Card (supplied with printer)

b. Centronics
Card: Centronics Printer Interface Card (Apple Product A2B0007

c. Printronix
Card: Parallel Interface Card (Apple Product A2B0002)

d. Qume Sprint 5, Diablo Hyterm, and NEC Spinwriter 5510R
Card: High Speed Serial Interface Card (Apple Product A2B0005) with P8-02 PROM

Some of the technical specifications of the Apple PILOT include:

1. Language—Written in Pascal; however the Apple Language System is not required to run Apple PILOT.

2. Diskettes—16-sector format

3. Commands:

A: Accept
AS: Accept Single
C: Compute
D: Dimension
E: End
FI: File Input
FO: File Output
G: Graphics
J: Jump
M: Match
PR: Problem
R: Remark
T: Type
TH: Type and Hang
U: Use
XI: Execute Indirect

In addition to providing all of the COMMON PILOT commands and facilities, Apple features the following extensions:

AP:	Accepts point on graphics screen.
FIX:n,var$	Opens diskette file< van $> for input and/or output with< n> records.
FOX:n,var$	Creates new diskette file< var$> with< n'> records.
G: C n	Sets pen color to< n>.
G:ES n	Erases the graphics screen color to< n>.
G:T	Prints text at the graphic cursor position.
G:VI,r,t,b	Sets graphic viewport coordinates.
GX:name	Draws previously defined graphic image < name> onto the screen.
L:name	
L:name,label	Links to PILOT lesson< name>, optionally at the specified point< label>.
PR:T nnn	Sets accept response time in seconds.
S:p,d	Generates a sound of pitch< p> for duration < d>.
SX:name	Plays previously defined sound effect < name>.

TX:name	Types output and accepts input using previously defined character set<name>.
W:nnn	Waits nnn seconds.
X=BTN(n)	Returns push button status.
X=KEY(0)	Returns keyboard status.
X=PDL(n)	Returns control paddle position.
X=RND(0)	Returns a random number between zero and one.
X=TIM(0)	Reads accept response time.

APPLE FORTRAN

FORTRAN is a powerful programming language, especially suitable for work in mathematics, engineering and the sciences. Apple FORTRAN, usable with the Apple Language System, is the ANSI Standard Subset of the recently defined FORTRAN 77 standard; in several areas, Apple FORTRAN contains enhanced features and capabilities.

Apple is providing FORTRAN for use by technical professionals and educators who are both familiar with the FORTRAN language and are using packages written in FORTRAN. Because FORTRAN is a well established language, large quantities of FORTRAN programs are already in existence, especially for engineering and scientific applications. Apple FORTRAN provides the sophisticated FORTRAN user with the capability to develop new and modify existing FORTRAN programs on an Apple.

The user of Apple FORTRAN will see many benefits including the following list:

1. Offers enhanced features and capabilities because it supports the newest computer industry standard, ANSI X3.9-1978.

2. Operates in the Apple Language System which provides a comprehensive software design environment including an editor, linker, file handler, assembler, Apple Pascal compiler, and system library.

3. Eliminates the need to recompile or reassemble existing code files when incorporating them into FORTRAN programs; compiled P-code and assembled machine code can be combined with a FORTRAN P-code file through the Apple Language System's linker facilities.

4. Allows you to take full advantage of Apple's Hires graphics capabilities by interfacing to graphics routines in the system library.

5. Gives programmers access to large libraries of material, since FORTRAN is a familiar, well established language.

6. Provides access to special Apple features, such as sound generation and control paddles, through its system library routines.

7. Permits you to combine several source files in a single compilation through compiler directives in the source code.

A closer look at Apple FORTRAN shows that the FORTRAN 77 contains significant additions and enhancements to the previous 1966 standard. For example, mixed-mode arithmetic expressions are allowed. Structured programming is supported through expanded IF statement constructs. Logical IF, Block IF, ELSE IF, ELSE, and END IF statements provide a vastly improved method of clearly and accurately specifying the flow of program control. CHARACTER data type replaces Hollerith; alphanumeric data can be represented as strings rather than array elements.

Apple FORTRAN is the ANSI Standard Subset FORTRAN 77. It also supports enhancements and facilities from the full FORTRAN 77 language. In particular.

1. Subscript expressions may include array elements and function calls.

2. DO statement limits may be defined by expressions, rather than just single variables.

3. I/O units may be specified by expressions, rather than just constants or simple variables.

4. The I/O list of a WRITE statement may include expressions.

5. All combinations of FORMATTED/UNFORMATTED and SEQUENTIAL/DIRECT files are allowed, with these restrictions: (1) BACKSPACE is supported only for files connected to the blocked devices; it is not supported for UNFORMATTED SEQUENTIAL files; DIRECT files must be connected to block devices.

Apple FORTRAN contains a number of enhancements beyond the full FORTRAN 77 specifications. In particular:

1. Compiler directives may be included in the source code.

2. An additional parameter to the OPEN statement allows you to specify whether the file is blocked or unblocked.

There are two minor differences between the ANSI Standard Subset FORTRAN 77 and Apple FORTRAN. They are:

1. Subprogram names cannot be passed as parameters.

2. INTEGER and REAL data types have different storage requirements—two bytes for INTEGER, four bytes for REAL.

To use Apple FORTRAN, you will need the Apple II or Apple II Plus with 48K of memory, the Apple Language System, and a video monitor or television. While a single drive system is adequate for very small programs, two drives are strongly recommended for ease of operation and more serious program development.

Chapter 8
Software for the Apple II

THE CONTROLLER—SMALL BUSINESS MANAGEMENT AND ACCOUNTING

The Controller Software package is a comprehensive accounting system that enables the small business owner to manage his business more effectively, allowing better planning of payments and faster cash collection. Furthermore, it generates timely reports which allow the owner to act quickly, if necessary, on items affecting the financial health of the business. The Controller system consists of three modules:

1. Accounts Receivable
2. Accounts Payable
3. General Ledger

The Controller also offers an easy effective alternative to manual bookkeeping. In general, the Apple Controller . . .

- allows you to trace any transaction because it automatically prints audit trails . . .
- warns you of data entry errors and prompts you further instructions through audio feedback ("beeps") . . .
- identifies and monitors slow paying customers through its account aging feature . . .
- assists you in planning cash needs for expenditures, and allows you to take advantage of discounts and net terms, because it tracks accounts payable by due data . . .
- shortens bookkeeping time required to maintain accurate records, because it automatically posts and updates . . .

• reduces bookkeeping errors by eliminating redundant writing, calculating and typing, and automatically prints management summaries, detailed reports, vendor and customer lists, mailing labels, account statements, and archival copies of each month's data for historical records . . .

• assists in maintaining complete, accurate and consistent records, because it encourages the use of standard bookkeeping practices . . .

• reduces the time required to process your accounts and makes information available to you when you need it . . .

• protects you from losing important business information by automatically making a back-up copy of all operational data after posting.

Here's a brief summary of how the Controller Software operates and handles accounting needs.

The Accounts Receivable, Accounts Payable and General Ledger menus include three common options. The first of these is *Customizing Features*, a program which allows you to configure the system to your business needs; for example, whether finance charges should be calculated and at what percentage rate. The second is *Utilities*, a set of computer programs that enable you to make back-up copies of your diskettes; restore diskettes that have been damaged in some way; and determine how many entries you have made and the amount of diskette space remaining. *Change Today's Date* allows you to change the date each time you use the selected module.

Accounts Receivable (A/R) System Module

After selecting Accounts Receivable from the Controller's main menu, your screen will display the Accounts Receivable menu.

Customer Master allows you to enter your sales by batch, and print reports for proofing. Sales adjustments can also be entered at this time.

Payment Entries permits you to record payments made by your customers. Payments may be entered in batches. As with Sales Entries, adjustments can also be made at this time.

As you post, both the Sales and Payment Entries are put into summarized forms, so that they may be later transferred automatically to the General Ledger should you choose to do so. One hundred Transfer Journal Entries may be made at any time from the A/R program to the General Ledger.

Aged Trial Balance keeps track of outstanding balances, appropriately distributing them among four aging periods: current, 31-60 days, 61-90 days, and over 90 days. It also prints three different reports. The first is a Summary Report, showing customer information, account balance by aging periods, and the total amount due. The second, Detail Report, includes the same information as the Summary Report, as well as the balance forward for the month and current monthly transactions. The Monthly Activity Report details the business's total activity for the month by transaction, including sales, taxes and other amount categories. For audit purposes, the Detail Report must be printed before you can close the month.

Finance Charges is an optional feature which automatically computes, on a monthly basis, the finance charge percentages against your customer's balances. You are prevented from running Finance Charges more than once a month, and before you have posted Sales and Payment entries.

With the Accounts Receivable module, the total of finance charges, sales, or payment entries should not exceed 750 per diskette per month.

Statements generates computer-printed customer account statements. You may print up to 250 per month; the largest single balance for any one customer per aging period is $90,000.00.

Sales commissions prints a report by salesman number detailing the amounts a business owes its commissioned salespeople, based on their individual sales for the month.

Close Month initiates the procedure that ends the monthly business cycle for billing. It eliminates all detailed transactions from Accounts Receivable and transfers the totals to the balance forward amount for the next month. Outstanding Accounts Receivable are aged automatically by one month.

Accounts Payable System Module

After the Accounts Payable has been selected from the Controller's main menu, the screen will display the Accounts Payable menu.

Vendor Master allows you to create a master file of all vendors with whom you do business. The vendors may be temporary or permanent, and you may have up to 125 vendors at one time. You can add, change, examine and remove vendors from the master file, and print a Vendor Master report and vendor labels at any time.

New Invoices enables you to enter data for up to 300 invoices with distribution to twelve General Ledger accounts. The number of available invoice records is decreased for distributions more than three in number. For example, if an invoice is distributed to nine accounts, the computer will subtract three invoice records from the total available. Processing options for New Invoices include adding, changing, displaying, and removing entries. Each invoice will be assigned a voucher number and you can print a proof report at any time to double-check the data before posting.

Pay Open Invoices directs the computer to print as many as 3000 checks in any one month for all invoices with a due date less than or equal to the date you enter as Check Date. It also prints a Paid Invoices Register to keep track of all checks printed and posted. Up to 300 open invoices may be in the A/P system at any time. If you have chosen not to use the computer to print checks, this selection can still be used to post the handwritten checks.

Distribution Journal allows you to post account distributions, print a report of all invoices by the respective accounts, and create all of the entries that will be transferred to the General Ledger. Up to 100 Transfer Journal Entries may be made to the General Ledger system at any one time. You will be required to post at least once before you close the month.

Disbursement Journal is a printed report that details what checks have been written, to whom, the check date/number/amount, and any discount received. The three accounts affected by the process are: Accounts Payable and Cash in Bank, which are reduced, and Vendor Discounts Taken, which increases (if a discount for prompt payment was offered).

Close Month is the process that ends each monthly business cycle. Before you are allowed to close the month, the system will check to be sure that certain processing functions have taken place, and that the corresponding reports have been printed. The system will also require you to make back-up copies of your data diskettes before and after closing the month.

General Ledger System Module

After selecting General Ledger from the Controller's main menu, your screen will displays the General Ledger menu.

Chart of Accounts permits you to add, change, and remove accounts, as well as to print and display them on your screen. The General Ledger system can handle up to 250 accounts, with a maximum recommended balance of $90,000,000 per account. This should certainly be enough for any homeowner!

Standard Entries is reserved for those same amounts posted to the same accounts each month, such as rent. Once these are established, you need only post them as a batch once each month, eliminating the need to retype individual entries every time. You can add, change, remove, print, and post the standard entries.

Journal Entries is used to make and adjust entries to the General Ledger. Processing options include adding, changing, removing, print, and posting entries. The General Ledger system can handle up to a total of 700 Journal Entry transactions and 50 Standard Entry transactions per month.

Transfer Journals transfers data from the Accounts Receivable and Payable systems into the General Ledger.

Trial Balance may be run to determine if total debits equal total credits. It may be run any time you choose provided there are no unposted Journal Entries. The Trial Balance option will also print summarized and detailed reports.

Balance Sheet is used to present the financial health or status of a business at any specific time. It prints both summarized and detailed reports.

Income Statement details the revenues and expenses of a company over a period of time. The Income Statement is often known as "the bottom line" or the Profit and Loss statement. This program prints both a summarized and detailed report.

Close Month begins the process that ends each monthly business cycle. Before you are allowed to close the month, you will be required to complete certain processes and print specific reports. Closing the month will also initiate closing the year when the month-end and fiscal year-end dates coincide.

If you are using either or both Accounts Receivable and Accounts Payable in conjunction with the General Ledger, the items you have customized and the date you have specified must be identical within the system modules.

THE APPLE CASHIER

This system offers the small business owner a store management system which can increase profits through improved inventory control and sales entry. Using this system will enable you to increase profits through improved inventory control and sales entry. You can also create and maintain customer/vendor files; process and monitor sales; order and receive stock; check profits, inventory, and cash; and generate management reports, invoices, and quotations. The benefits of THE APPLE CASHIER Software include the following:

● Increased sales revenue and profit by reducing losses caused by theft, since only authorized personnel can access the program to change inventory and financial transaction data . . .

● Eliminate tedious, time consuming record keeping, since it allows you to expense lost items out of inventory and print expense vouchers; prepare and print purchase orders; and quickly update your inventory file, customer list, and vendor information . . .

● Allows you to easily determine your income from sales, since it automatically tallies daily, monthly and yearly cash and sales totals . . .

● Saves time and labor costs, because it processes sales and updates inventory records after each transaction . . .

● Assists you in determining your optimal inventory levels and reorder quantities, becauuse it analyzes sales rates by item and tracks changes in inventory levels . . .

● Prevents loss of sales from stockouts by prompting you to reorder when inventory levels become low . . .

● Simplifies the process of updating accounting records by automatically providing total inventory value . . .

● Increases employee productivity by allowing a clerk to check item availability and verify price without ever leaving the sales desk.

After initializing the Apple Cashier System's master diskettes, the system is ready for use. The Store Management Menu is the main menu of The Apple Cashier; it allows access to the seven main programs available in the system.

Access CREATE NEW DATA FILES to establish your inventory and/or customer master files. Preformatted screens allow you to insert appropriate information quickly and easily.

After the master files have been created, other programs may be used in the system. By selecting the DAILY TRANSACTIONS program from the Store Management Menu, sales may be processed, quotations prepared, print and record orders, receive and add new inventory to stock, expense items, and update sales and cash totals.

If the MAIN INVENTORY FILE program is accessed, new items may be added or existing products changed in the inventory file. The MAINTAIN CUSTOMER FILE program allows individual access of records in the Customer Master File. Names and addresses of new customers may be added, information on current customers may be changed, search for and locate a particular name, or delete any name wished.

To guard against the remote possibility of loss or destruction of your master diskette files, this system offers the COPY DATA FILES program which allows you to make back-up copies of your index, inventory, and customer files. You can make copies as often as they are needed.

Printing information on inventory value, turnover, backorders, item movement, and customers is accomplished by using the PRINT FILES program. There's no lengthy typing time required, since information is automatically printed quickly and letter-perfect.

If you make a system input error while using any one of the programs, the computer will stop, display an error code and, in some cases, explain the error to you. It then waits for your correction of the problem before continuing.

APPLE WRITER

The Apple Writer Software turns your computer into a sophisticated text editor providing you with the capability to write, revise, edit, and print all types of documents quickly and inexpensively. You can easily perform every editing task, from correcting typographical errors to moving whole paragraphs. And you can precisely format and print your text letter-perfect every time. In general, the Apple Write Program:

1. Saves time often spent modifying, moving, and formatting text, with its extensive editing and printing commands.
2. Increases productivity by eliminating retyping because corrections can be made character-by-character, so there's no need to retype an entire line when only minor changes are required.
3. Is easy to learn and operate with its simplified command structure.
4. Saves paper costs and filing space with floppy diskette storage.
5. Reduces paperwork costs with its powerful editing capabilities.
6. Allows you to write in any order you choose, so text can be stored in sections and later combined in any order for printing.
7. Protects files from accidental loss through its program/system recovery and audible prompt features.

The Apple Writer program diskette contains a tutorial text file which you can view on your screen. It introduces you to some of the features of the Apple Writer editor, so that you'll feel more comfortable using the program for the first time. Just follow the simple instructions in the Apple Writer program manual to access the tutorial.

The Apple Writer program is ready to use when the Editor Menu is displayed on your monitor or television screen.

By selecting INITIALIZE NEW FILE, for example, and pressing the RETURN key, you may begin a new document. Simply enter your text on the Apple's keyboard, and it will be displayed simultaneously on your screen. Although only upper case letters will appear, Apple Writer will automatically translate them into lower case during printing. To capitalize a letter or word, use the ESC key. Capitals will appear as inverse video on your screen and upper case when printed.

When typing your text, pressing the return key is necessary only at the end of paragraphs. Apple Writer will automatically insert all other RETURNS during printing. You can type continuously—and faster—since there's no need to press the RETURN key at the end of every line.

If you want to insert a new word or sentence within your text, move the cursor to the desired location and begin typing. To delete information, use one of the commands that allow you to edit out by word, sentence, or block of text. Or simply position the cursor after the data to be deleted and backspace.

The program also provides an automatic or manual search and and replace feature. If you've misspelled a word through-out the text, for example enter the misspelled word and its correct spelling. Then type two simple commands, and the computer will change every misspelling of the word instantly. If you've overused a word and wish to change it only in specific locations, enter the word and an appropriate synonym. The computer will lead you through the text, stopping at each occurrence of the word. You can then specify where you wish each substitution to be made.

To format text, just type one of the four commands that center, left-, right-, or fill-justify lines during printing.

When connected to a compatible printer, the system will print your finished documents automatically. The Apple Writer Print Menu will be displayed after you have selected PRINT FILE from your Editor Menu.

To print your document, select PRINT NEW DOCUMENT and press the RETURN key. Apple Writer will then display a listing of printer parameters. Specify desired line spacing, number of lines per page, page numbering, and margins. Then press the RETURN key once more. Apple Writer will print your document exactly as you've specified. In other words, a first draft can be the final copy every time!

APPLE PLOT

The Apple Plot program allows you to use your Apple Computer System to create, revise, and print highly detailed charts and graphs quickly and easily. Any information, from sales and stock activities to caloric intake and miles per gallon, can be presented in a visually appealing, comprehensive bar, line or scatter chart.

The program allows you to specify each axis, update and change information, and label the charts exactly as you wish. Graphs can be colored for differentiation and effect. With the Apple Graphics Tablet, you can further customize any graph with a company logo or other marking. Transparencies of finished graphs can be used for presentations; hard copy can be printed for reports and later analysis. Apple Plot . . .

- helps you understand numerical information by displaying it graphically . . .
- offers the capability for displaying externally generated data, because it can be used with other data base programs . . .
- saves countless hours of design and drawing time by producing a finished chart automatically; you only provide data points and choose the format . . .
- offers versatility in presenting material, because it provides six graph forms from which to choose . . .
- allows data to be differentiated on the screen through your Apple's color capability . . .
- permits design of custom plots because the user controls every graph parameter . . .
- provides for comparisons because two graphs can be displayed on the same axis, and each graph can contain up to 100 points.

It's easy to put the Apple Plot to work for you. The program diskette contains sample data sets to help you learn to create custom plots. Following the step-by-step instructions in the Apple Plot manual, you can chart your way, selecting functions from the program's main menu.

Graph Format Selection

The Apple Plot option offers a choice of six graph formats for plotting up to two separate data sets in a single display. If you're plotting more than two, there is a special overlay capability which allows additional data sets to be placed on the same graph. You can also physically exchange the coordinate data of the two data sets automatically, as well as specify colors.

X-Axis and Y-Axis Parameters

These options let you specify the limits, resolution and labeling of the axes. Apple Plot will ask questions about the data, display a possible reply, and wait for you to either confirm its answer or type in a different one.

Data Entry and Editing

This option is used for entering the number of data points in a graph, specifying where they are to be placed, changing information if necessary, or displaying a list of the data points in the current data set.

Display Graph

This option actually produces the graph on the screen.

Save Data to Disk

There are two forms in which you can save Apple Plot data onto an Apple diskette; Data and Picture. Data saves the data point in both data sets, the selected graph format, and all of the X- and Y-axis parameters. Picture save the Apple's high-resolution screen image of the most recently displayed graph when other graphs have been overlayed.

Although there are only two ways to store Apple Plot data onto a diskette, there are three in which to recall it; Data, Data (Raw) and Picture. When you call Data, the computer will display all stored data; when you recall Data (Raw), it will provide only the data points. Picture recall simply redraws a previously developed high resolution screen image, exactly as it looked when it was saved.

Clear for New Graph

Resets all parameters and data to begin a new graph.

Print the Graph

Provides hard copy printout of graphs when an Apple Silentype or Qume Sprint 5 is connected to the system. Additionally, there is a special program on the Apple Plot diskette that allows you to use your stored charts and graphs in a slide show on your monitor or television screen. This unique capability is ideal both for reviewing different graphs and for making presentations without the need for hardcopy or other printed visuals.

APPLE POST

Apple Post is a mailing list system designed to allow entry, editing and storing names, addresses and telephone numbers. When the Apple Computer System is attached to a compatible printer, Apple Post will also print mailing labels, address and telephone lists, and your personal zip code directory.

The main purpose of the Apple Post is to allow small business to take advantage of direct mail to customers, because it uses the power of the Apple computer to maintain customer lists and print mailing labels, locate names that you wish to modify or which may have been misspelled during data entry, through its phonetic search routines, provide you with the capability to perform demographic mailings quickly and easily, because it will print addresses by specified zip codes or other identifiers through its special search routines, offers you the option of printing complete or specified portions of any list for your review or files through its select routine and automatically prints mailing labels of completed or selected mailing lists through its labels routine.

An Apple Post list will hold approximately 500 name and address records on a single diskette, for use with a two drive system. A maximum of 2,590 records, or five full diskettes, may be kept online at the same time with a six-drive system. If you are going to be creating large lists, consider the possibility of breaking them up into smaller lists. For example, a subscription list for a monthly magazine could be broken into one list for the subscriptions that would expire in January, a second for those that would expire in February, etc. This would allow Apple Post to handle over 30,000 subscriptions with six drives, or 6,000 with two drives.

Learning the function of each Apple Post command is all it takes to begin using the system. These commands appear in the VALID COMMAND LIST at the beginning of the program. A few are detailed here to give you a feeling for the program.

EXPLAIN may be used to display a brief three line summary of any listed command in the system. It's especially helpful if you forget what a certain command will do.

The ENTER command permits you to add new entries to the name and address list. After selecting this command, your screen will display the NEW ENTRY preformatted screen.

Most of the entries are self-explanatory. The ATTENTION line is a free line of 20 characters. It is printed before the name line on a mailing label. If the name line contains the name of a company, for example, the attention line could contain the name of an individual or department within the company.

The SORT KEY is the line used by the system to decide where on the diskette to file the entry. All entries are stored in alphabetical order by sort key. The sort key line cannot be empty. When a name and address is first entered, a default reply will appear on the sort key line. If you wish to change the sort key, type the new entry and the default reply will disappear as you type over it.

To "flag" or identify some names as belonging to special groups, Apple Post provides the UTILITY line. It will be referenced when you use the SELECT command to specify a group or groups for which you need to print a listing or mailing labels.

The EDIT command allows you to modify any line of a name and address record, except for the sort key line, or delete the entire entry. If you are trying to locate a certain name and you're not sure of the way you spelled it during entry, you will use the FIND command. The spelling and spacing of the name need not be identical to what was entered; the system will search for any entries that are phonetically similar to the one you have specified.

The ZIPFIND command selects name and address records by Zip Code and permits you to modify any line of the names and addresses in the list.

DOW JONES SERIES PORTFOLIO EVALUATOR

The Apple Portfolio Evaluator program allows you to store, modify, and update approximately 100 individual portfolios of up to 50 stocks each on a single diskette. Additionally, by connecting your Apple Computer System to a telephone, the Portfolio Evaluator program permits you to access quotes for more than 6,000 companies using the Dow Jones News Retrieval System.

This system is a convenient, time saving way to keep your finger on the pulse of the stockmarket.

The Portfolio Evaluator saves time usually spent obtaining quotes from a broker by giving you access to information about stocks, preferred stocks, and warrants listed by Dow Jones. Furthermore, it eliminates the need for time consuming math, because it instantly tabulates the current value—gains or losses—of each portfolio, and displays it on the screen or on paper via a printer. Therefore, the system increases your efficiency, because it automatically catalogs the portfolios by name and displays the complete catalog for your review upon command.

The main menu of the Portfolio Evaluator contains three program options. To create a portfolio, select EDIT. The edit module will be loaded from the diskette, and the Portfolio Evaluator program will lead you through the data entry process step-by-step.

Preformatted screens assist you in entering stock symbol, number of shares, purchase date, and purchase price for each stock in a portfolio.

Perhaps the most exciting aspect of the Portfolio Evaluator is its ability to let you log on to the Dow Jones News/Retrieval Service. With your password, you will be able to access the Dow Jones computer and fetch current quotes in real time. You'll need a working telephone, a modem, and a special interface to take advantage of this part of the program.

To access Dow Jones, select FETCH CURRENT QUOTATIONS from the main menu; the log on module will be loaded into your Apple. Once again, the Portfolio Evaluator will lead you through this part of the program step-by-step. You'll be instructed to dial a Dow Jones telephone number and insert your telephone receiver into the modem. After you have satisfied the Dow Jones computer with an acceptable password, you'll be able to update every quote in every portfolio on your diskette.

You can review a revised portfolio simply by choosing DISPLAY OR EVALUATE STOCKS from the main menu. The display module will be loaded from the diskette, and you will be asked for the name of the portfolio you wish to review. Type the name and press the RETURN key. If you've forgotten the name of the portfolio, simply type a question mark (?) and press the RETURN key to view the diskette catalog.

After identifying the desired portfolio from the catalog, press the space bar and enter its name. **SEARCHING FOR PORTFOLIO** will appear on your screen. In a few seconds, you will be presented with a list of four options. The first three options listed allow you to obtain previously-stored information within the specific portfolio. The fourth option—Printer ON/OFF—allows you to print information.

DOW JONES NEWS & QUOTES REPORTER

This Software package available for the Apple II is another business program, designed especially for investors, busy managers, and executives who need fast access to stock market news and information. It allows users to retrieve—over telephone lines—past and current news stories and headlines from the Dow Jones News/Retrieval Service, The Wall Street Journal, and Barron's, as well as quotations for more than 6,000 companies traded on the major exchanges.

News & Quotes Reporter can also be used in conjunction with

Portfolio Evaluator, another Dow Jones program from Apple. Portfolio Evaluator allows you to store, modify, and update approximately 100 individual portfolios of up to 50 stocks each on a single diskette. This capability—coupled with News & Quotes Reporter's access to late-breaking financial news and stock quotations—provides the tools and information needed for sophisticated portfolio creation and management.

The Dow Jones News & Quotes Reporter is your personal key to making sound investment decisions in a rapidly changing world. Additional benefits of the Dow Jones Software include:

1. Saves time spent skimming and searching through business media, by putting financial headlines and news stories at your fingertips.

2. Keeps you informed of stock price fluctuations, by providing fast access to stock quotations for more than 6,000 companies listed on the major stock exchanges.

3. Renders concise records for business or tax purposes through a monthly Dow Jones billing.

The main menu of this Software Package contains five program selections. You can access, display, and print news headlines and entire stories from the worldwide network of the Dow Jones News/Retrieval Service, The Wall Street Journal, and Barron's. You can also access timely stock and composite quotes on corporate stocks and bonds, options, mutual funds, and treasury notes and bonds on the New York, the American, the Mid West, and the Pacific Stock Exchanges, plus the Over-the-Counter market.

You can log on to the Dow Jones News/Retrieval Service over telephone lines, using either an autodial or acoustic modem and a special password. To access news items, select NEWS RETRIEVAL SERVICE from the main menu. Your Apple II system automatically initiates the log-on procedure, even automatically dialing the correct phone number if you have a autodial modem.

You can obtain news either by category or company. For example, you may be interested in up-to-the-minute foreign news—say, from the Mid-East—or in current stories concerning aerospace, mining, or a particular company. Using the NEWS RETRIEVAL SERVICE, simply enter the appropriate symbol. Then choose the most recent news story, or the first page of subject-related headlines. There may be less than a page or many pages of headlines, listing some stories as far back as three months.

Using one of several suggested printers, you can also print news stories in their entirety, or the full list of headlines. Simply type the ! symbol, and the news item or list of headlines that you're reading on the video monitor will be printed.

Another selection option available from the main menu is STOCK QUOTE SERVICE, which allows you to access Dow Jones' securities quote data base and obtain current stock quotations. As it does with NEWS RETRIEVAL SERVICE, News & Quotes Reporter leads you step-by-step through the STOCK QUOTE SERVICE procedures.

The third option on News & Quotes Reporter's main menu, CUSTOMIZING FEATURES, allow you to print news stories either at 40 or 80 characters wide. You can switch easily from 80 character/line hardcopy for news stories, to 40 character/line hardcopy for the Dow Jones Industrial Averages. CUSTOMIZING FEATURES also lets you enter and maintain your password, and enter and maintain two telephone numbers for use with an autodial modem.

Selection 4, DISCONNECT DOW JONES, simply disconnects your line from the Dow Jones phone number. With this option, you hang up the phone and don't continue paying connect-time charges, but your system is left running, connected and ready to log back on, as soon as you need News & Reporter again. Selection 5 terminates the program.

TAX PLANNER

This Apple Software package allows you to determine the federal income tax advantages or liabilities that result from personal financial decisions. It provides you with the capability to construct various income scenarios, and then compare the federal income tax impact of each. Additionally, Tax Planner instantly computes the financial consequences of income-affecting decisions for up to nine years in the future. This means you can determine the best time to make a financial move. And you can print out your tax strategies, or store them on diskettes, ready for fast retrieval and modification. It's a package that can help you better manage your personal income and the tax mechanisms that affect it.

In general, the Tax Planner Software Package offers the following benefits:

1. Provides you with the capability to optimize the federal income tax advantages available to you, because it lets you quickly compare the tax consequences of various financial decisions.

2. Assists you in choosing the best time to make certain financial moves, by instantly computing their impact on income taxes in current and future years.

3. Helps clarify current federal tax regulations, because you can experiment with various financial scenarios and observe how tax mechanisms apply to each.

4. Increases your productivity, by allowing you to quickly develop or change tax strategies.

The main menu of this Software package consists of four options. To begin using the program, select TAX PLANNING. Before tax computations can be performed, you will be asked to provide some information, including how far into the future you wish to plan, and your taxable income for each of the four preceding years. If you choose to plan only for next year, you may specify the number of alternative scenarios to be examined for that year. After you've provided this information, your screen will display the Tax Matrix, a skeletal list of items which affect your federal income tax situation. These include your tax filing status, long- and short-term capital gains, income, deductions, and adjustments.

Suppose, for example, your base year is 1980 and you wish to do some planning for 1981 and 1982. On the screen, the matrix will display three columns labeled 1980, 1981, and 1982. Tax Planner will automatically compute your adjusted gross income, your estimated tax, and your tax bracket, once you've filled in the information above ADJ GROSS INC.

Setting up your matrix usually requires some time and careful thought. But once it's complete, Tax Planner does all the rest of the work—the tedious tax calculations—for you. To compute your adjusted gross income, taxable income, taxes, and other figures, just press the C key. The computer automatically computes your tax by income averaging as well as by the regular method. It also computes the maximum tax on personal service income, the minimum tax on preference items, and the alternative minimum tax. In addition, your tax bracket and the tax computation method most advantageous to you are determined for each year or financial scenario.

You can create a matrix with as many as nine columns, each containing alternative sets of tax data for a single year. Although the screen displays only three columns at a time, up to nine can be stored with any single scenario. The additional columns are moved, or scrolled, on movement keys.

With Tax Planner, you can use a matrix to quickly perform "what if" experiments that otherwise would consume hours of tedious calculations. Suppose, for instance, that you're thinking about selling your home, and you wonder if it would be more advantageous in tax savings to sell it this year rather than next. Simply include the expected sale price in this and next year's cell, letting Tax Planner compute the results in each case. A quick comparison will reveal the more advantageous timing for the sale.

Once you have developed a tax scenario you want to keep, save it on your diskette by selecting FILE CLERK from the main menu, and following the step-by-step instructions displayed on your monitor. Or choose the PRINTER option to set your printing parameters and print out the strategy.

Because Tax Planner incorporates the current federal tax laws, you can be assured of the validity of its computational results. In addition, if you fill out and mail the user registration card that accompanies the program. Apple Computer Inc. will keep you informed of any product changes corresponding to tax law revisions.

Whether you're a financial advisor who wants to bring the latest technology to bear on your client's tax situations, or an individual with substantial opportunities for advantageous tax treatment of income, you'll find that Tax Planner will become an indispensable tool for quickly generating dollar-saving financial strategies.

ELEMENTARY, MY DEAR APPLE

This Software package is a collection of four programs designed to help youngsters learn to spell, understand arithmetic concepts, and sharpen problem-solving skills. Recommended for children 12 years of age and up, it's an entertaining way to learn some basic educational concepts.

The first program on the package diskette is Lemonade, a business simulation game for one or two players. The remaining three, each designed for a single player, are Darts, Supermath, and Don't Fall. Respectively, they help students understand fractions, solve basic arithmetic problems, and improve word recognition and spelling.

Elementary, My Dear Apple is simple and fun to play the games. Just insert the program diskette into your disk drive. A colorful title page welcomes you to the program and leads directly to the program selection chart menu.

Lemonade

This is a business simulation game that combines math drills with business acumen. The player tries to make profits each day from his lemonade stand by estimating the number of glasses that will be sold, setting the price per glass, forecasting the cost of material and advertising, and anticipating the effect on sales of changes in the weather.

Darts

This teaches fractions and fraction estimation in a game that simulates throwing darts at balloons. Every time the player hits a balloon, a fraction is displayed. The player then uses the displayed fraction as a reference for his next throw.

Supermath

This is a drill and practice program that teaches addition, subtraction, multiplication, and division at several difficulty levels. The player can concentrate on specific drills, and can specify whether only integers should be used, or integers with remainders. The program will also help the player determine his difficulty level and will automatically increase or decrease the difficulty as required.

Don't Fall

This is a variation on the traditional game Hangman and tests word recognition and spelling. The player tries to guess and spell the correct word before the character displayed on the screen falls over a cliff. Don't Fall incorporates one of Apple's Shell Games editors, which makes it simple for teachers and parents to supply special words to work with and to guess. In this way, the game can be quickly customized for a particular age group, or to teach a specific terminology.

With this Software package, youngsters can use the Apple II with little training and guidance to discover how much fun learning can be.

Apple Music Theory

Apple Music Theory is a series of clever programs that make it interesting to learn music fundamentals. Developed for Apple by music teachers from the Minnesota Educational Computing Consortium, the programs use the superb graphic and sound capabilities of your Apple II to generate tones and display sheet music on a video monitor. Because you can both hear and see the music, as well as repeat and practice lessons easily, you can quickly learn what otherwise might take dozens of private lessons to master.

This system is designed for teenagers and up and is an excellent teacher, whether you're starting from scratch or simply reviewing forgotten concepts. The programs provide challenging drill and practice exercises for scales, chords, sharps and flats, half-tones, intervals, and other music elements. Apple Music Theory also keeps track of performance, so you can identify weak areas and gauge your progress.

Apple Music Theory lets you learn at your own pace, at home or in a classroom. And anyone can use it easily. Just insert the program diskette into your disk drive, turn on the system, and class begins.

The program provides fundamental exercises in aural intervals, counting, harmonics, key signatures, naming notes, note types, visual intervals, music terms, halves, rhythm, scales, sevenths, triads, and whole and half-step intervals.

The Apple II will generate clear tones and passages of music that demonstrate a wide range of music concepts. Bars of music are displayed on your screen, exactly as they would appear on a sheet of music. By matching the note and other music symbols with their corresponding sounds, you can quickly learn to read and hear music, so that you can interpret both played and written passages.

Whether you're considering it for your school, your child, or yourself, the Software package provides a truly convenient and effective way to learn music fundamentals.

THE SHELL GAMES

Apple's Shell Games turn your Apple II into an excellent teaching aid for the home or classroom. The Shell Games diskette contains four programs. The first is an introductory color cartoon called *The Animated Apple*. The remaining three are the *Match Machine, Mr. Multiple*, and *Professor True.* They offer matching, multiple choice, and true/false quizzes, respectively, on a variety of subjects. Combined, these three programs contain over 180 ready-to-solve problems. And that's not all.

Because the Shell Games diskette also contains its own Editor, you can choose your own quiz problems to place into each Shell. You don't have to be a programmer in order to create highly successful quizzes. In a few short minutes, you can enter a complete quiz into any one of the three quiz programs; revisions can be made just as quickly.

Playing the Shell Games is fun and simple. Insert the program diskette into your disk drive. Then sit back and enjoy the Animated Apple, a brief, colorful cartoon that will lead you directly into the program selection chart menu.

Because the Shell Games were designed with children in mind, no complicated commands are necessary. Just select one of the three games and then follow the instructions on the screen. Correct responses to questions are rewarded, and scoring is performed automatically by each program.

Use the Shell Games Editor to enter new questions and answers into existing games, delete material you don't wish to use or create entire quizzes on your own. You'll quickly build up large libraries of material that you can use over and over again.

DOS TOOLKIT

Apple's DOS Toolkit is a collection of programs and subroutines designed to aid the Apple II user in the development of Applesoft BASIC and 6502 Assembly Language programs. The Toolkit simplifies program development by providing a number of handy features that make programming easier.

Included are an assembler and source editor for use under DOS on Apple II or Apple II Plus systems, as well as an assembly language program that renumbers, merges, and deletes remarks from Applesoft Basic programs. In addition, there are two special high resolution graphics programs in the Toolkit—one that helps you create and edit high resolution character sets, and another that lets you display characters on the high resolution graphics screen. Also included are three graphics demo programs, and character sets for editing high resolution characters.

Apple's DOS Toolkit reduces programming time, by providing the user with such powerful program editing capabilities as character search, line search, and string replace. Other benefits:

- Allows the user to assemble, arbitrarily, large sources files, because its disk-based operation requires that only the symbol table be held in RAM.
- Makes the assembler easier to learn, since its fully compatible with 6502 syntax.
- Increases programming flexibility, because its text files feature provides a degree of compatibility with other assemblers.
- Simplifies the creation of relocatable modules by providing the user with relocating loader.
- Speeds program development, because its multiple applications assist users in accomplishing many time-consuming and difficult programming tasks.
- Aids in the design of high-resolution graphics characters through the use of a special graphics editor.

The four programs and subroutines that make up the DOS Toolkit were designed to meet a variety of programming needs.

The Editor/Assembler is an integrated assembler and source editor designed for the creation of 6502 assembly language programs. After accessing the Editor/Assembler from the Toolkit diskette, you can create and edit source code files in RAM, store and retrieve programs as text files, assemble disk source files into disk object files, and create your own symbol table summary. The Editor/Assembler program also features relocatable or absolute code output, as well as a relocating loader.

The Hi-Res Character Generator is an assembly language program for displaying text on the high-resolution graphics screen. Using the Generator, you can mix text with high-resolution graphics, write text over an existing background, automatically downshift alphabetic characters for displaying lower case text, and animate figures. The Generator also allows alternate character sets for user-defined characters and features a text wrap-around within the text window. Additionally, it provides example of graphic implementation through three graphics-oriented demos and several alphabetic fonts.

Animatrix (Character Editor) is a special Applesoft BASIC program which makes it easy for you to create and edit character sets for the Hi-Res Character Generator.

Applesoft Programmer's Assistant is an assembly language program that helps you write your own programs in Applesoft BASIC. The Assistant can determine program length, renumber and merge several programs, and delete remarks. Its automatic line numbering feature makes program entry easier, and—since it allows you to cross reference variables—takes some of the confusion out of programming. The Assistant also provides you with the use of three, non-standard keys; underscore, left bracket, and backslash. In addition, it will print non-visible characters when listing a program.

To use the DOS Toolkit, you will need the Apple II (with Applesoft Firmware Card) or Apple II Plus each with 48K of memory and the Apple Language System. You will also need the Apple Disk II with controller and 16-sector PROMs, and a video monitor or television.

The DOS Toolkit is written in Applesoft BASIC and Machine Language.

Glossary Of Apple Terms

6502—The manufacturer's name for the microprocessor at the heart of your Apple.

address—As a noun: the particular number associated with each memory location. On the Apple, an address is a number between 0 and 65535 ($0000 to $FFFF hexadecimal). As a verb: to refer to a particular memory location.

address bus—The set of wires which carries the binary-encoded address from the microprocessor to the rest of the computer.

addressing mode—The Apple's 6502 microprocessor has thirteen distinct ways of referring to most locations in memory. These thirteen methods of forming addresses are called addressing modes.

analog—Analog measurements, as opposed to digital measurements, use a continuously variable physical quantity (such as length, voltage, or resistance) to represent values. Digital measurements use precise, limited quantities (such as presence or absence of voltages or magnetic fields) to represent values.

AND—A binary function which is "on" if and only if all of its inputs are "on".

Apple—A brand of personal computer.

ASCII—An acronym for the American Standard Code for Information Interchange (often called "USASCII" or misinterpreted as "ASC-II"). This standard code assigns a unique value from 0 through 127 to each of 128 numbers, special characters, and control characters.

assembler—A program which converts the mnemonics and symbols of assembly language into the opcodes and operands of machine language.

assembly language—A language similar in structure to machine language, but made up of mnemonics and symbols. Programs written in assembly language are slightly less difficult to write and understand than programs in machine language.

BASIC—Acronym for "Beginner's All-Purpose Symbolic Instruction Code". BASIC is a higher-level language, similar in structure to FORTRAN but somewhat easier to learn. It was invented by Kemney and Kurtz at Dartmouth College in 1963 and has proved to be the most popular language for personal computers.

binary—A number system with two digits, "0" and "1", with each digit in a binary number representing a power of two. Most digital computers are binary, deep down inside. A binary signal is easily expressed by the presence or absence of something, such as an electrical potential or a magnetic field.

binary function—An operation performed by an electronic circuit which has one or more inputs and only one output. All inputs and outputs are binary signals. See AND, OR, and Exclusive-OR.

bit—A Binary digIT. The smallest amount of information which a computer can hold. A single bit specifies a single value; "0" or "1". Bits can be grouped to form larger values.

board—See Printed Circuit Board

boot—To get a system running from a cold start. The name comes from the machine's attempts to "pull itself off the ground by tugging on its own bootstraps".

buffer—A device or area of memory which is used to hold something temporarily. The "picture buffer" contains graphic information to be displayed on the video screen. The "input buffer" holds a partially formed input line.

bug—An error. A hardware bug is a physical or electrical malfunction or design error. A software bug is an error in programming, either in the logic of the program or typographical in nature.

byte—A basic unit of measure of a computer's memory. A byte comprises eight bits. Thus, it can have a value from 0 to 255. Each character in the ASCII can be represented in one byte. The Apple's memory locations are all one byte, and the Apple's addresses of these locations consist of two bytes.

call—As a verb: to leave the program or subroutine which is currently executing and to begin another, usually with the intent to return to the original program or subroutine. As a noun: an instruction which calls a subroutine.

character—Any graphic symbol which has a specific meaning to people. Letters (both upper and lower case), numbers, and various symbols (such as punctuation marks) are all characters.

chip—*See* Integrated Circuit.

code—A method of representing something in terms of something else. The ASCII code represents characters as binary numbers, the BASIC language represents algorithms in terms of program statements. "Code" is also used to refer to programs, usually in low-level languages.

cold-start—To begin to operate a computer which has just been turned on.

color burst—A signal which color television sets recognize and convert to the colored dots you see on a color TV screen. Without the color burst signal, all pictures would be black-and-white.

computer—Any device which can receive and store a set of instructions, and then act upon those instructions in a predetermined and predictable fashion. The definition implies that both the instruction and the data upon which the instructions act can be changed. A device whose instructions cannot be changed is not a computer.

control (CTRL) character—Characters in the ASCII character set which usually have no graphic representation, but are used to control various functions. For example, the RETURN control character is a signal to the Apple that you have finished typing an input line and you wish the computer to act upon it.

CRT—Acronym for "Cathode Ray Tube", meaning any television screen, or a device containing such a screen.

cursor—A special symbol which reminds you of a certain position on something. The cursor on a slide rule lets you line up numbers. The cursor on the Apple's screen reminds you of where you are when you are typing.

data—Information of any type. Plural: datum.

debug—To find bugs and eliminate them.

DIP—Acronym for "Dual In-line Package", the most common container for an Integrated Circuit. DIPs have two parallel rows of pins, spaced on one-tenth of an inch centers. DIPs usually come in 14, 16, 18, 20, 24, and 40 pin configurations.

disassembler—A program which converts the opcodes of machine language to the mnemonics of assembly language. The opposite of an assembler.

display—As a noun: any sort of output device for a computer, usually a video screen. As a verb: to place information on such a screen.

edge connector—A socket which mates with the edge of a printed circuit board in order to exchange electrical signals.

entry point—The location used by a machine language subroutine which contains the first executable instruction in that subroutine. Consequently, it is often the beginning of the subroutine.

exclusive-OR—A binary function whose value is "off" only if all but one of its inputs are "off".

execute—To perform the intention of a command or instruction. Also, to run a program or a portion of a program.

format—As a noun: the physical form in which something appears. As a verb: to specify such a form.

graphic—Visible as a distinct, recognizable shape or color.

graphics—A system to display graphic items or a collection of such items.

hardware—The physical parts of a computer.

hexadecimal—A number system which uses the ten digits 0 through 9 and the six letters A through F to represent values in base 16. Each hexadecimal digit in a hexadecimal number represents a power of 16. Preceded by a dollar sign on the Apple monitor.

high level language—A language which is more intelligible to humans than it is to machines.

high order—The most important, or item with the highest value, of a set of similar items. The high order bit of a byte is that which has the highest place value.

high part—The high order byte of a two byte address. In decimal, the high part of an address is the quotient of the address divided by 256. In the 6502, as in many other microprocessors, the high part of an address comes last when that address is stored in memory.

hz (Hertz)—Cycles per second. A bicycle wheel which makes two revolutions in one second is running at 2Hz. The Apple's microprocessor runs at 1,023,000 Hz.

I/O—*See* Input/Output

IC—*See* Integrated Circuit.

input—As a noun, data which flows from the outside world into the computer. As a verb: to obtain data from the outside world.

instruction—The smallest portion of a program that a computer can execute. In 6502 machine language, an instruction comprises one, two, or three bytes. In a higher level language, instructions may be many characters long.

integrated circuit—A small (less than the size of a fingernail and about as thin) wafer of a glassy material (usually silicon) into which has been etched an electronic circuit. A single IC can contain from ten to ten thousand discrete electronic components. ICs are usually housed in DIPs, and the term IC is sometimes used to refer to both the circuit and its package.

interface—An exchange of information between one thing and another, or the mechanisms which make such an exchange possible.

interpreter—A program, usually written in machine language, which understands and executes a higher level language.

interrupt—A physical effect which causes the computer to jump to a special interrupt-handling subroutine. When the interrupt has been taken care of, the computer resumes execution of the interrupted program with no noticeable change. Interrupts are used to signal the computer that a particular device wants attention.

K—Stands for the Greek prefix "Kilo", meaning one thousand. In common computer language "K" usually represents the quantity 2^{10}, or 1024 (hexadecimal $400).

kilobyte—1,024 bytes.

language—A computer language is a code which (hopefully) both a programmer and his computer understand. The programmer expresses what he wants to do in this code, and computer understands the code and performs the desired actions.

line—On a video screen, a "line" is a horizontal sequence of graphic symbols extending from one edge of the screen to the other. To the Apple, an input line is a sequence of up to 254 characters, terminated by the control character RETURN.

low level language—A language which is more intelligible to machines than it is to humans.

low order—The least important, or item with the least value, of a set of items. The low order bit in a byte is the bit with the least place value.

low part—The low order byte of a two-byte address. In decimal, the low part of an address is the remainder of the address divided by 256, also called the "address modulo 256." In the 6502, as in many other microprocessors, the low part of an address comes first when that address is stored in memory.

machine language—The lowest level language which a computer understands. Machine languages are usually binary in nature. Instructions in machine language are single byte opcodes sometimes followed by various operands.

memory address—A memory address is a two byte value which selects a single memory location out of the memory map. Memory addresses in the Apple are stored with their low order bytes first, followed by their high order bytes.

memory location—The smallest subdivision of the memory map to which the computer can refer. Each memory location has associated with it a unique address and a certain value. Memory locations on the Apple comprise one byte each.

memory map—This term is used to refer to the set of all memory locations which the microprocessor can address directly. It is also used to describe a graphic representation of a system's memory.

microcomputer—A term used to describe a computer which is based upon a microprocessor.

microprocessor—An integrated circuit which understands and executes machine language programs.

mnemonic—An acronym (or any other symbol) used in the place of something more difficult to remember. In Assembly Language, each machine language opcode is given a three letter mnemonic.

mode—A condition or set of conditions under which a certain set of rules apply.

modulo—An arithmetic function with two operands. Modulo takes the first operand, divides it by the second, and returns the remainder of the division.

monitor—1) A closed-circuit television receiver; 2) A program which allows you to use your computer at a very low level; often with the values and addresses of individual memory locations.

multiplexer—An electronic circuit which has many data inputs, a few selector inputs, and one output. A multiplexer connects one of its many data inputs to its output. The data input it chooses to connect to the output is determined by the selector inputs.

mux—*See* Multiplexer.

nybble—Colloquial term for half of a byte or four bits.

opcode—A machine language instruction, numerical (often binary) in nature.

OR—A binary function whose value is "on" if at least one of its inputs are "on".

output—As a noun: data generated by the computer whose destination is the real world. As a verb: the process of generating or transmitting such data.

page—1) A screenful of information on a video display. 2) A quantity of memory locations, addressable with one byte. On the Apple, a page of memory contains 256 locations.

Pascal—1) A noted French scientist; 2) A structured, high level language.

PC board—*See* Printed Circuit Board.

peripheral—Something attached to the computer which is not part of the computer itself. Most peripherals are input and/or output devices.

personal computer—A computer with memory, languages, and peripherals which are well suited for use in a home, office, or school.

pinout—A description of the function of each pin on an IC; often presented in the form of a diagram.

potentiometer—An electronic component whose resistance to the flow of electrons is proportional to the setting of a dial or knob. Also known as a "pot" or "variable resistor".

printed circuit board—A sheet of fiberglass or epoxy onto which a thin layer of metal has been applied, then etched away to form traces. Electronic components can then be attached to the board with molten solder, and they can exchange electronic signals via the etched traces on the board. Small printed circuit boards are often called "cards", especially if they are meant to connect with edge connectors.

program—A sequence of instructions which describes a process

PROM—Acronym for Programmable Read-Only Memory. A PROM is a ROM whose contents can be altered by electrical means. Information in PROMs does not disappear when the power is turned off. Some PROMs can be erased by ultraviolet light and be reprogrammed.

RAM—*See* Random Access Memory.

random access memory—This is the main memory of a computer. The acronym RAM can be used to refer either to the integrated circuits which make up this type of memory or to the memory itself. The computer can store values in distinct locations in RAM and recall them again, or alter and re-store them if it wishes. On the Apple, as with most small computers, the values which are in RAM memory are lost when the power to the computer is turned off.

read-only memory (ROM)—This type of memory is usually used to hold important programs or data which must be available to the computer when the power is first turned on. Information in ROMs is placed there in the process of manufacturing the ROMs and is unalterable. Information stored in ROMs does not disappear when the power is turned off.

reference—1) A source of information, such as a book, a signal, or a label; 2) As a verb, the action of examining or using this information.

return—To exit a subroutine and go back to the program which called it.

ROM—*See* Read-Only Memory.

run—To follow the sequence of instructions which comprise a program, and to complete the process outlined by the instructions.

scan line—A single sweep of a cathode beam across the face of a cathode ray tube.

schematic—A diagram which represents the electrical interconnections and circuitry of an electronic device.

scroll—To move all the text on a display (usually upwards) to make room for more (usually at the bottom).

soft switch—A two position switch which can be "thrown" either way by the software of a computer.

software—The programs which give the hardware something to do.

stack—A reserved area in memory which can be used to store information temporarily. The information in a stack is referenced not by address, but in the order in which it was placed on the stack. The last datum which was "pushed" onto the stack will be the first one to be "popped" off it in the 6502.

strobe—A momentary signal which indicates the occurrence of a specific event.

subroutine—A segment of a program which can be executed by a single call. Subroutines are used to perform the same sequence of instructions at many different places in one program.

syntax—The structure of instructions in a given language. If you make a mistake in entering an instruction and garble the syntax, the computer sometimes calls this a "SYNTAX ERROR."

text—Characters, usually letters and numbers. Text usually refers to large chunks of English, rather than computer language.

toggle switch—A two position switch which can only flip from one position to the other and back again, and cannot be directly set either way.

trace—An etched conductive path on a Printed Circuit Board which serves to electronically connect components.

video—1) Anything visual; 2) Information presented on the face of a cathode ray tube.

warm-start—To restart the operation of a computer after you have lost control of its language or operating system.

window—A reserved area on a display which is dedicated to some special purpose.

Mini Encyclopedia of Computing

absolute address—An address which indicates the exact storage location where the referenced operand is to be found or stored in the actual machine code address numbering system. *Synonymous with* specific address. *Related to* absolute code.

absolute code—A code using absolute addresses and absolute operation codes; i.e., a code which indicates the exact location where the referenced operand is to be found or stored. *Synonymous with* one level code *and* specific code. *Related to* absolute address.

absolute error—The magnitude of the error disregarding the algebraic sign or if a vectorial error, disregarding its direction.

absolute value computer—A computer which processes all data expressed in full values of all variables at all times. *Contrasted with* computer, incremental.

ac dump—The removal of all alternating current power intentionally, accidentally or conditionally from a system or component. An ac dump usually results in the removal of all power, since direct current is usually supplied through a rectifier or converter.

acceleration time—The time between the interpretation of instructions to read or write on tape and the transfer of information to or from the tape into storage, or from storage into tape, as the case may be. *Synonymous with* start time.

accumulator—(1) The register and associated equipment in the arithmetic unit of the computer in which arithmetical and logical operations are performed. (2) A unit in a digital computer where numbers are totaled; i.e., accumulated. Often the accumulator stores one operand and upon receipt of any second operand, it forms and stores the result of performing the indicated operation on the first and second operands. *Related to* adder.

accuracy—The degree of exactness of an approximation or measurement. High accuracy thus implies low error. Accuracy normally denotes absolute quality of computed results; precision usually refers to the amount of detail used in representing those results. Thus, four place results are less precise than six place results; nevertheless a four place table might be more accurate than an erroneously computed six place table.

acoustic delay line—A delay line using a medium providing acoustic delay; such as, mercury or quartz delay lines. *Synonymous with* sonic delay line. *Related to* line, mercury delay.

action, rate—*See* rate action.

add subtract time—The time required to perform an addition or subtraction, exclusive of the time required to obtain the quantities from storage and put the sum or difference back into storage.

adder—A device which forms, as output, the sum of two, or more numbers presented as inputs. Often no data retention feature is included; i.e., the output signal remains only as long as the input signals are present. *Related to* accumulator, 2.

address—(1) An identification, represented by a name, label or number, for a register or location in storage. Addresses are also a part of an instruction word along with commands, tags, and other symbols. (2) The part of an instruction which specifies an operand for the instruction.

addressing system—The procedure used to label storage locations in a computer; e.g., on a magnetic storage drum, storage locations might be identified by four digit addresses which are numbered consecutively in each band as follows:

First band	0000-0199
Second band	0200-0399
Third band	0400-0599
* * * * * * * * *	
Twenty-fourth band	4600-4799
Twenty-fifth band	4800-4999

The consecutively numbered band addresses begin with 0000, to which increments of 200 are added until the address of the last band, 4800 is reached. Within each band, particular locations might be consecutively numbered from 0 to 199 to give each location an address indicative of a position on the drum or drum level. This level is added to the band address to produce the address of a particular storage location. In a magnetic core storage unit, the locations might be addressed consecutively from 0000 to 4095.

ADP—(*A*utomatic *D*ata *P*rocessing), Data processing performed by a system of electronic or electrical machines so interconnected and interacting as to reduce to a minimum the need for human assistance or intervention.

advance, item—*See* item advance.

algebra, Boolean—*See* Boolean algebra.

ALGOL *(ALGOrithmic Language)*—An arithmetic language by which numerical procedures may be precisely presented to a computer in a standard form. The language is intended not only as a means of directly presenting any numerical procedure to any suitable computer for which a compiler exists, but also as a means of communicating numerical procedures among individuals. The language itself is the result of international cooperation to obtain a standardized algorithmic language. The International Algebraic Language is the forerunner of ALGOL.

algorithm translation—A specific, effective, essentially computational method for obtaining a translation from one language to another.

algorithmic—Pertaining to a constructive calculating process usually assumed to lead to the solution of a problem in a finite number of steps.

algorithmic language—*Same as* ALGOL.

allocation storage—*See* storage allocation.

alphabet—A specific kind of character set excluding numerals; i.e., the character set most frequently used in a natural language. *Clarified by* set, character.

alphabetic code—A system of alphabetic abbreviations used in preparing information for input into a machine; e.g., Boston, New York, Philadelphia, and Washington may in alphabetical coding be reported as BS, NY, PH, WA. *Contrasted with* numeric code.

alphabetic-numeric—The characters which include letters of the alphabet, numerals, and other symbols such as punctuation or mathematical symbols.

alphameric—A contraction of alphanumeric.

alphanumeric instruction—The name given to instructions which can be used equally well with alphabetic or numeric kinds of fields of data.

ALU *(A*rithmetic and *L*ogical *U*nit)—The portion of the hardware of a computer in which arithmetic and logical operations are performed. The arithmetic unit generally consists of an accumulator, some special registers for the storage of operands and results supplemented by shifting and sequencing circuitry for implementing multiplication, division, and other desired operations.

analog—The representation of numerical quantities by means of physical variable; e.g., translation, rotation, voltage, or resistance. *Contrasted with* digital.

analog computer—A computer which represents variables by physical analogies. Thus any computer which solves problems by translating physical conditions such as flow, temperature, pressure, angular position, or voltage into related mechanical or electrical quantities and uses mechanical or electrical equivalent circuits as an analog for the physical phenomenon being investigated. In general it is a computer which uses an analog for each variable and produces analogs as output. Thus an analog computer measures continuously whereas a digital computer counts discretely. *Related to* machine, data processing.

analog device—A mechanism which represents numbers by physical quantities; e.g., by lengths, as in a slide rule, or by voltage currents as in a differential analyzer or a computer of the analog type.

analog network—A circuit or circuits which represent(s) physical variables in such a manner as to permit the expression and solution of mathematical relationships between the variables or permits the solution directly by electric or electronic means.

analog representation—A representation which does not have discrete values but is continuously variable.

analysis, numerical—*See* numerical analysis.

analysis, systems—*See* systems analysis.

analyst—A person skilled in the definition of and the development of techniques for the solving of a problem; especially those techniques for solutions on a computer.

analytic relationship—The relationship which exists between concepts, and corresponding terms, by virtue of their definition and inherent scope of meaning.

analyzer—A computer routine whose purpose is to analyze a program written for the same or a different computer. This analysis may consist of summarizing instruction references to storage and tracing sequences of jumps.

analyzer, differential—*See* differential analyzer.

analyzer, digital differential—*See* digital differential analyzer.

analyzer, electronic differential—*See* electronic differential analyzer.

analyzer, mechanical differential—*See* mechanical differential analyzer.

analyzer, network—*See* network analyzer.

AND—*Same as* and operator.

AND circuit—*Same as* and gate.

AND gate—A signal circuit with two or more input wires in which the output wire gives a signal, if and only if, all input wires receive coincident signals. *Synonymous with* and circuit. *Clarified by* conjunction.

AND operator—(1) A logical operator which has the property that if P is a statement and Q is a statement, then P and Q is true if both statements are true, false if either is false or both are false. Truth is normally expressed by the value 1, falsity by 0. The AND operator is often represented by a centered dot (P.Q), by no sign (PQ), by an inverted "u" or logical product symbol (P.Q), or by the letter "X" or multiplication symbol (P×Q). Note that the letters AND are capitalized to differentiate between the logical operator AND the word "and" in common usage. (2) The logical operation which makes use of the AND operator or logical product. *Synonymous with* and; logical multiply. *Clarified* by conjunction.

application—The system or problem to which a computer is applied. Reference is often made to an application as being either of the computational type, wherein arithmetic computations predominate, or of the data processing type, wherein data handling operations predominate.

application, standby—*See* standby application.

application study—The detailed process of determining a system or set of procedures for using a computer for definite functions or operations, and establishing specifications to be used as a base for the selection of equipment suitable to the specific needs.

area, constant—*See* constant area.

area, input—*Same as* input block (1).

argument—(1) An independent variable, e.g., in looking up quantity in a table, the number or any of the numbers which identifies the location of the desired value; or in a mathematical function the variable which when a certain value is substituted for it the value of the function is determined. (2) An operand in an operation on one or more variables.

arithmetic check—A check which uses mathematical identities or other properties, occasionally with some degree of discrepancy being acceptable, e.g., checking multiplication by verifying that $A \times B = B \times A$.

arithmetic shift—To multiply or divide a quantity by a power of the number base; e.g., if binary 1101, which represents decimal 13, is arithmetically shifted twice to the left, the result is 110100, which represents 52, which is also obtained by multiplying 13 by 2 twice; on the other hand, if the decimal 13 were to be shifted to the left twice, the result would be the same as multiplying by 10 twice, or 1300. *Related to* shift *and* shift, cyclic.

arithmetic unit—*Same as* ALU.

arithmetic operation—A computer operation in which the ordinary elementary arithmetic operations are performed on numerical quantities. *Contrasted with* operation, logical.

artificial intelligence—The study of computer and related techniques to supplement the intellectual capabilities of man. As man has invented and used tools to increase his physical powers, he now is beginning to use artificial intelligence to increase his mental powers. In a more restricted sense, the study of techniques for more effective use of digital computers by improved programming techniques.

array—A series of items arranged in a meaningful pattern.

artificial language—A language specifically designed for ease of communication in a particular area of endeavor, but one that is not yet natural to that area. This is contrasted with a natural language which has evolved through long usage.

aspect card—A card on which is entered the accession numbers of documents in an information retrieval system. The documents are judged to be related in an important fashion to the concept for which the card is established. *Related to* system, peek-a-boo; system, uniterm; docuterm; and uniterm.

assemble—(1) To integrate subroutines that are supplied, selected, or generated into the main routine, by means of preset parameters, by adapting, or changing relative and symbolic addresses to absolute form, or by placing them in storage; (2) to operate, or perform the functions of an assembler.

assembler—A computer program which operates on symbolic input data to produce from such data machine instructions by carrying out such functions as: translation of symbolic operation codes into computer operating instructions; assigning locations in storage for successive instructions; or computation of absolute addresses from symbolic addresses. An assembler generally translates input symbolic codes into machine instructions time for item, and produces as output the same number of instructions or constants which were defined in the input symbolic codes. *Synonymous with* assembly routine; assembly program. *Related to* compiler.

assembly list—A printed list which is the by-product of an assembly procedure. It lists in logical instruction sequence all details of a routine showing the coded and symbolic notation next to the actual notations established by the assembly procedure. This listing is highly useful in the debugging of a routine.

assembly program—*Same as* assembler.

assembly routine—*Same as* assembler.

assembly unit—(1) A device which performs the function of associating and joining several parts or piecing together a program, (2) a portion of a program which is capable of being assembled into a larger whole program.

asynchronous—Pertaining to a lack of time coincidence in a set of repeated events where this term is applied to a computer to indicate that the execution of one operation is dependent on a signal that the previous operation is completed.

asynchronous computer—A computer in which the performance of each operation starts as a result of a signal either that the previous operation has been completed; or that the parts of the computer required for the next operation are now available. *Contrasted with* computer, synchronous.

attenuation, signal—*See* signal attenuation.

audit, trail—*See* trail audit.

auto-abstract—(1) A collection of words selected from a document, arranged in a meaningful order, commonly by an automatic or machine method; (2) to select an assemblage of key words from a document, commonly by an automatic or machine method.

automatic check—A provision constructed in hardware for verifying the accuracy of information transmitted, manipulated, or stored by any unit or device in a computer. *Synonymous with* built in check; built in automatic check; hardware check. *Related to* check program, 2.

automatic code—A code which allows a machine to translate or convert a symbolic language into a machine language for automatic machine or computer operations.

automatic computer—A computer which performs long sequences of operations without human intervention.

automatic data processing—*See* ADP.

automatic data processing equipment—(1) A machine, or group of interconnected machines, consisting of input, storage, computing, control, and output devices, which uses electronic circuitry in the main computing element to perform arithmetic and/or logical operations automatically by means of internally stored or externally controlled programmed instructions. *Synonymous with* (equipment,electronic data processing). (2) The data processing equipment which directly supports or services the central computer operation. *Clarified by* equipment, peripheral.

automatic data processing system—The term descriptive of an interacting assembly of procedure, processes, methods, personnel and automatic data processing equipment to perform a complex series of data processing operations.

automatic dictionary—The component of a language translating machine which will provide a word for word substitution from one language to another. In automatic searching systems, the automatic dictionary is the component which substitutes codes for words or phrases during the encoding operation. *Related to* translation, machine.

automatic error correction—A technique, usually requiring the use of special codes and or automatic retransmission, which detects and corrects errors occurring in transmission. The degree of correction depends upon coding and equipment configuration.

automatic feed punch—A card punch having a hopper, a card track and a stacker. The movement of cards through the punch is automatic.

automatic programming—The method or technique whereby the computer itself is used to transform or translate programming from a language or form that is easy for a human being to produce, into a language that is efficient for the computer to carry out. Examples of automatic programming are compiling, assembling, and interpretive routines.

automatic routine—A routine that is executed independently of manual operations, but only if certain conditions occur within a program or record, or during some other process.

automatic stop—An automatic halting of a computer processing operation as the result of an error detected by built in checking devices.

automation—(1) The implementation of processes by automatic means; (2) the theory, art, or technique of making a process more automatic; (3)

the investigation, design, development, and application of methods of rendering processes automatic, self-moving, or self controlling.

automation, source data—*See* source data automation.

automonitor—To make an electronic computer prepare a record of its own data processing operations, or a program or routine for this purpose.

auxiliary equipment—*Same as* equipment, off line.

auxiliary routine—A routine designed to assist in the operation of the computer and in debugging other routines.

auxiliary storage—A storage device in addition to the main storage of a computer; e.g., magnetic tape, disk or magnetic drum. Auxiliary storage usually holds much larger amounts of information than the main storage, and the information is accessible less rapidly. *Contrasted with* storage, main.

available machine time—*Same as* available time.

available time—(1) The number of hours a computer is available for use. (2) The time during which a computer has the power turned on, is not under maintenance, and is known or believed to be operating correctly. *Synonymous with* available machine time.

average effectiveness level—A percentage figure determined by subtracting the total computer down time from the total performance period hours, and dividing the difference by the total performance period hours. For this computation, equipment down time can be measured by those intervals during the performance period between the time that the contractor or other person having maintenance responsibility is notified of equipment failure, and the time the equipment is returned to the user in proper operating condition.

balanced error (range of)—(1) A range of error in which the maximum and minimum possible errors are opposite in sign and equal in magnitude, (2) a range of error in which the average value is zero.

band—(1) The gamut or range of frequencies; (2) the frequency spectrum between two defined limits; (3) the frequencies which are within two definite limits and are used for a different purpose; (4) a group of channels. *Same as* channel, 3.

band, dead— *See* dead band.

band, proportional—*See* proportional band.

bandwidth— (1) A group of consecutive frequencies constituting a band which exists between limits of stated frequency attenuation. A band is normally defined as more than 3.0 decibels greater than the mean attenuation across the band. (2) A group of consecutive frequencies constituting a band which exists between limits of stated frequency delay.

base—*Same as* radix.

base address—(1) A number which appears as an address in a computer instruction, but which serves as the base, index, initial or starting point for subsequent addresses to be modified. *Synonymous with* presumptive address; reference address. (2) A number used in symbolic coding in conjunction with a relative address.

base notation—*Same as* notation, radix.

base number—*Same as* radix.

batch processing—A technique by which items to be processed must be coded and collected into groups prior to processing.

batch total—The sum of certain quantities, pertaining to batches of unit records, used to verify accuracy of operations on a particular batch of records; e.g., in a payroll calculation, the batches might be departments and batch totals would be number of employees in the department, total hours worked in the department, total pay for the department. Batches, however, may be arbitrary, such as orders received from 9 a.m. to 11 a.m. on a certain day.

batten system—*Same as* system, peek-a-boo.

baud—(1) A unit of signalling speed equal to the number of code elements per second; (2) the unit of signalling speed equal to twice the number of Morse code dots continuously sent per second. *Clarified by* rate, bit; capacity, channel.

B-box—*Same as* index register.

benchmark problem—A routine used to determine the speed performance of a computer. One method is to use one tenth of the time required to perform nine complete additions and one complete multiplication. A complete addition or a complete multiplication time includes the time required to procure two operands from storage, perform the operation and store the result, and the time required to select and execute the required number of instructions to do this.

bias—(1) An unbalanced range of error; i.e., having an average error that is not zero. (2) The average dc voltage maintained between certain elements of a circuit, such as between the cathode and the control grid of a vacuum tube.

binary—A characteristic, property, or condition in which there are but two possible alternatives; e.g., the binary number system using 2 as its base and using only the digits zero (0) and one (1). *Related to* decimal, binary coded. *Clarified by* systems, number.

binary cell—(1) A cell of one binary digit capacity, (2) a one bit register or bit position.

binary code—(1) A coding system in which the encoding of any data is done through the use of bits; i.e., 0 or 1. (2) A code for the ten decimal digits, 0, 1, . . ., 9 in which each is represented by its binary, radix 2, equivalent; i.e., straight binary.

binary coded character—One element of a notation system representing alphameric character such as decimal digits, alphabetic letters, and punctuation marks by a predetermined configuration of consecutive binary digits.

binary coded decimal—Describing a decimal notation in which the individual decimal digits are represented by a pattern of ones and zeros; e.g., in the 8-4-2-1 coded decimal notation, the number twelve is represented as 0001 0010 for 1 and 2, respectively, whereas in pure or straight binary notation it is represented as 1100. *Related to* binary.

binary coded decimal notation—A method of representing each figure in a decimal number by a four figured binary number.

binary coded decimal number—A number usually consisting of successive groups of figures, in which each group of four figures is a binary number that represents but does not necessarily equal arithmetically, a particular figure in an associated decimal number; e.g., if the three rightmost figures of a decimal number are 262, the three rightmost figure groups of the binary coded decimal number might be 0010, 0110, and 0010.

binary counter—(1) A counter which counts according to the binary number system, (2) a counter capable of assuming one of two stable states.

binary digit—A numeral in the binary scale of notation. This digit may be zero (0), or one (1). It may be equivalent to an on or off condition, a yes, or a no. Often *abbreviated to* bit.

binary notation—A number system written to the base two notation.

binary number—A number, usually consisting of more than one figure, representing a sum, in which the individual quantity represented by each figure is based on a radix of two. The figures used 0 and 1.

binary number system—*Same as* system, number, 2.

binary point—The radix point in a binary number system; i.e., the dot that marks the position between the integral and fractional, or units and halves in a binary number.

binary search—A search in which the series of items is divided into two parts, one of which is rejected, and the process repeated on the unrejected part until the item with the desired property is found. This process usually depends upon the presence of a known sequence in the series. *Synonymous with* dichotomizing search.

binary signalling—A communications mode in which information is passed by the presence and absence or plus and minus variations of one parameter of the signaling medium only.

binary to decimal conversion—The process of converting a number written to the base of two to the equivalent number written to the base of ten.

binary variable—*Same as* two valued variable.

bionics—The application of knowledge gained from the analysis of living systems to the creation of hardware that will perform functions in a manner analogous to the more sophisticated functions of the living system.

bi-stable—The capability of assuming either of two stable states, hence of storing one bit of information.

bit—(1) An abbreviation of *bi*nary digi*t*. (2) A single character in a binary number. (3) A single pulse in a group of pulses. (4) A unit of information capacity of a storage device. The capacity in bits is the logarithm to the base two of the number of possible states of the device. *Related to* capacity, storage.

bit check—A binary check digit; often a parity bit. *Related to* check, parity number, self checking.

bit location—A storage position on a record capable of storing one bit.

bit, parity—*See* parity bit.

bit rate—The rate at which binary digits, or pulses representing them pass a given point on a communications line or channel. Clarified by (baud) and (capacity, channel).

bit, sign—*See* sign bit.

bit, zone—*See* zone bit.

blank—(1) A regimented place of storage where data may be stored; e.g., a location in a storage medium. *Synonymous with* space. (2) A character used to indicate an output space on a printer in which nothing is printed.

blank, switching—*Same as* dead band.

block—(1) A group of computer words considered as a unit of virtue of their being stored in successive storage locations. (2) The set of locations or tape positions in which a block of words, as defined above, is stored or recorded. (3) A circuit assemblage which functions as a unit; e.g., a circuit building block of standard design, and the logic block in a sequential circuit.

block diagram—(1) A graphical representation of the hardware in a computer system. The primary purpose of a block diagram is to indicate the paths along with information and/or control flows between the various parts of a computer system. It should not be confused with the term flowchart. (2) A coarser and less symbolic representation than a flowchart.

block, input— *See* input block.

block length—The total number of records, words or characters contained in one block.

block, output—*See* output block.

block sort—A sort of one or more of the most significant characters of a key to serve as a means of making workable sized groups from a large volume of records to be sorted.

block, standby—*See* standby block.

block transfer—The conveyance of a group of consecutive words from one place to another.

blockette—A subdivision of a group of consecutive machine words transferred as a unit, particularly with reference to input and output.

blocking—The combining of two or more records into one block.

bookkeeping operation—A computer operation which does not directly contribute to the result; i.e., arithmetical, logical, and transfer operations used in modifying the address section of other instructions, in counting cycles and in rearranging data. *Synonymous with* red tape operation.

Boolean algebra—A process of reasoning, or a deductive system of theorems using a symbolic logic, and dealing with classes, propositions, or on-off circuit elements. It employs symbols to represent operators such as AND, OR, NOT, EXCEPT, IF . . . THEN, etc., to permit mathematical calculation. Named after George Boole, famous English mathematician (1815-1864).

bootstrap—A technique for loading the first few instructions of a routine into storage; then using these instructions to bring in the rest of the routine. This usually involves either the entering of a few instructions manually or the use of a special key on the console.

borrow—An arithmetically negative carry. It occurs in direct subtraction by raising the low order digit of the minuend by one unit of the next higher order digit; e.g., when subtracting 67 from 92, a tens digit is borrowed from the 9, to raise the 2 to a factor of 12; the 7 of 67 is then subtracted from the 12 to yield 5 as the units digit of the difference; the 6 is then subtracted from 8, or 9 − 1, yielding 2 as the tens digit of the difference. *Related to* carry (3).

box, B—*Same as* index register.

box, decision—*See* decision box.

branch—The selection of one or two or more possible paths in the flow of control based on some criterion. The instructions which mechanize this concept are sometimes called branch instructions; however, the terms transfer of control and jump are more widely used. *Related to* transfer, conditional.

branch instruction—An instruction to a computer that enables the programmer to instruct the computer to choose between alternative subprograms depending upon the conditions determined by the computer during the execution of the program. *Synonymous with* transfer instruction.

branch, conditional—*See* transfer conditional.

branch, unconditional—*Same as* transfer, unconditional.

branchpoint—A point in a routine where one of two or more choices is selected under control of the routine.

breakpoint—A point in a computer program at which conditional interruption, to permit visual check, printing out, or other analyzing, may occur. Breakpoints are usually used in debugging operations.

breakpoint instruction—(1) An instruction which will cause a computer to stop or to transfer control in some standard fashion to a supervisory routine which can monitor the progress of the interrupted program; (2) an instruction which, if some specified switch is set, will cause the computer to stop or take other special action.

breakpoint switch—A manually operated switch which controls conditional operation at breakpoints, used primarily in debugging.

breakpoint symbol—A symbol which may be optionally included in an instruction, as an indication, tag, or flag, to designate it as a breakpoint.

B-register—(1) *Same as* index register; (2) a register used as an extension of the accumulator during multiply and divide processes.

broadband noise—The thermal noise which is uniformally distributed across the frequency spectrum at a wide range of energy levels.

brush—An electrical conductor for reading data from a punch card.

bucket—A slang expression used to indicate some portion of storage specifically reserved for accumulating data, or totals; e.g., "throw it in bucket #1." is a possible expression. Commonly used in initial planning.

buffer—(1) An internal portion of a data processing system serving as intermediary storage between two storage or data handling systems with different access times or formats; usually to connect an input or output device with the main or internal highspeed storage. *Clarified by* storage, buffer (4). (2) A logical OR circuit. (3) An isolating component designed to eliminate the reaction of a driven circuit on the circuits driving it; e.g., a buffer amplifier. (4) A diode.

buffer storage—(1) A synchronizing element between two different forms of storage, usually between internal and external. (2) An input device in which information is assembled from external or secondary storage and stored ready for transfer to internal storage. (3) An output device into which information is copied from internal storage and held for transfer to secondary or external storage. Computation continues while transfers between buffer storage and secondary or internal storage or vice versa take place. (4) Any device which stores information temporarily during data transfers. *Clarified by* buffer.

buffer computer—A computing system with a storage device which permits input and output data to be stored temporarily in order to match the slow speed of input-output devices with the higher speeds of the computer. Thus, simultaneous input-output computer operations are possible. A data transmission trap is essential for effective use of buffering since it obviates frequency testing for the availability of a data channel.

bug—A mistake in the design of a routine or a computer, or a malfunction.

built in check—*Same as* check, automatic.

built in automatic check—*Same as* check, automatic.

bus—(1) A circuit over which data or power is transmitted. Often one which acts as a common connection among a number of locations. *Synonymous with* trunk. (2) A communications path between two switching points.

byte—(1) A generic term to indicate a measurable portion of consecutive binary digits; e.g., an 8 bit or 6 bit byte. (2) A group of binary digits usually operated upon as a unit.

calculation, fixed point—*See* fixed point calculation.

calculation, floating point—*See* floating point calculation.

calculator—(1) A device that performs primarily arithmetic operations based upon data and instructions inserted manually or contained on punch cards. It is sometimes used interchangeability with computer. (2) A computer.

calculator, network—*Same as* network analyzer.

call in—To transfer control of a digital computer temporarily from a main routine to a subroutine, which is inserted in the sequence of calculating operations to fulfill a subsidiary purpose.

call number—(1) A group of characters identifying a subroutine and containing (a) information concerning parameters to be inserted in the subroutine, (b) information to be used in generating the subroutine, or (c) information related to the operands. (2) A call word, if the quantity of characters in the call number is equal to the length of a computer word.

calling sequence—The instructions used for linking a closed subroutine with a main routine; i.e., standard linkage and a list of the parameters.

card feed—A mechanism which moves cards serially into a machine.

card field—A set of card columns, either fixed as to number and position or, if variable, then identifiable by position relative to other fields. Corresponding fields on successive cards are normally used to store similar information.

card image—A representation in storage of the holes punched in a card, in such a manner that the holes are represented by one binary digit and the unpunched spaces are represented by the other binary digit.

card jam—A pile up of cards in a machine.

card, master—*See* master card.

card, ninety (90) column—*See* ninety (90) column card.

card programmed—(1) The capability of being programmed by punch cards, (2) the capability of performing sequences of calculating operations according to instructions contained in a stack of punch cards.

card, punch—*See* punch card.

card punch unit—*Same as* punch card.

card reader—(1) A mechanism that senses information punched into cards. (2) An input device consisting of a mechanical punch card reader and related electronic circuitry which transcribes data from punch cards to working storage or magnetic tape. *Synonymous with* card reader unit.

card reader unit—*Same as* card reader, 2.

card reproducer—A device that reproduces a punch card by punching another similar card.

card stacker—(1) A receptacle that accumulates cards after they have passed through a machine. (2) A hopper. *Synonymous with* hopper.

card to tape converter—A device which converts information directly from punched cards to punched or magnetic tape.

card, transfer—*Same as* card, transition.

card, transfer of control—*Same as* card, transition.

card, transition—*See* transition card.

carrier wave—The basic frequency or pulse repetition rate of a signal, bearing no intrinsic intelligence until it is modulated by another signal which does bear intelligence. A carrier may be amplitude, phase, or frequency modulated; e.g., in a typical mercury delay line storage of a digital computer, the 8 megacycle/second sound wave carrier is amplitude or pulse modulated by a 1 megacycle/second pulse code signal, the presence or absence of a pulse determining whether or not a one or a zero is present in the binary number being represented.

carry—(1) A signal, or expression, produced as a result of an arithmetic operation on one digit place of two or more numbers expressed in positional notation and transferred to the next higher place for processing there. (2) A signal or expression as defined in (1) above which arises in adding, when the sum of two digits in the same digit place equals or exceeds the base of the number system in use. If a carry into a digit place will result in a carry out of the same digit place, and if the normal adding circuit is by-passed when generating this new carry, it is called a high speed carry, or standing on nines carry. If the normal adding circuit is used in such a case, the carry is called a cascaded carry. If a carry resulting from the addition of carries is not allowed to propagate; e.g., when forming the partial product in one step of a multiplication process, the process is called a partial carry. If it is allowed to propagate, the process is called a complete carry. If a carry generated in the most significant digit place is sent directly to the least significant place; e.g., when adding two negative numbers using nine complements, that carry is called an end around carry. *Synonymous with* cascaded carry; complete carry; end around carry; high-speed carry; and partial carry. (3) A signal or expression in direct subtraction, as defined in (1) above which arises when the difference between the digits is less than zero. Such a carry is frequently called a borrow. *Related* to borrow. (4) The action of forwarding a carry. (5) The command directing a carry to be forwarded.

carry, cascaded—*Same as* carry, 2.

carry, complete—*Same as* carry, 2.

carry complete signal—A signal generated by a digital parallel adder, indicating that all carries from an adding operation have been generated and propagated and the addition operation is completed.

carry, end around—*Same as* carry, 2.

carry, high speed—*Same as* carry, 2.

carry, partial—*Same as* carry, 2.

carry, standing on nines—*See* standing-on-nines carry.

carry time—(1) The time required for transferring a carry digit to the higher column and there add it, (2) the time required for transferring all the carry digits to higher columns and adding them for all digits in the number.

cascade control—An automatic control system in which various control units are linked in sequence, each control unit regulating the operation of the next control unit in line.

cascaded carry—*Same as* carry, 2.

cathode follower—A vacuum tube circuit in which the input signal is applied to the control grid and the output is taken from the cathode. Electrically, such a circuit possesses high input impedance and low output impedance characteristics. The equivalent circuit using a transistor is called an emitter follower.

cell—(1) The storage for one unit of information, usually one character or one word. (2) A location specified by whole or part of the address and possessed of the faculty of store. Specific terms such as column, field, location, and block, are preferable when appropriate.

centralized data processing—Data processing performed at a single, central location on data obtained from several geographical locations or managerial levels. Decentralized data processing involves processing at various managerial levels or geographical points throughout the organization.

chad—A small piece of paper tape or punch card removed when punching a hole to represent information.

chaded paper tape—A paper tape with the holes fully punched.

chadless—A type of punching of paper tape in which each chad is left fastened by about a quarter of the circumference of the hole, at the leading edge. This mode of punching is useful where it is undesirable to destroy information written or printed on the punched tape or it is undesirable to produce chads. Chadless punched paper tape must be sensed by mechanical fingers, for the presence of chad in the tape would interfere with reliable electrical or photoelectric reading of the paper tape.

chadless paper tape—A paper tape with the holes partially punched. It is commonly used in teletype operations.

chain—(1) Any series of items linked together; (2) pertaining to a routine consisting of segments which are run through the computer in tandem, only one being within the computer at any one time and each using the output from the previous program as its input.

change dump—A print out or output recording of the contents of all storage locations in which a change has been made since the previous change dump.

change tape—A paper tape or magnetic tape carrying information that is to be used to update filed information. This filed information is often on a master tape. *Synonymous with* transaction tape.

change, step—*See* step change.

channel—(1) A path along with information, particularly a series of digits or characters, may flow. (2) One or more parallel tracks treated as a unit.

(3) In a circulating storage, a channel is one recirculating path containing a fixed number of words stored serially by word. *Synonymous with* band. (4) A path for electrical communication. (5) A band of frequencies used for communication.

channel capacity—(1) The maximum number of binary digits or elementary digits to other bases which can be handled in a particular channel per unit time. (2) The maximum possible information transmission rate through a channel at a specified error rate. The channel capacity may be measured in bits per second or bauds. *Clarified by* bit rate; baud.

channel reliability—The percentage of time the channels meet the arbitrary standards established by the user.

character—(1) One symbol of a set of elementary symbols such as those corresponding to the keys on a typewriter. The symbols usually include the decimal digits 0 through 9, the letters A through Z, punctuation marks, operation symbols, and any other single symbols which a computer may read, store, or write. (2) The electrical, magnetic, or mechanical profile used to represent a character in a computer, and its various storage and peripheral devices. A character may be represented by a group of other elementary marks, such as bits or pulses.

character, binary coded—*See* binary coded character.

character density—The number of characters that can be stored per unit of length; e.g., on some makes of magnetic tape drives, 200 or 556 bits can be stored serially, linearly, and axially to the inch.

character, illegal—*See* illegal character.

character reader—A specialized device which can convert data represented in one of the type fonts or scripts read by human beings directly into machine language. Such a reader may operate optically; or if the characters are printed in magnetic ink, the device may operate magnetically or optically.

character recognition—The technology of using a machine to sense and encode into a machine language characters which are written or printed to be read by human beings.

character, redundant—*See* redundant character.

character set—An agreed set of representations, called characters from which selections are made to denote and distinguish data. Each character differs from all others, and the total number of characters in a given set is fixed; e.g., a set may include the numerals 0 to 9, the letters A to Z, punctuation marks and a blank or space. *Clarified by* alphabet.

characteristic impedance—(1) The ratio of voltage to current at every point along a transmission line on which there are no standing waves. (2) The square root of the product of the open and short circuit impedance of the line. When a transmission line is terminated in its characteristic impedance, energy is not reflected, but is fully absorbed in the terminating impedance.

chart, logical flow—*See* logical flowchart.

chart, process—*Same as* flowchart.

check—A process of partial or complete testing of the correctness of machine operations, the existence of certain prescribed conditions within the computer, or the correctness of the results produced by a program. A check of any of these conditions may be made automatically by the equipment or may be programmed. *Related to* marginal check.

check, arithmetic—*Same as* mathematical check.

check, automatic—*See* automatic check.

check bit—A binary check digit; often a parity bit. *Related to* parity check; self-checking number.

check, built in—*Same as* automatic check.

check, built in automatic—*Same as* automatic check.

check code—To isolate and remove mistakes from a routine.

check digit—One or more redundant digits carried along with a machine word and used in relation to the other digits in the word as a self checking or error detecting code to detect malfunctions of equipment in data transfer operations. *Related to* forbidden combination check; parity check.

check indicator—A device which displays or announces that an error has been made or that a checking operation has determined that a failure has occurred.

check indicator instruction—An instruction which directs that a signal device which is turned on to call operators' attention to the fact that there is some discrepancy in the instruction now in use.

check number—A number composed of one or more digits and used to detect equipment malfunctions in data transfer operations. If a check number consists of only one digit, it is synonymous with check digit. *Related to* check digit.

check, odd-even—*Same as* parity check.

check, parity—*See* parity check.

checkpoint—A point in time in a machine run at which processing is momentarily halted to make a magnetic tape record of the condition of all the variables of the machine run such as the position of input and output tapes and a copy of working storage. Checkpoints are used in conjunction with a restart routine to minimize reprocessing time occasioned by functional failures.

check problem—A problem chosen to determine whether the computer or a program is operating correctly.

check, program—*See* program check.

check sum—The sum used in a summation check.

check, summation—*See* summation check.

check, system—*See* system check.

check, transfer—*See* transfer check.

check, twin—*See* twin check.

check, validity—*See* validity check.

chinese binary—*Same as* column binary code.

circuit—(1) A system of conductors and related electrical elements through which electrical current flows, (2) a communications link between two or more points.

circuit capacity—The number of communications channels which can be handled by a given circuit at the same time.

circuit, AND—*Same as* and gate.

circuit dropout—The momentary interruption of a transmission because of the complete failure of a circuit.

circuit, Eccles-Jordan—*Same as* flip-flop.

circuit, four wire—*See* four wire circuit.

circuit, OR—*Same as* or gate.

circuit reliability—The percentage of time the circuit meets arbitrary standards by the user.

circular shift—*Same as* cyclic shift.

circulating register—(1) A shift register in which the stored information is moved right or left, and the information from one end is reinserted at the other end. In the case of a one character right shift, the rightmost character reappears as the new leftmost character, and every other character is shifted one position to the right. (2) A register in which the process, as in 1, is continuously occurring. This can be used as a delaying mechanism.

circulating storage—A device or unit which stores information in a train or pattern of pulses, where the pattern of pulses issuing at the final end are sensed, amplified, reshaped and reinserted into the device at the beginning end.

clear—To erase the contents of a storage device by replacing the contents with blanks, or zeros. *Contrasted with* hold. *Clarified by* erase.

clock—(1) A master timing device used to provide the basic sequencing pulses for the operation of a synchronous computer; (2) a register which automatically records the progress of real time, or perhaps some approximation to it, records the number of operations performed, and whose contents are available to a computer program.

clock frequency—The master frequency of periodic pulses which schedules the operation of the computer. *Clarified by* computer, synchronous.

clock rate—The time rate at which pulses are emitted from the clock. The clock rate determines the rate at which logical or arithmetic gating is performed with a synchronous computer.

clock, real time—*See* real time clock.

closed loop—Pertaining to a system with feedback type of control, such that the output is used to modify the input.

closed routine—A routine which is not inserted as a block of instructions within a main routine but is entered by basic linkage from the main routine.

closed shop—The operation of a computer facility where programming service to the user is the responsibility of a group of specialists, thereby effectively separating the phase of task formulation from that of computer implementation. The programmers are not allowed in the computer room to run or oversee the running of their programs. *Contrasted with* open shop.

closed subroutine—A subroutine not stored in the main path of the routine. Such a subroutine is entered by a jump operation and provision is made to return control to the main routine at the end of the operation. The instructions related to the entry and re-entry function constitute a linkage. *Synonymous with* linked subroutine.

COBOL—*CO*mmon *B*usiness *O*riented *L*anguage, *see* language; common business oriented.

code—(1) A system of symbols for meaningful communications. *Related to* instruction, (1). (2) A system of symbols for representing data or instructions in a computer or a tabulating machine. (3) To translate the program for the solution of a problem on a given computer into a sequence of machine language or pseudo instructions and addresses acceptable to that computer. *Related to* encode. (4) A machine language program.

code element—The elemental unit from which a code is constructed; e.g., Baudot code is a binary representation of the alphabet and numerals in which a grouping, presence or absence, of five elements expresses the code information.

coded decimal—Describing a form of notation by which each decimal digit separately is expressed in some other number system; e.g., in the 8-4-2-1 coded decimal notation, the number twelve is represented as 1100. Other coded decimal notations used are the 5-4-2-1, the excess three, and the 2-3-2-1 codes.

coded decimal number—A number consisting of successive characters or a group of characters in which each character or group of characters usually represents a specific figure in an associated decimal number; e.g., if the figures of a decimal number are 45, the coded decimal number might be represented as GQ, or LLZZ, or 1101 0110.

coded program—A program which has been expressed in the code or language of a specific machine or programming system.

coded stop—A stop instruction built into the routine.

coder—A person who prepares instruction sequences from detailed flow charts and other algorithmic procedures prepared by others, as *contrasted with* a programmer who prepares the procedures and flowcharts.

coding—The ordered list in computer code or pseudo code, of the successive computer instructions representing successive computer operations for solving a specific problem.

coding, minimum access—*See* minimum access coding.

coincidence gate—A circuit with the ability to produce an output which is dependent upon a specified type of or the coincident nature of the input; e.g., an AND gate has an output pulse when there are pulses in time coincidence at all inputs; an OR gate has an output when any one or any combination of input pulses occur in time coincidence. Any gate may contain a number of inhibits, in which there is no output under any condition of input if there is time coincidence of an inhibit or except signal.

collate—To merge two or more ordered sets of data, or cards in order to produce one or more ordered sets which still reflect the original ordering relations. The collation process is the merging of two sequences of cards, each ordered on some mutual key, into a single sequence ordered on the mutual key.

collation sequence—The sequence in which the characters acceptable to a computer are ordered.

collator—A device used to collate or merge sets or decks of cards or other units into a sequence. A typical example of a card collator has two input feeds, so that two ordered sets may enter into the process, and four output stackers, so that four ordered sets can be generated by the process. Three comparison stations are used to route the cards to one stacker or the other on the basis of comparison of criteria as specified by plugboard wiring.

column—(1) A character or digit position in a positional information format, particularly one in which characters appear in rows, and the rows are placed one above another; e.g., the rightmost column in a five decimal place table, or in a list of data. (2) A character or digit position in a physical device, such as punch card or a register, corresponding to a position in a written table or list; e.g., the rightmost place in a register; or the third column in an eighty column punch card.

column-binary code—A code used with punch cards in which successive bits are represented by the presence or absence of punches on contiguous positions in successive columns as opposed to rows. Column binary code is widely used in connnection with 36 bit word computers where each group of 3 columns is used to represent a single word. *Synonymous with* chinese binary code.

command—(1) An electronic pulse, signal or set of signals to start, stop or continue some operation. It is incorrect to use command as a synonym for instruction. (2) The portion of an instruction word which specifies the operation to be performed.

comment—An expression which explains or identifies a particular step in a routine, but which has no effect on the operation of the computer in performing the instructions for the routine.

COmmon Business Oriented Language—A specific language by which business data processing procedures may be precisely described in a standard form. The language is intended not only as a means for directly presenting any business program to any suitable computer, for which a compiler exists, but also as a means of communicating such procedures among individuals. *Synonymous with* COBOL.

common machine language—A machine sensible information representation which is common to a related group of data processing machines.

comparator—(1) A device for comparing two different transcriptions of the same information to verify the accuracy of transcription, storage, arithmetic operation, or other processes, in which a signal is given dependent upon some relation between two items; i.e., one item is larger than, smaller than, or equal to the other. (2) A form of verifier.

compare—To examine the representation of a quantity to discover its relationship to zero, or to examine two quantities usually for the purposes of discovering identity or relative magnitude.

comparison—The act of comparing and, usually, acting on the result of the comparison. The common forms are comparison of two numbers for identity, comparison of two numbers for relative magnitude, and comparison of two signs plus or minus.

compatibility, equipment—*See* equipment compatibility.

compile—To produce a machine language routine from a routine written in source language by selecting appropriate subroutines from a subroutine library, as directed by the instructions or other symbols of the original routine, supplying the linkage which combines the subroutines into a workable routine and translating the subroutines and linkage into machine language. The compiled routine is then ready to be loaded into storage and run; i.e., the compiler does not usually run the routine it produces.

compiler—A computer program more powerful than an assembler. In addition to its translating function which is generally the same process as that used in an assembler it is able to replace certain items of input with series of instructions, usually called subroutines. Thus, where an assembler translates item for item, and produces as output the same number of instructions or constants which were put into it, a compiler will do more than this. The program which results from compiling is a translated and expanded version of the original. *Synonymous with* compiling routine. *Related to* assembler.

compiling routine—*Same as* compiler.

complement—(1) A quantity expressed to the base N, which is derived from a given quantity by a particular rule; frequently used to represent the negative of the given quantity. (2) A complement on N, obtained by subtracting each digit of the given quantity from N–1, adding unity to the least significant digit, and performing all resultant carrys; e.g., the twos complement of binary 11010 is 00110; the tens complement of decimal 456 is 554. (3) A complement on N–1, obtained by subtracting each digit of the given quantity from N–1; e.g., the ones complement of binary 11010 is 00101; the nines complement of decimal 456 is 543. *Synonymous with* radix minus 1 complement; radix complement.

complement, radix—*Same as* complement, 3.

complement, radix, minus 1—*Same as* complement, 2.

complete carry—*Same as* carry, 2.

complete operation—An operation which includes obtaining the instruction, obtaining all the operands from storage, performing the operation, and returning the results to storage.

computer—A device capable of accepting information, applying prescribed processes to the information, and supplying the results of these processes. It usually consists of input and output devices, storage, arithmetic, and logical units, and a control unit.

computer code—(1) A system of combinations of binary digits used by a given computer. *Synonymous with* machine code. (2) A repertoire of instructions.

computer limited—Pertaining to a situation in which the time required for computation exceeds the time required to read inputs and write outputs.

computer operation—The electronic action resulting from an instruction. In general it is a computer manipulation required to secure results.

computer parallel—*See* parallel computer.

concept coordination—A term used to describe the basic principles of various punched card and mechanized information retrieval systems which involve the multidimensional analysis of information and coordination retrieval. In concept coordination, independently assigned concepts are used to characterize the subject contents of documents and the latter are identified during searching by means of either such assigned concepts or a combination of the same.

condensed instruction deck—The card output from an assembly program in which several instructions per card are punched in machine language. Input to the assembly program may consist of one instruction per card, thus, the name condensed is used for output.

conditional branch—*Same as* conditional transfer.

conditional breakpoint instruction—A conditional jump instruction which, if some specified switch is set or situation exists, will cause the computer to stop; after which either the routine may be continued as coded, or a jump may be forced.

conditional jump—*Same as* conditional transfer.

conditional transfer—An instruction which, if a specified condition or set of conditions is satisfied, is interpreted as an unconditional transfer.

If the condition is not satisfied, the instruction causes the computer to proceed in its normal sequence of control. A conditional transfer also includes the testing of the condition. *Synonymous with* conditional jump *and* conditional branch. *Related to* branch.

conditional transfer of control—A computer instruction which when reached in the course of a program will cause the computer either to continue with the next instruction in the original sequence or to transfer control to another stated instruction, depending on a condition regarding some property of a number or numbers which has then been determined.

conditional, signal—*See* signal conditioning.

configuration—A group of machines which are interconnected and are programmed to operate as a system.

conjunction—The logical operation which makes use of the AND operator or logical product. The conjunction of two variables, or expressions, may be written as A.B, A∨B, A∧B, or just plain AB. These may also be described as an intersection when using Venn diagrams. *Clarified by* Operator, and; gate, and. *Contrasted with* disjunction.

conjunctive search—A search defined in terms of a logical product; i.e., conjunctive form, in contrast to a disjunctive form, or logical sum.

connectives, logical—*See* logical connectives.

connector, variable—*See* variable connector.

console—A portion of the computer which may be used to control the machine manually, correct errors, determine the status of machine circuits, registers, and counters, determine the contents of storage, and manually revise the contents of storage.

constant area—A part of storage designated to store the invariable quantities required for processing.

constant instruction—An instruction not intended to be executed as an instruction, written in the form of a constant. *Related to* instruction, dummy.

constant(s)—The quantities or messages, which will be present in the machine and available as data for the program and which, usually, are not subject to change with time.

content(s)—The data contained in any storage medium. Quite prevalently, the symbol ( ) is used to indicate the contents of; e.g., (M) indicates the contents of the storage location whose address is M; or (T2) may indicate the contents of the tape on input-output unit two.

control—(1) The part of a digital computer or processor which determines the execution and interpretation of instructions in proper sequence, including the decoding of each instruction and the application of the proper signals to the arithmetic unit and other registers in accordance with the decoded information. (2) Frequently, it is one or more of the components in any mechanism responsible for interpreting and carrying out manually initiated directions. Sometimes it is called manual control.

(3) In some business applications, a mathematical check. (4) In programming, instructions which determine conditional jumps are often referred to as control instructions, and the time sequence of execution of instructions is called the flow of control.

control card—A card which contains input data or parameters for a specific application of a general routine.

control, cascade—*See* cascade control.

control counter—A device which records the storage location of the instruction word, which is to be operated upon following the instruction word in current use. The control counter may select storage locations in sequence, thus obtaining the next instruction word from the subsequent storage location, unless a transfer or special instruction is encountered.

control data—The items of data, one or more of which is used to identify, select, execute or modify another routine, record, file, operation or data value.

control, feedback—*See* feedback control.

control field—A constant location where information for control purposes is placed; e.g., in a set of punch cards, if columns 79 and 80 contain various codes which control whether or not certain operations will be performed on any particular card, then columns 79 and 80 constitute a control field.

control grid—The electrode of a vacuum tube other than a diode upon which a signal voltage is impressed in order to regulate the plate current, usually electrode or grid number 1.

control, manual—*See* manual control.

control, master—*See* master control.

control panel—(1) An interconnection device, usually removable, which employs removable wires to control the operation of computing equipment. It is used on punch card machines, to carry out functions which are under control of the user. On computers it is used primarily to control input and output functions. (2) A device or component of some data processing machines, which permits the expression of instructions in a semi-fixed computer program by the insertion of pins, plugs, or wires into sockets, or hubs in the device, in a pattern to represent instructions, and thus making electrical interconnections which may be sensed by the data processing machine. *Synonymous with* plugboard. *Related to* pinboard.

control register—A register which holds the identification of the instruction word to be executed next in time sequence, following the current operation. The register is often a counter which is incremented to the address of the next sequential storage location, unless a transfer or other special instruction is specified by the program. *Synonymous with* program counter. *Contrasted with* register, program (1).

control sequence—The normal order of selection of instructions for execution. In some computers one of the addresses in each instruction specifies the control sequence. In most other computers, the sequence is consecutive except where a transfer occurs.

control total—A sum of numbers in a specified record field of a batch of records, determined repetitiously, during the processing operation so that any discrepancy from the control indicates an error. A control total often has some significance in itself, but may not, as for example, when a control total is determined as the sum of identification numbers of records. *Related to* total, hash.

control unit—The portion of a computer which directs the sequence of operations, interprets the coded instructions, and initiates the proper commands to the computer circuits preparatory to execution.

control word—A word, usually the first or last of a record, or first or last word of a block which carries indicative information for the following words, records, or blocks.

conversion—(1) The process of changing information from one form of representation to another; such as, from the language of one type of machine to that of another or from magnetic tape to the printed page. *Synonymous with* conversion, data. (2) The process of changing from one data processing method to another, or from one type of equipment to another; e.g., conversion from punch card equipment to magnetic tape equipment.

conversion, binary to decimal—*See* binary to decimal conversion.

conversion, data—*Same as* conversion, 1.

conversion, decimal to binary—*See* decimal to binary conversion.

conversion equipment—The equipment that is capable of transposing or transcribing the information from one type of data processing medium to render it acceptable as input to another type of processing medium.

convert—(1) To change numerical information from one number base to another (2) to transfer information from one recorded medium to another.

converter—A device which converts the representation of information, or which permits the changing of the method for data processing from one form to another; e.g., a unit which accepts information from punch cards and records the information on magnetic tape, and possibly including editing facilities.

converter, card to tape—*See* card to tape converter.

converter, tape to card—*See* tape to card converter.

coordinate indexing—An indexing scheme by which descriptors may be correlated or combined to show any interrelationships desired to purposes of more precise information retrieval.

coordinate paper—Marginally punched, continuous form graph paper normally used for printout on an XY plotter.

copy—To reproduce information in a new location, replacing whatever was previously stored there, and usually leaving the information unchanged at the original location.

copy, hard—*See* hard copy.

Cordonnier system—*Same as* peek-a-boo system.

core dump—*Same as* storage dump.

core storage—*Same as* magnetic core storage.

correction, automatic error—*See* automatic error correction.

counter—A device, register, or location in storage for storing numbers or number representations in a manner which permits these numbers to be increased or decreased by the value of another number, or to be changed or reset to zero or to an arbitrary value.

CPU—*C*entral *P*rocessing *U*nit. *Same as* main frame, **1**.

crippled leap frog test—A variation of the leapfrog test, modified so that it repeats its tests from a single set of storage locations rather than a changing set of locations. *Related to* leapfrog test.

cross bar—An automatic telephone switching system using movable switches mounted on bars. The dialed information is received and stored by common circuits which select and test the switching paths and control the operation of the switching mechanisms.

crosstalk—(1) The unwanted signals in a channel which originate from one or more other channels in the same communications system; (2) signals electrically coupled from another circuit, usually undesirably, but sometimes for useful purposes.

cryogenics—The field of technology in which the use of devices utilizing properties assumed by metals at absolute zero. At these temperatures large current changes can be obtained by relatively small magnetic field changes.

cybernetics—The field of technology involved in the comparative study of the control and intracommunication of information handling machines and nervous systems of animals and man in order to understand and improve communication.

cycle—(1) The *same as* loop, **1**. (2) A nonarithmetic shift in which digits dropped off at one end of a word are returned at the other end in circular fashion; e.g., cycle left and cycle right. (3) To repeat a set of operations, indefinitely or until a stated condition is met. The set of operations may be subject to variation on each repetition, as by address changes obtained by programmed computation or by use of devices such as an index register. (4) An occurrence, phenomena, or interval of space or time that recurs regularly and in the same sequence; e.g., the interval required for completion of one operation in a repetitive sequence of operations.

cycle-index—The number of times a cycle has been executed or the difference, or the negative of the difference, between the number that has been executed and the number of repetitions desired.

cycle-reset—To return a cycle index to its initial value.

cyclic code—*See* gray code.

cyclic shift—A shift in which the digits dropped off at one end of a word are returned at the other in a circular fashion; e.g., if, register holds eight digits, 23456789, the result of a cyclic shift two columns to the left would be to change the contents of the register to 45678923. *Synonymous with* circular shift; end around shift; logical shift; non arithmetic shift; and ring shift.

damping—A characteristic built into electrical circuits and mechanical systems to prevent rapid or excessive corrections which may lead to instability or oscillatory conditions; e.g., connecting a register on the terminals of a pulse transformer to remove natural oscillations or placing a moving element in oil or sluggish grease to prevent mechanical overshoot of the moving parts.

data—A general term used to denote any or all facts, numbers, letters and symbols, or facts that refer to or describe an object, ideal, condition, situation, or other factors. It connotes basic elements of information which can be processed or produced by a computer. Sometimes data is considered to be expressible only in numerical form, but information is not so limited. *Related to* information.

data, control—*See* control data.

data conversion—*Same as* conversion, 1.

data element—A specific item of information appearing in a set of data; e.g., in the following set of data, each item is a data element: the quantity of a supply item issued, a unit rate, an amount, and the balance of stock items on hand.

data error—A deviation from correctness in data, usually an error, which occurred prior to processing the data.

data handling—*Same as* processing, data 2.

data, master—*See* master data.

data origination—The act of creating a record in a machine sensible form, directly or as a by-product of a human readable document.

data phone—A generic term to describe a family of devices available to facilitate data communication.

data processing—(1) The preparation of source media which contain data or basic elements of information, and the handling of such data according to precise rules of procedure to accomplish such operations as classifying, sorting, calculating, summarizing, and recording. (2) The production of records and reports. *Synonymous with* data handling.

data processing center—A computer installation providing data processing service for others, sometimes called customers, on a reimbursable or non-reimbursable basis.

data processing machine—A general name for a machine which can store and process numeric and alphabetic information. *Related to* analog computer; digital computer; automatic data processing equipment.

data purification—The reduction of the number of errors as much as possible prior to using data in an automatic data processing system.

data, raw—*See* raw data.

data reduction—The process of transforming masses of raw test or experimentally obtained data, usually gathered by automatic recording equipment, into useful, condensed, or simplified intelligence.

data reduction, on-line—*See* on-line data reduction.

data, test—*See* test data.

data, transaction—*See* transaction data.

data transmission equipment—The communications equipment used in direct support of data processing equipment.

data word—A word which may be primarily regarded as part of the information manipulated by a given program. A data word may be used to modify a program instruction, or to be arithmetically combined with other data words.

datamation—A shortened term for automatic data processing; taken from data and automation.

date, delivery—*See* delivery date.

date, installation—*See* installation date.

dc coupled—The connection by a device which passes the steady state characteristics of a signal and which largely eliminates the transient or oscillating characteristics of the signal.

dc dump—The removal of all direct current power, intentionally, accidentally or conditionally, from a system or component.

DDA—*D*igital *D*ifferential *A*nalyzer An incremental differential analyzer, usually electronic.

dead band—A specific range of values in which the incoming signal can be altered without also changing the outgoing response. *Synonymous with* dead space; dead zone; switching blank. *Similar to* zone, neutral.

dead halt—*Same as* drop dead halt.

dead space—*Same as* dead band.

dead time—Any definite delay deliberately placed between two related actions in order to avoid overlap that might cause confusion or to permit a particular different event such as a control decision, switching event or similar action to take place.

dead zone—*Same as* dead band.

debug—(1) To locate and correct any errors in a computer program. (2) To detect and correct malfunctions in the computer itself. *Related to* diagnostic routine.

debugging aid routine—A routine to aid programmers in the debugging of their routines. Some typical routines are: storage, print out, tape print out and drum print out routines.

decade—A group of assembly of ten units, e.g., a counter which counts to ten in one column or a resistor box which inserts resistance quantities in multiples of powers of 10.

decay time—The time in which a voltage or current pulse will decrease to one tenth of its maximum value. Decay time is proportional to the time constant of the circuit.

deceleration time—The time which elapses between completion of reading or writing of a tape record and the time when the tape stops moving. *Synonymous with* stop time.

decimal, binary coded—*See* binary coded decimal.

decimal, coded—*See* coded decimal.

decimal coded digit—A digit or character defined by a set of decimal digits, such as a pair of decimal digits specifying a letter or special character in a system of notation.

decimal number—A number, usually of more than one figure, representing a sum, in which the quantity represented by each figure is based on the radix of ten. The figures used are 0, 1, 2, 3, 4, 5, 6, 7, 8, and 9.

decimal numbering system—A system of reckoning by 10 or the powers of 10 using the digits 0-9 to express numerical quantities.

decimal to binary conversion—The process of converting a number written in the base of two from the equivalent number written in the base of ten.

decision—The computer operation of determining if a certain relationship exists between words in storage or registers, and taking alternative courses of action. This is effected by conditional jumps or equivalent techniques. Use of this term has given rise to the misnomer "magic brain;" actually the process consists of making comparisons by use of arithmetic to determine the relationship of two terms (numeric, alphabetic or a combination of both); e.g., equal, greater than, or less than.

decision box—The symbol used in flowcharting to indicate a choice or branching in the information processing path.

decision, logical—*See* logical decision.

deck—A collection of cards, commonly a complete set of cards which have been punched for a definite service or purpose.

deck, condensed instruction—*See* condensed instruction deck.

decode—(1) To apply a code so as to reverse some previous encoding; (2) to determine the meaning of individual characters or groups of characters in a message; (3) to determine the meaning of an instruction from the set of pulses which describes the instruction, command, or operation to be performed.

decoder—(1) A device which determines the meaning of a set of signals and initiates a computer operation based thereon. (2) A matrix of switching elements which selects one or more output channels according to the combination of input signals present. *Contrasted with* encoder. *Clarified by* matrix.

decoding—(1) Performing the internal operations by which a computer determines the meaning of the operation code of an instruction; also sometimes applied to addresses. In interpretive routines and some subroutines, an operation by which a computer determines the meaning of parameters in the routine. (2) Translating a secretive language into the clear.

decrement—(1) The quantity by which a variable is decreased. (2) A specific part of an instruction word in some binary computers, thus a set of digits.

decrement field—A portion of an instruction word set aside specifically for modifying the contents of a register or storage location.

definition—(1) The resolution and sharpness of an image, or the extent to which an image is brought into sharp relief; (2) the degree with which a communication system reproduces sound images or messages.

definition, problem—*See* problem definition.

deflection sensitivity—Used in connection with cathode ray tubes, the quotient of the change in displacement of the electron beam at the place of impact, divided by the change in the deflecting field. It is usually expressed in millimeters per volt applied between the deflection electrode plates for electrostatic field deflection, or in millimeters per gauss for magnetic field deflection.

delay—(1) The length of time after the close of a reporting period before information pertaining to that period becomes available. Delay may also cover the time to process data, and prepare and distribute reports. (2) The retardation of the flow of information in a channel for a finite period of time.

delay, differential—*See* differential delay.

delay line—A device capable of retarding a pulse of energy between input and output, based on the properties of materials, or circuit parameters or mechanical devices. Examples of delay lines are material media such as mercury, in which sonic patterns may be propagated in time; lumped constant electrical lines; coaxial cables, transmission lines and recirculating magnetic drum loops. *Related to* magnetic delay line.

delimiter—A character which limits a string of characters, and therefore cannot be a member of the string.

delivery date—The data of physical delivery on site of the components of the computer configuration without regard to whether or not they have been unpacked, placed in final position, or interconnected. Delivery of equipment carries no connotation of operational status.

demodulator—(1) A device which receives tones from a transmission circuit and converts them to electrical pulses, or bits, which may be accepted by a business machine. (2) A device which detects the modulating signals, thus removes the carrier signal and reconstitutes the intelligence. *Clarified by* modulation code. *Contrasted with* modulator.

density, character—*See* character density.

density, packing—*See* packing density.

descriptor—An elementary term, word, or simple phrase used to identify a subject, concept, or idea.

design, item—*See* item design.

design, logical—*See* logical design.

detail file—A file of information which is relatively transient. This is contrasted with a master file which contains relatively more permanent information; e.g., in the case of weekly payroll for hourly employees, the detail file will contain employee number, regular time, and overtime, the hours such employee has worked in a given week, and other information changing weekly. The master file will contain the employee's name, number, department, rate of pay, deduction specifications, and other information which regularly stays the same from week to week.

diagnostic routine—A routine used to locate a malfunction in a computer, or to aid in locating mistakes in a computer program. Thus, in general any routine specifically designed to aid in debugging or trouble shooting. *Synonymous with* malfunction routine. *Related to* debugging (2).

diagnostic test—The running of a machine program or routine for the purpose of discovering a failure or a potential failure of a machine element, and to determine its location or its potential location.

diagnotor—A combination diagnostic and edit routine which questions unusual situations and notes the implied results.

diagram—(1) A schematic representation of a sequence of subroutines designed to solve a problem. (2) A coarser and less symbolic representation than a flow chart, frequently including descriptions in English words. (3) A schematic or logical drawing showing the electrical circuit or logical arrangements within a component.

di-cap storage—A device capable of holding data in the form of an array of charged capacitors, or condensers, and using diodes for controlling information flow.

dichotomizing search—*Same as* binary search.

dictionary—A list of code names used in a routine or system and their intended meaning in that routine or system.

dictionary, automatic—*See* automatic dictionary.

dictionary code—An alphabetic arrangement of English words and terms, associated with their code representations. *Related to* reverse code dictionary.

difference, logical—*See* logical difference.

differential analyzer—A computer (usually analog) designed and used primarily for solving many types of differential equations.

differential delay—The difference between the maximum and the minimum frequency delays occurring across a band.

differentiator—A device whose output function is proportional to a derivative; i.e., the rate of change, of its input function with respect to one or more variables.

digit—A sign or symbol used to convey a specific quantity of information either by itself or with other numbers of its set; e.g., 2, 3, 4, and 5 are digits. The base or radix must be specified and each digit's value assigned.

digital—Pertaining to the utilization of discrete integral numbers in a given base to represent all the quantities that occur in a problem or a calculation. It is possible to express in digital form all information stored, transferred, or processed by a dual state condition; e.g., on-off, open-closed, and true-false.

digital computer—A computer which processes information represented by combinations of discrete or discontinuous data as compared with an analog computer for continuous data. More specifically, it is a device for performing sequences of arithmetic and logical operations, not only on data but its own program. Still more specifically it is a stored program digital computer capable of performing sequences of internally stored instructions, as opposed to calculators, such as card programmed calculators, on which the sequence is impressed manually. *Related to* machine, data processing.

digital differential analyzer—An incremental differential analyzer, usually electronic.

digitize—To convert an analog measurement of a physical variable into a numerical value, thereby expressing the quantity in digital form. *Synonymous with* quantize.

digitizer—A device which converts an analog measurement into digital form. *Synonymous with* quantizer.

digit(s), equivalent binary—*See* equivalent binary digit.

digit(s), significant—*See* significant digit.

diode—A device used to permit current flow in one direction in a circuit and to inhibit current flow in the other. In computers, these are primarily germanium or silicon crystals.

direct address—An address which indicates the location where the referenced operand is to be found or stored with no reference to an index register or B-Box. *Synonymous with* first level address.

direct code—A code which specifies the use of actual computer command and address configurations.

direct insert subroutine—*Same as* open subroutine.

directory—A file with the layout for each field of the record which it describes; thus a directory describes the layout of a record within a file.

disjunction—The logical operation which makes use of the OR operator or the logical sum. The disjunction of two variables, or expressions, may be written as A+B, A∨B, or A∧B. These may also be described as a union when using Venn diagrams. *Clarified by* or operator; gate, or. *Contrasted with* conjunction.

disjunctive search—A search defined in terms of a logical sum; i.e., disjunctive form, ***in contrast to*** a conjunctive form or logical product.
disk, magnetic—*See* magnetic disk.
disk storage—The storage of data on the surface of magnetic disks. *Related to* magnetic disk; magnetic disk storage.
disperse—A data processing operation in which input items or fields are distributed or duplicated in more than one output item or field.
display tube—A cathode ray tube used to display information.
distributor—The electronic circuitry which acts as an intermediate link between the accumulator and drum storage.
distributor, time pulse—*See* time pulse distributor.
document—(1) A form, voucher, or written evidence of a transaction; (2) to instruct, as by citation of references; (3) to substantiate, as by listing of authorities.
document, source—*See* source document.
documentation—The group of techniques necessary for the orderly presentation, organization and communication of recorded specialized knowledge, in order to maintain a complete record of reasons for changes in variables. Documentation is necessary not so much to give maximum utility as to give an unquestionable historical reference record.
docuterm—A word or phrase descriptive of the subject matter or concept of an item of information and considered important for later retrieval of information. Related to aspect card.
double length number—A number having twice as many figures as are normally handled in a particular device. *Synonymous with* double precision number.
double precision—The retention of twice as many digits of a quantity as the computer normally handles; e.g., if a computer, whose basic word consists of 10 decimal digits is called upon to handle 20 decimal digit quantities, then double precision arithmetic must be resorted to.
double precision number—*Same as* double length number.
double precision quantity—A quantity having twice as many digits as are normally carried in a word of a fixed word length computer.
down time—The period during which a computer is malfunctioning or not operating correctly due to mechanical or electronic failure, as opposed to available time, idle time, or stand-by time, during which the computer is functional. *Contrasted with* up time.
drive, tape—*Same as* tape transport. *Synonymous with* tape unit. *Clarified by* magnetic tape unit; paper tape unit.
drop dead halt—A machine halt from which there is no recovery. Such a halt may be deliberately programmed. A drop dead halt may occur through a logical error in programming. Examples in which a drop dead halt could occur are division by zero and transfer to a nonexistent

instruction word. *Synonymous with* dead halt.

drops, false—*See* false drops.

drum, magnetic—*See* magnetic drum.

drum mark—A character used to signify the end of a record on a drum.

dummy—An artificial address, instruction, or record of information inserted solely to fulfill prescribed conditions, such as to achieve a fixed word length or block length, but without itself affecting machine operations except to permit the machine to perform desired operations.

dummy instruction—An artificial instruction or address inserted in a list to serve a purpose other than the execution as an instruction. *Related to* constant instruction.

dump check—A check which usually consists of adding all the digits during dumping, and verifying the sum when retransferring.

duodecimal number—A number, consisting of successive characters, representing a sum, in which the individual quantity represented by each character is based on a radix of twelve. The characters used are 0, 1, 2, 3, 4, 5, 6, 7, 8, 9, T (for ten), and E (for eleven). *Related to* number systems.

duoprimed word—A computer word containing a representation of the 6, 7, 8, and 9 rows of information from an 80-column card.

duplex—Pertaining to a twin, a pair or a two-in-one situation; e.g., a channel providing simultaneous transmission in both directions or a second set of equipment to be used in event of the failure of the primary or either device.

duplication check—A check which requires that the results of two independent performances, either concurrently on duplicate equipment or at different times on the same equipment, of the same operation, be identical.

dynamic memory—*Same as* dynamic storage.

dynamic storage—The storage of data on a device or in a manner that permits the data to move or vary with time, and thus the data is not always available instantly for recovery; e.g., acoustic delay line, magnetic drum, or circulating or recirculating of information in a medium.

dynamic subroutine—A subroutine which involves parameters, such as decimal point position or item size, from which a relatively coded subroutine is derived. The computer itself is expected to adjust or generate the subroutine according to the parametric values chosen.

EAM—*E*lectrical *A*ccounting *M*achine. The set of conventional punch card equipment including sorters, collators and tabulators. *Synonymous with* EAM. *Clarified by* tabulating equipment.

Eccles-Jordan circuit—*Same as* flip-flop.

Eccles-Jordan Trigger—*Same as* flip-flop.

echo check—A check of accuracy of transmission in which the information which was transmitted to an output device is returned to the information source and compared with the original information to insure accuracy of output.

edge notched card—A card of any size provided with a series of holes on one or more edges for use in coding information for a simple mechanical search technique. Each hole position may be coded to represent an item of information by notching away the edge of the card into the hole. Cards containing desired information may then be mechanically selected from a deck by inserting a long needle in a hole position and lifting the deck to allow the notched cards to fall from the needle. Unwanted cards remain in the deck.

edge punched card—A card of fixed size into which information may be recorded or stored by punching holes along one edge in a pattern similar to that used for punch tape. Hole positions are arranged to form coded patterns in 5, 6, 7, or 8 channels and usually represent data by a binary coded decimal system.

edit—To rearrange data or information. Editing may involve the deletion of unwanted data, the selection of pertinent data, the application of format techniques, the insertion of symbols such as page numbers and typewriter characters, the application of standard processes such as zero suppression, and the testing of data for reasonableness and proper range. Editing may sometimes be distinguished between input edit (rearrangement of source data) and output edit (preparation of table formats).

edit, post—*See* post edit.

editor—A routine which performs editing operations.

EDP—*E*lectronic *D*ata *P*rocessing. Data processing performed largely by electronic equipment.

effective address—(1) A modified address. (2) The address actually considered to be used in a particular execution of a computer instruction.

eighty (80) column card—A punch card with 80 vertical columns representing 80 characters. Each column is divided into two sections, one with character positions labeled zero through nine, and the other labeled eleven (11) and (12) twelve. The 11 and 12 positions are also referred to as the X and Y zone punches, respectively. *Related to* punch card; ninety column card.

electric delay line—A delay line using properties of lumped or distributed capacitive and inductive elements.

electrical accounting machine—*Same as* EAM.

electronic—Pertaining to that branch of science which deals with the motion, emission and behavior of currents of free electrons, especially in vacuum, gas or phototubes and special conductors or semiconductors. This is *contrasted with* electric which pertains to the flow of large currents in metal conductors.

electronic calculating punch—A card punch machine which reads a punch card, performs arithmetic and other operations sequentially and punches the result in a card.

electronic data processing—*Same as* EDP.

electronic data processing equipment—*Same as* automatic data processing equipment, (1).

electronic data processing machine—*Same as* automatic data processing equipment.

electronic data processing system—The general term used to define a system for data processing by means of machines utilizing electronic circuitry at electronic speed, as opposed to electromechanical equipment.

electronic differential analyzer—A form of analog computer using interconnected electronic integrators to solve differential equations.

electronic switch—A circuit element causing a start and stop action or a switching action electronically, usually at high speeds.

electrostatic printer—*Same as* xerographic printer.

electrostatic storage—(1) The storage of data on a dielectric surface such as the screen of a cathode ray tube, in the form of the presence or absence of spots bearing electrostatic charges, that can persist for a short time after the electrostatic charging force is removed. (2) A storage device so used.

element, data—*See* data element.

element, logical—*See* logical element.

eleven punch (11-punch)—*Same as* punch, x, (2).

encipher—*Same as* encode, (1) and (2).

encode—(1) To apply a code, frequently one consisting of binary numbers, to represent individual characters or groups of characters in a message. *Synonymous with* encipher. *Inverse of* decode. (2) To substitute letters, numbers, or characters for other numbers, letters, or characters, usually to intentionally hide the meaning of the message except to certain individuals who know the enciphering scheme. *Synonymous with* encipher.

encoded question—A question set up and encoded in a form appropriate for operating, programming or conditioning a searching device.

encoder—A device capable of translating from one method of expression to another method of expression, e.g., translating a message, "add the contents of A to the contents of B", into a series of binary digits. *Contrasted with* decoder. *Clarified by* matrix.

end around carry—*Same as* carry, (2).

end around shift—*Same as* cyclic shift.

end of file—Termination or point of completion of a quantity of data. End of the file marks are used to indicate this point. *Synonymous with* EOF.

end of file indicator—A device associated with each input and output unit that makes an end of file condition known to the routine and operator controlling the computer.

end mark—An indicator to signal the end of a word or the end of a unit of data.

engineering time—The total machine down time necessary for routine testing, good or bad, for machine servicing due to breakdowns, or for preventive servicing measures; e.g., block tube changes. This includes all test time, good or bad, following breakdown and subsequent repair or preventive servicing. *Synonymous with* servicing time.

English, ruly—*See* ruly English.

entry—(1) A statement in a programming system. In general each entry is written on one line of a coding form and punched on one card, although some systems permit a single entry to overflow several cards. (2) A member of a list.

entry, keyboard—*See* keyboard entry.

EOF—End Of File. *See* end of file.

equation solver—A calculating device, usually analog, which solves systems of linear simultaneous non-differential equations or determines the roots of polynomials or both.

equipment, automatic data processing—*See* automatic data processing equipment.

equipment, auxiliary—*See* auxiliary equipment.

equipment compatibility—The characteristic of computers by which one computer may accept and process data prepared by another computer without conversion or code modification.

equipment, conversion—*See* conversion equipment.

equipment, data transmission—*See* data transmission equipment.

equipment, electronic data processing—*Same as* automatic data processing equipment, (1).

equipment failure—A fault in the equipment, excluding all external factors, which prevents the accomplishment of a scheduled job.

equipment, input—*See* input equipment.

equipment, off line—*See* off line equipment.

equipment, on-line—*See* on-line equipment.

equivalent binary digits—The number of binary digits required to express a number in another base with the same precision; e.g., approximately 3-1/3 binary digits are required to express in binary form each digit of a decimal number. For the case of coded decimal notation, the number of binary digits required is usually 4 times the number of decimal digits.

erasable storage—(1) A storage device whose data can be altered during the course of a computation; e.g., magnetic tape, drum and cores. (2) An area of storage used for temporary storage.

erase—To replace all the binary digits in a storage device by binary zeros.

In a binary computer, erasing is equivalent to clearing, while in a coded decimal computer where the pulse code for decimal zero may contain binary ones, clearing leaves decimal zero while erasing leaves all zero pulse codes in all storage locations. *Clarified by* clear.

error—(1) The general term referring to any deviation of a computed or a measured quantity from the theoretically correct or true value. (2) The part of the error due to a particular identifiable cause; e.g., a truncation error, or a rounding error. In a restricted sense, that deviation due to unavoidable random disturbances, or to the use of finite approximations to what is defined by an infinite series. *Contrasted with* mistake. (3) The amount by which the computed or measured quantity differs from the theoretically correct or true value.

error, absolute—*See* absolute error.

error, balanced (range of)—*See* balanced error, range of.

error correcting code—An error detecting code in which the forbidden pulse combination produced by gain or loss of a bit indicates which bit is wrong.

error, data—*See* data error.

error detecting code—A code in which errors produce forbidden combinations. A single error detecting code produces a forbidden combination if a digit gains or loses a single bit. A double error detecting code produces a forbidden combination if a digit gains or loses either one or two bits and so forth. *Synonymous with* self checking code. *Related to* self checking number.

error detection routine—A routine used to detect whether or not an error has occurred, usually without special provision to find or indicate its location.

error range—(1) The range of all possible values of the error of a particular quantity, (2) the difference between the highest and the lowest of these values.

error rate—The total amount of information in error, due to the transmission media, divided by the total amount of information received.

evaluation, performance—*See* performance evaluation.

except gate—A gate in which the specified combination of pulses producing an output pulse is the presence of a pulse on one or more input lines and the absence of a pulse on one or more other input lines.

exception principle system—An information system or data processing system which reports on situations only when actual results differ from planned results. When results occur within a normal range they are not reported.

excess fifty—A binary representation in which the decimal number 'n' is represented by the binary equivalent of (n+50).

exchange—To interchange the contents of two storage devices or locations.

exchange message—*See* message exchange.

exclusive OR operator—A logical operator which has the property that if P and Q are two statements, then the statement P*Q, where the * is the Exclusive OR operator, is true if either P or Q, but not both are true, and false if P and Q are both false or both true, according to the following table, wherein the figure 1 signifies a binary digit or truth.

P	Q	P*Q	
0	0	0	(Even)
0	1	1	(odd)
1	0	1	(odd)
1	1	0	(even)

Note that the Exclusive OR is the same as the Inclusive OR, except that the case with both inputs true yields no output; i.e., P*Q is true if P or Q are true, but not both. Primarily used in compare operations.

execute—To interpret a machine instruction and perform the indicated operation(s) on the operand(s) specified.

execution of an instruction—The set of elementary steps carried out by the computer to produce the result specified by the operation code of the instruction.

execution time—The portion of an instruction cycle during which the actual work is performed or operation executed; i.e., the time required to decode and perform an instruction. *Synonymous with* instruction time, (2).

executive routine—A routine which controls loading and relocation of routines and in some cases makes use of instructions which are unknown to the general programmer. Effectively, an executive routine is part of the machine itself. *Synonymous with* monitor routine, supervisory routine, supervisory program, and operating system.

executive system—*Same as* operating system.

exit—A way of momentarily interrupting or leaving a repeated cycle of operations in a program.

expression—Any symbol representing a variable or a group of symbols representing a group of variables possibly combined by symbols representing operators in accordance with a set of definitions and rules.

external memory—*Same as* external storage.

external storage—(1) The storage of data on a device which is not an integral part of a computer, but in a form prescribed for use by the computer. (2) A facility or device, not an integral part of a computer, on which data usable by a computer is stored such as, off line magnetic tape units, or punch card devices. *Synonymous with* external memory. *Contrasted with* internal storage.

extract—(1) To copy from a set of items all those items which meet a specified criterion. (2) To remove only a given set of digits or characters occupying certain specified locations in a computer word, such as extract the 8, 9, and 10 binary digits of a 44-bit word, as specified by the filter. *Clarified by* filter. (3) To derive a new computer word from part of another word, usually by masking. *Related to* unpack.

extractor—*Same as* filter.

factor, scale—*See* scale factor.

false drops—The documents spuriously identified as pertinent by an information retrieval system, but which do not satisfy the search requirements, due to cause such as improper coding, punching spurious or wrong combinations of holes, or improper use of terminology. *Related to* noise.

false retrievals—The library references which are not pertinent to but are vaguely related to the subject of the library search and are sometimes obtained by automatic search methods.

fast access storage—The section of the entire storage from which data may be obtained most rapidly.

feed—(1) To supply the material to be operated upon to a machine. (2) A device capable of feeding as in definition **#1**.

feed, card—*See* card feed.

feed, tape—*See* tape feed.

feedback—The part of a closed loop system which automatically brings back information about the condition under control.

feedback control—A type of system control obtained when a portion of the output signal is operated upon and fed back to the input in order to obtain a desired effect.

feedback control signal—That portion of the output signal which is returned to the input in order to achieve a desired effect, such as fast response.

ferroelectric—Pertaining to a phenomenon exhibited by certain materials in which the material is polarized in one direction or the other, or reversed in direction by the application of a positive or negative electric field of magnitude greater than a certain amount. The material retains the electric polarization unless it is disturbed. The polarization can be sensed by the fact that a change in the field induces an electromotive force which can cause a current.

ferromagnetic—Pertaining to a phenomenon exhibited by certain materials in which the material is polarized in one direction or the other, or reversed in direction by the application of a positive or negative magnetic field of magnitude greater than a certain amount. The material retains the magnetic polarization unless it is disturbed. The polarization can be sensed by the fact that a change in the field induces an electromotive force, which can cause a current.

fetch—To obtain a quantity of data from a place of storage.

field—An assigned area in a record to be marked with information.

field length—The physical extent of a field. On a punch card it refers to the number of columns. On a tape it refers to bit positions.

file—An organized collection of information directed toward some purpose. The records in a file may or may not be sequenced according to a key contained in each record.

file, detail—*See* detail file.

file gap—An interval of space or time associated with a file to indicate or signal the end of the file. *Related to* gap (2).

file identification—The coding required to identify each physical unit of the outputs of electronic data processing machine runs.

file maintenance—The periodic modification of a file to incorporate changes which occurred during a given period.

file, master—*See* master file.

file protection—A device or method which prevents accidental erasure of operative data on magnetic tape reels.

film optical sensing device—A piece of equipment capable of reading the contents of a film by optical methods; i.e., a system consisting of a light source, lenses, photo cells and a film moving mechanism. The output of the device is digitized and transferred directly to an electronic computer. An example of such a device is the FOSDIC system developed jointly by the Bureau of Census and the National Bureau of Standards.

filmorex system—A system for the electronic selection of microfilm cards devised by Jacques Samain. Each card has a micro reproduction of the document or abstract and a field of twenty 5 digit code numbers giving the bibliographic references and the subjects treated.

filter—A machine word that specifies which parts of another machine word are to be operated upon, thus the criterion for an external command. *Synonymous with* extractor mask. *Clarified by* extract (2).

first level address—*Same as* direct address.

fixed cycle operation—(1) A type of computer performance whereby a fixed amount of time is allocated to an operation. (2) A synchronous or clock type arrangement within a computer in which events occur as a function of measured time. *Contrasted with* variable cycle operation.

fixed field—A given field on punch cards or a given number of holes along the edge of an edge punched card, set aside for the recording of a given type or classification of information.

fixed length record—A record whose number of characters is fixed. The restriction may be deliberate to simplify and speed processing or may be caused by the characteristics of the equipment used.

fixed point arithmetic—(1) A method of calculation in which operations take place in an invariant manner, and in which the computer does not consider the location of the radix point. This is illustrated by desk calculators or slide rules, with which the operator must keep track of the decimal point. Similarly with many automatic computers, in which the location of the radix point is the programmer's responsibility. *Contrasted with* arithmetic, floating point. (2) A type of arithmetic in which the operands and results of all arithmetic operations must be properly scaled so as to have a magnitude between certain fixed values.

fixed point calculation—A calculation made with fixed point arithmetic.

fixed program computer—A computer in which the sequence of instructions are permanently stored or wired in, and perform automatically and are not subject to change either by the computer or the programmer except by rewiring or changing the storage input. *Related to* wired program computer.

fixed word length—Having the property that a machine word always contains the same number of characters or digits.

flag—(1) A bit of information attached to a character or word to indicate the boundary of a field. (2) An indicator used frequently to tell some later part of a program that some condition occurred earlier. (3) An indicator used to identify the members of several sets which are intermixed. *Synonymous with* sentinel.

flip-flop—(1) A bi-stable device; i.e., a device capable of assuming two stable states. (2) A bi-stable device which may assume a given stable state depending upon the pulse of history of one or more input points and having one or more output points. The device is capable of storing a bit of information. (3) A control device for opening or closing gates; i.e., a toggle. *Synonymous with* Eccles-Jordan circuit; Eccles-Jordan trigger.

floating address—Formerly, an address written in such a way that it can easily be converted to a machine address by indexing, assembly, or by some other means.

floating decimal arithmetic—A method of calculation which automatically accounts for the location of the radix point. This is usually accomplished by handling the number as a signed mantissa times the radix raised to an integral exponent; e.g. the decimal number +88.3 might be written as $+.883 \times 10^2$; the binary number $-.0011$ as $-.11 \times 2^{-2}$. *Synonymous with* floating decimal arithmetic. *Contrasted with* fixed point arithmetic (1).

floating point arithmetic—*Same as* floating decimal arithmetic.

floating point calculation—A calculation made with floating point arithmetic.

floating point routine—A set of subroutines which cause a computer to execute floating point arithmetic. These routines may be used to simulate floating point operations on a computer with no built in floating point hardware.

flowchart—A graphic representation of the major steps of work in process. The illustrative symbols may represent documents, machines, or actions taken during the process. The area of concentration is on where or who does what rather than how it is to be done. *Synonymous with* process chart; flow diagram.

flow diagram—*Same as* flowchart.

flying spot—A small, rapidly moving, spot of light, usually generated by a cathode ray tube and used to illuminate successive spots of a surface containing dark and light areas. The varying amount of light reflected is detected by a phototube and used to produce a time succession of electronic signals which effectively describe the surface.

forbidden combination check—A check, usually an automatic check, which tests for the occurrence of a nonpermissible code expression. A self checking code, or error detecting code, uses code expressions such that one or more errors in a code expression produces a forbidden combination. A parity check makes use of a self-checking code employing binary digits in which the total number of 1's, or 0's in each permissible code expression is always even or always odd. A check may be made either for even parity or odd parity. A redundancy check employs a self checking code which makes use of redundant digits called check digits. Some of the various names that have been applied to this type of check are: forbidden pulse combination, unused order, improper instruction, unallowable digits, improper command, false code, forbidden digit, nonexistent code, and unused code.

force—To intervene manually in a routine and cause the computer to execute a jump instruction.

form stop—The automatic device on a printer which stops the machine when paper has run out.

formal logic—A branch of logic that deals with the study of the structure and forms of valid argument without regard to content.

format—The predetermined arrangement of characters, fields, lines, page numbers, and punctuation marks, usually on a single sheet or in a file. This refers to input, output and files.

FORTRAN—A programming language designed for problems which can be expressed in algebraic notation, allowing for exponentation and up to three subscripts. The FORTRAN compiler is a routine for a given machine which accepts a program written in FORTRAN source language and produces a machine language routine object program. FORTRAN II added considerably to the power of the original language by giving it the ability to define and use almost unlimited hierarchies of subroutines, all sharing a common storage region if desired. Later improvements have added the ability to use Boolean expressions, and some capabilities for inserting symbolic machine language sequences within a source program.

FOSDIC—*F*ilm *O*ptical *S*ensing *D*evice for *I*nput to *C*omputers. *Same as* film optical sensing device.

four address—A method of specifying the location of operands and instructions in which the storage location of the two operands and the storage location of the results of the operation are cited, and the storage location of the next instruction to be executed are cited.

four address instruction—A machine instruction usually consisting of the addresses of two operands, the address for storing the result, the address of the next instruction, the command to be executed, and miscellaneous indices. *Synonymous with* three plus one address instruction.

four wire circuit—A two way circuit using two paths so arranged that communication currents are transmitted in one direction only on one path, and in the opposite direction on the other path. The transmission path may or may not employ four wires.

frame, main—*See* main frame.

free field—A property of information processing recording media which permit recording of information without regard to a preassigned or fixed field; e.g., in information retrieval devices information may be dispersed in the record in any sequence or location.

frequency, clock—*See* clock frequency.

frequency response—A measure of the ability of a device to take into account, follow or act upon a varying condition; e.g., as applied to amplifiers, the frequencies at which the gain has fallen to the one-half power point or to 0.707 of the voltage gain, either at the high or low end of the frequency spectrum. When applied to a mechanical controller, the maximum rate at which changes in condition can be followed and acted upon, since it is implied that the controller can follow slow changes.

function switch—A circuit having a fixed number of inputs and outputs designed such that the output information is a function of the input information, each expresses in a certain code, signal configuration, or pattern.

function table—(1) The two or more sets of information so arranged that an entry in one set selects one or more entries in the remaining sets; (2) a dictionary; (3) a device constructed of hardware, or a subroutine, which can either decode multiple inputs into a single output or encode a single input into multiple outputs; (4) a tabulation of the values of a function for a set of values of the variable.

function, transfer—*See* transfer function.

functor—An improper term to be avoided. This term is sometimes used to designate a logic element which performs a specific function or provides a linkage between variables.

gain—The ratio between the output signal and the input signal of a device.

game theory—A mathematical process developed by Von Neumann of selecting an optimum strategy in the face of an opponent who has a strategy of his own.

gang punch—To punch identical or constant information into all of a group of punch cards.

gap—(1) An interval of space or time used as an automatic sentinel to indicate the end of a word, record, or file of data on a tape; e.g., a word gap at the end of a word, a record or item gap at the end of a group of words, and a file gap at the end of a group of records or items. (2) The absence of information for a specified length of time or space on a recording medium, as contrasted with marks and sentinels which are the presence of specific information to achieve a similar purpose. Marks are used primarily internally in variable word length machines. Sentinels achieve similar purposes either internally or externally; however, sentinels are programmed rather than inherent in the hardware. *Related to* file gap; symbol, terminating. (3) The space between the reading or recording head and the recording medium, such as tape, drum, or disk. *Related to* head gap.

gate—A circuit which yields an output signal that is dependent on some function of its present or past input signals.

gate pulse—A pulse which enables a gate circuit to pass a signal; usually, the gate pulse is of longer duration than the signal, to make sure that coincidence in time occurs.

general program—A program expressed in computer code designed to solve a class of problems, or specializing on a specific problem when appropriate parametric values are supplied. *Synonymous with* general routine.

general purpose computer—A computer designed to solve a large variety of problems, e.g., a stored program computer which may be adapted to any of a very large class of applications.

general routine—*Same as* general program.

generate—To produce or prepare a specific item in accordance with a specific and defined rule or program over a period of time.

generating routine—A form of compiling routine, capable of handling less fully defined situations.

gigacycle—A kilomegacycle per second, 10^9 cycles per second. *Synonymous with* kilomegacycle.

grandfather cycle—The period during which magnetic tape records are retained before reusing so that records can be reconstructed in the event of loss of information stored on a magnetic tape.

graphic panel—A master control panel which, pictorially and usually colorfully, traces the relationship of control equipment and the process operation. It permits an operator at a glance, to check on the operation of a far flung control system by noting dials, valves, scales, and lights.

grid, control—*See* control grid.

group mark—A special character used to designate the end of a record in storage for a write instruction.

grouping of records—The combining of two or more records into one block of information on tape, to decrease the wasted time due to tape acceleration and deceleration and to conserve tape space. This is also called blocking of records.

gulp—Several bytes, thus a part of a word.

half adder—A circuit having two output points, S and C, representing sum and carry; and two input points, A and B, representing addend and augend, such that the output is related to the input according to the following table:

Input		Output	
A	B	S	C
0	0	0	0
0	1	1	0
1	0	1	0
1	1	0	1

A and B are arbitrary input pulses, and S and C are sum without carry and carry, respectively. Two half-adders, properly connected, may be used for performing binary addition and form a full serial adder.

half adjust—A kind of rounding in which the value of the least significant digit of a number determines whether or not a one shall be added to the next higher significant digit, or, in which the two least significant digits determine whether or not a one is to be added to the next higher significant digit. If the least significant digits represent less than one-half, nothing is added to the next higher significant digit, if the least significant digits represent one-half or more than a one is added to the next higher significant digit.

half duplex service—A type of communication channel which is capable of transmitting and receiving signals, but is not capable for simultaneous and independent transmission and reception.

halt, dead—*Same as* drop dead halt.

halt, drop dead—*See* drop dead halt.

handling, data—*Same as* data processing (2).

hang up—A nonprogrammed stop in a routine. It is usually an unforeseen or unwanted halt in a machine pass. It is most often caused by improper coding of a machine instruction or by the attempted use of a non-existent or improper operation code.

hard copy—A printed copy of machine output; e.g., printed reports, listings, documents, and summaries.

hardware—The physical equipment or devices forming a computer and peripheral equipment. *Contrasted with* software.

hardware check—*Same as* automatic check.

hash total—A sum of numbers in a specified field of a record or of a batch of records used for checking purposes. No attention is paid to the significance of the total. Examples of such numbers are customer numbers or part numbers. If alphabetic characters have a numerical interpretation to a computer, they also could be added. *Related to* control total.

head—A device which reads, records or erases information in a storage medium, usually a small electromagnet used to read, write or erase information on a magnetic drum or tape or the set of perforating or reading fingers and block assembly for punching or reading holes in paper tape or cards.

head gap—(1) The space between the reading or recording head and the recording medium, such as tape, drum or disk; (2) the space or gap intentionally inserted into the magnetic circuit of the head in order to force or direct the recording flux into the recording medium.

head, read write—*See* read write head.

heuristic—Pertaining to trial and error methods of obtaining solutions to problems.

heuristic program—*Same as* heuristic routine.

heuristic routine—A routine by which the computer attacks a problem not by a direct algorithmic procedure, but by a trial and error approach frequently involving the act of learning. *Synonymous with* heuristic program.

hexadecimal number—*Same as* sexadecimal number.

hi-erarchy—A specified rank or order of items, thus, a series of items classified by rank or order.

high-low bias test—*Same as* marginal check.

high order—Pertaining to the weight or significance assigned to the digits of a number; e.g., in the number 123456, the highest order digit is one; the lowest order digit is six. One may refer to the three high order bits of a binary word, as another example. *Clarified by* order (3).

high speed carry— *Same as* carry (2).

high speed printer— A printer which operates at a speed more compatible with the speed of computation and data processing so that it may operate on-line. At the present time a printer operating at a speed of 250 lines per minute, 100 characters per line is considered high-speed. *Synonymous with* HSP.

high speed reader—A reading device capable of being connected to a computer so as to operate on-line without seriously holding up the computer. A card reader reading more than 250 cards per minute would be called a high speed reader. A reader which reads punched paper tape at a rate greater than 50 characters per second could also be called a high speed reader. *Synonymous with* HSR.

hold—The function of retaining information in one storage device after also transferring it to another device. *Contrasted with* clear.

Hollerith—A widely used system of encoding alphanumeric information onto cards, hence Hollerith cards is synonymous with punch cards. Such cards were first used in 1890 for the U.S. Census and were named after Herman Hollerith, their originator.

homostasis—The dynamic condition of a system wherein the input and output are balanced precisely, thus presenting an appearance of no change, hence a steady state.

hopper—*Same as* card stacker.

horizontal system—A programming system in which instructions are written horizontally; i.e., across the page.

housekeeping—Pertaining to administrative or overhead operations or functions which are necessary in order to maintain control of a situation; e.g., for a computer program, housekeeping involves the setting up of constants and variables to be used in the program. *Synonymous with* red tape.

housekeeping operation—A general term for the operation which must be performed for a machine run usually before actual processing begins. Examples of housekeeping operations are: establishing controlling marks, setting up auxiliary storage units, reading in the first record for processing, initializing, set up verification operations, and file identification.

housekeeping routine—The initial instructions in a program which are executed only one time; e.g., clear storage.

HSP—High Speed Printer.

HSR—High Speed Reader.

hub—A socket on a control panel or plugboard into which an electrical lead or plug wire may be connected in order to carry signals, particularly to distribute the signals over many other wires.

hunting—A continuous attempt on the part of an automatically controlled system to seek a desired equilibrium condition. The system usually contains a standard, a method of determining deviation from this standard and a method of influencing the system such that the difference between the standard and the state of the system is brought to zero. *Clarified by* servomechanism (2).

hystersis—(1) The lagging in the response of a unit of a system behind an increase or a decrease in the strength of a signal, (2) a phenomenon demonstrated by materials which make their behavior a function of the history of the environment to which they have been subjected.

IAL—*I*nternational *A*lgebraic *L*anguage. *See* language, international algebraic.

identification, file—*See* file identification.

idle time—(1) The period between the end of one programmed computer run and the commencement of a subsequent programmed run; (2) the time normally used to assemble cards, paper, tape reels, and control panels required for the next computer operation; (3) the time between operations when no work is scheduled.

IDP—*I*ntegrated *D*ata *P*rocessing. *See* integrated data processing.

ignore—(1) A typewriter character indicating that no action whatsoever be taken; e.g., in teletype or flexowriter code, a character code consisting of holes punched in every hole position is an ignore character; this convention makes possible erasing any previously punched character. (2) An instruction requiring non performance of what normally might be executed;' i.e., not to be executed. This instruction should not be confused with a NO OP or Do Nothing instruction, since these generally refer to an instruction outside themselves.

illegal character—A character or combination of bits which is not accepted as a valid representation by the machine design or by a specific routine. Illegal characters are commonly detected and used as an indication of machine malfunction.

image—An exact duplicate array of information or data stored in, or in transit to, a different medium.

image, card—*See* Card image.

immediate access—Pertaining to the ability to obtain data from or place data in a storage device, or register directly without serial delay due to other units of data, and usually in a relatively short period of time.

immediate address—An instruction address in which the address part of the instruction is the operand. *Synonymous with* zero level address.

impedance, characteristic—*See* characteristic impedance.

Inclusive OR operator—A logical operator which has the property that P or Q is true, if P or Q or both is true; when the term OR is used alone, as in OR gate, the Inclusive OR is usually implied.

impulse noise—A pulse appearing at the output of a circuit which was not transmitted from the originating input to the circuit. These pulses usually are induced from circuit functioning or from sources outside the circuit and its associated input-output equipment.

incremental computer—A computer in which changes in the variables rather than the variables themselves are represented. Those changes correspond to a change in an independent variable as defined by the equations being solved. *Contrasted with* absolute value computer.

index—A symbol or a number used to identify a particular quantity in an array of similar quantities; e.g., X5 is the fifth item in an array of X's.

index register—A register which contains a quantity which may be used to modify addresses. *Synonymous with* B-register (1); B-box.

index, word—*See* word index.

index word—A storage position or register the contents of which may be used to modify automatically the effective address of any given instruction.

indexed address—An address that is to be modified or has been modified by an index register or similar device. *Synonymous with* variable address.

indicators—The devices which register conditions, such as high or equal conditions resulting from a comparison of plus or minus conditions resulting from a computation. A sequence of operations within a procedure may be varied according to the position of an indicator.

indirect address—An address in a computer instruction which indicates a location where the address of the referenced operand is to be found. In some computers the machine address indicated can itself be indirect. Such multiple levels of addressing are terminated either by prior control or by a termination symbol. *Synonymous with* second level address.

information—A collection of facts or other data especially as derived from the processing of data. *Related to* data.

information processing—A less restrictive term than data processing, encompassing the totality of scientific and business operations performed by a computer.

information requirements—The actual or anticipated questions which may be posed to an information system.

information retrieval—The recovering of desired information or data from a collection of documents or other graphic records.

information retrieval system—A system for locating and selecting, on demand, certain documents, or other graphic records relevant to a given information requirement from a file of such material. Examples of information retrieval systems are classification, indexing, and machine searching systems.

information system—The network of all communication methods within an organization. Information may be derived from many sources other than a data processing unit, such as by telephone, by contact with other people, or by studying an operation.

information theory—The mathematical theory concerned with information rate, channels, channel width, noise and other factors affecting information transmission. Initially developed for electrical communications, it is now applied to business systems, and other phenomena which deal with information units and flow of information in networks.

information word—An ordered set of characters bearing at least one meaning and handled by a computer as a unit, including separating and spacing, which may be contrasted with instruction words. *Related to* machine word.

inherent error—*Same as* inherited error.

inherited error—The error in the initial values. Especially the error inherited from the previous steps in the step-by-step integration. This error could also be the error introduced by the inability to make exact measurements of physical quantities. *Synonymous with* inherent error.

inhibiting input—A gate input which, if in its prescribed state, prevents any output which might otherwise occur.

inhibiting signal—A signal, which when entered into a specific circuit will prevent the circuit from exercising its normal function; e.g., an inhibit signal fed into an AND gate will prevent the gate from yielding an output when all normal input signals are present.

initialize—(1) To set various counters, switches and addresses to zero or other starting values, at the beginning of, or at the prescribed points in a computer routine; (2) Used as an aid to recovery and restart during a long computer run.

in line processing—*Same as* on line (2).

in line subroutine—A subroutine inserted directly into the linear operational sequence. Such a subroutine must be recopied at each point that it is needed in a routine.

input—(1) Information or data transferred or to be transferred from an external storage medium into the internal storage of the computer, (2) describing the routines which direct input as defined in (1) or the devices from which such information is available to the computer.(3)The device or collective set of devices necessary for input as defined in (1).

input area—*Same as* input block (1).

input block—(1) A section of internal storage of a computer reserved for the receiving and processing of input information. *Synonymous with* input area. (2) An input buffer. (3) A block of computer words considered as a unit and intended or destined to be transferred from an external source or storage medium to the internal storage of the computer.

input device—The mechanical unit designed to bring data to be processed into a computer; e.g., a card reader, a tape reader, or a keyboard.

input equipment—(1) The equipment used for transferring data and instructions into an automatic data processing system, (2) the equipment by which an operator transcribes original data and instructions to a medium that may be used in an automatic data processing system.

input, inhibiting—*See* inhibiting input.

input magazine—The card feed magazine in a reader, or read-punch unit. *Synonymous with* input stacker.

input-output—A general term for the equipment used to communicate with a computer and the data involved in the communication. *Synonymous with* I/O.

input-output limited—Pertaining to a system or condition in which the time for input and output operation exceeds other operations.

input routine—A routine, sometimes stored permanently in a computer, to allow reading of programs and data into the machine.

input stacker—*Same as* input magazine.

inquiry—A technique whereby the interrogation of the contents of a computer's storage may be initiated at a keyboard.

inquiry station—The remote terminal device from which an inquiry into computing or data processing equipment is made.

installation date—The date new equipment is ready for use. The commencement of rental normally begins on the day following the date on which the contractor officially notifies the using organization that the equipment is installed and ready for use, subject to the acceptance and standard of performance provisions of the applicable contract.

instruction—(1) A set of characters which defines an operation together with one or more addresses, or no address, and which, as a unit, causes the computer to perform the operation on the indicated quantities. The term instruction is preferable to the terms command and order; command is reserved for a specific portion of the instruction word; i.e., the part which specifies the operation which is to be performed, order is reserved for the ordering of the characters, implying sequence, or the order of the interpolation, or the order of the differential equation. *Related to* code, 1. (2) The operation or command to be executed by a computer, together with associated addresses, tags and indices.

instruction, alphanumeric—*See* alphanumeric instruction.

instruction area—(1) A part of storage allocated to receive and store the group of instructions to be executed; (2) the storage locations used to store the program.

instruction, branch—*See* branch instruction.

instruction, breakpoint—*See* breakpoint instruction.

instruction, check indicator—*See* check indicator instruction.

instruction code—The list of symbols, names and definitions of the instructions which are intelligible to a given computer or computing system.

instruction, quasi—*Same as* pseudo instruction.

instruction register—*Same as* program register, (2).

instruction repertory—(1) The set of instructions which a computing or data processing system is capable of performing, (2) the set of instructions which an automatic coding system assembles.

instruction, skip—*See* skip instruction.

instruction, symbolic—*See* symbolic instruction.

instruction time—(1) The portion of an instruction cycle during which the control unit is analyzing the instruction and setting up to perform the indicated operation; (2) *same as* execution time.

instruction, three plus one address—*Same as* four address instruction.

instruction, transfer—*See* transfer instruction.

instruction, two, three or four address—*See* two, three or four address instruction.

instruction, waste—*See* waste instruction.

instruction, zero address—*See* zero address instruction.

integrated data processing—(1) A system that treats as a whole, all data processing requirements to accomplish a sequence of data processing steps, or a number or related data processing sequences, and which strives to reduce or eliminate duplicating data entry or processing steps. (2) The processing of data by such a system. *Synonymous with* IDP.

integrator—A device whose output is proportional to the integral of the input variable with respect to time.

intelligence, artificial—*See* artificial intelligence.

interface—A common boundary between automatic data processing systems or parts of a single system.

interfix—A technique which allows the relationships of key words in an item or document to be described so that very specific inquiries can be answered without false retrievals due to crosstalk.

interlace—To assign successive storage locations; e.g., on a magnetic drum, usually for the purpose of reducing access time.

interlock—To arrange the control of machines or devices so that their operation is interdependent in order to assure their proper coordination.

internal arithmetic—The computations performed by the arithmetic unit of a computer.

internal memory—*Same as* internal storage.

internal storage—(1) The storage of data on a device which is an integral part of a computer. (2) The storage facilities forming an integral physical part of the computer and directly controlled by the computer. In such facilities all data are automatically accessible to the computer; e.g., magnetic core, and magnetic tape on-line. *Synonymous with* internal memory. *Contrasted with* external storage.

internally stored program—A sequence of instructions, stored inside the computer in the same storage facilities as the computer data, as opposed to external storage on punched paper tape and pinboards.

international algebraic language—The forerunner of ALGOL. *Synonymous with* IAL. *Clarified by* algorithmic language.

interpret—(1) To print on a punch card the information punched in that card, (2) to translate non-machine language into machine language instructions.

interpreter—(1) A punch card machine which will take a punch card with no printing on it, read the information in the punched holes, and print a translation in characters in specified rows and columns on the card. (2) An executive routine which, as the computation progresses, translates a stored program expressed in some machine like pseudo code into machine code and performs the indicated operations, by means of subroutines, as they are translated. An interpreter is essentially a closed subroutine which operates successively on an indefinitely long sequence of program parameters, the pseudo instructions and operands. It may usually be entered as a closed subroutine and left by a pseudo code exit instruction.

interpretive code—*Same as* interpretive routine.

interpretive programming—The writing of programs in a pseudo machine language, which is precisely converted by the computer into actual machine language instructions before being performed by the computer.

interpretive routine—A routine which decodes and immediately executes instructions written as pseudo codes. This is contrasted with a compiler which decodes the pseudo codes into a machine language routine to be executed at a later time. The essential characteristic of an interpretive routine is that a particular pseudo code operation must be decoded each time it is executed. *Synonymous with* interpretive code.

inter-record gap—An interval of space or time deliberately left between recording portions of data or records. Such spacing is used to prevent errors through loss of data or overwriting, and permits tape stop-start operations.

interrupt—To temporarily disrupt the normal operation of a routine by a special signal from the computer. Usually the normal operation can be resumed from that point at a later time.

interstage punching—A system of punching in which only odd numbered rows of cards are used. *Contrasted with* normal stage punching.

inverter—A circuit which takes in a positive pulse and puts out a negative one, or takes in a negative pulse and puts out a positive one. The physical meaning of positive and negative depends on the specific circuit and the conventions established for it.

I/O—The abbreviation for input-output.

item—(1) A set of one or more fields containing related information, (2) a unit of correlated information relating to a single person or object, (3) the contents of a single message.

item advance—A technique in the grouping of records for operating successively on different records in storage.

item design—The specification of what fields make up an item, the order in which the fields are to be recorded, and the number of characters to be allocated to each field.

item size—(1) The magnitude of an item, usually expressed in numbers of words, characters or blocks; (2) the number of characters in an item.

iterative—Describing a procedure or process which repeatedly executes a series of operations until some condition is satisfied. An iterative procedure can be implemented by a loop in a routine.

iterative process—A process for calculating a desired result by means of a repeating cycle of operations, which comes closer and closer to the desired result; e.g., the arithmetical square root of N may be approximated by an iterative process using additions, subtractions, and divisions only.

key—(1) A group of characters which identifies or is part of a record or item, thus any entry in a record or item can be used as a key for collating or sorting purposes. (2) A marked lever manually operated for copying a character; e.g., a typewriter, paper tape perforator, card punch, manual keyboard, digitizer or manual word generator. (3) A lever or switch on a computer console for the purpose of manually altering computer action.

keyboard entry—(1) An element of information inserted manually, usually via a set of switches or marked punch levers, called keys, into an automatic data processing system; (2) a medium as in (1) above for achieving access to or entrance into an automatic data processing system.

keypunch—(1) A special device to record information in cards or tape by punching holes in the cards or tape to represent letters, digits, and special characters; (2) to operate a device for punching holes in cards or tape.

key verify—To use the punch card machine known as a verifier, which has a keyboard, to make sure that the information supposed to be punched in a punch card has actually been properly punched. The machine signals when the punched hole and the depressed key disagree.

kilocycle—A thousand cycles per second, or 10^3 cycles per second. *Clarified by* megacycle; gigacycle; teracycle.

kilomegacycle—*Same as* gigacycle.

label—A set of symbols used to identify or describe an item, record, message, or file. Occasionally it may be the same as the address in storage.

lacing—Extra multiple punching in a card column to signify the end of a specific card run. The term is derived from the lace work appearance of the card.

lag—A relative measure of the time delay between two events, states, or mechanisms.

language—A system for representing and communicating information or data between people, or between people and machines. Such a system consists of a carefully defined set of characters and rules for combining them into larger units, such as words or expressions, and rules for word arrangement or usage to achieve specific meanings.

latency time—(1) The time lag between completion of instruction staticizing and the initiation of the movement of data from its storage location, (2) the rotational delay time from a disc file or a drum file.

leader—(1) A record which precedes a group of detail records, giving information about the group not present in the detail records; e.g., beginning of batch 17. (2) An unused or blank length of tape at the beginning of a reel of tape preceding the start of the recorded data.

leapfrog test—A program designed to discover computer malfunction, characterized by the property that it performs a series of arithmetical or logical operations on one group of storage locations, transfers itself to another group of storage locations, checks the correctness of the transfer, then begins the series of operations again. Eventually, all storage positions will have been occupied and the test will be repeated. *Related to* crippled leapfrog test.

library—(1) A collection of information available to a computer, usually on magnetic tapes; (2) a file of magnetic tapes.

line printer—A device capable of printing one line of characters across a page; i.e., 100 or more characters simultaneously as continuous paper advances line by line in one direction past type bars or a type cylinder that contains all characters in all positions.

linear programming—A technique of mathematics and operations research for solving certain kinds of problems involving many variables where a best value or set of best values is to be found. This technique is not to be confused with computer programming, although problems using the technique may be programmed on a computer. Linear programming is most likely to be feasible when the quantity to be optimized, sometimes called the objective function, can be stated as a mathematical expression in terms of the various activities within the system, and when this expression is simply proportional to the measure of the activities; i.e., is linear, and when all the restrictions are also linear.

linkage—A technique for providing interconnections between program runs or between routines.

linked subroutine—*Same as* closed subroutine.

load—(1) To put data into a register or storage; (2) to put a magnetic tape onto a tape drive, or to put cards into a card reader.

load-and-go—Refers to an automatic coding procedure which not only compiles the program, creating machine language, but also proceeds to execute the created program. Load and go procedures are usually part of a monitor.

load point—A preset point at which magnetic tape is initially positioned under the read-write head to start reading or writing.

loading routine—A routine which, once it's itself in storage, is able to bring other information into storage from cards or tape.

location—A storage position in the main internal storage which can store one computer word and which is usually identified by an address.

location, bit—*See* bit location.

location counter—(1) The control section register which contains the address of the instruction currently being executed. (2) A register in which the address of the current instruction is recorded. *Synonymous with* instruction counter; program address counter.

log—A record of everything pertinent to a machine run including: identification of the machine run, record of alteration switch settings, identification of input and output tapes, copy of manual key ins, identification of all stops, and a record of action taken on all stops.

logger—A device which automatically records physical processes and events, usually chronologically.

logic—(1) The science dealing with the criteria or formal principles of reasoning and thought. (2) The systematic scheme which defines the interactions of signals in the design of an automatic data processing system. (3) The basic principles and application of truth tables and interconnection between logical elements required for arithmetic computation in an automatic data processing system. *Related to* symbolic logic.

logical connectives—The operators or words, such as AND, OR, OR ELSE, IF THEN, NEITHER NOR, and EXCEPT, which make new statements from given statements and which have the property that the truth or falseness of the new statements can be calculated from the truth or falsity of the given statements and the logical meaning of the operator.

logical decision—The choice or ability to choose between alternatives. Basically this amounts to an ability to answer yes or no with respect to certain fundamental questions involving equality and relative magnitude; e.g., in an inventory application, it is necessary to determine whether or not there has been an issue of a given stock item.

logical diagram—A diagram which represents the logical elements of a system and their interconnections without necessarily expressing construction, engineering or electrical schematic circuit details.

logical difference—All elements belonging to class A but not to class B, when two classes of elements, class A and class B, are given.

logical element—The smallest building block in a computer or data processing system, which can be represented by logical operators in an appropriate system of symbolic logic. Typical logical elements are the AND-gate and the OR-gate, which can be represented as operators in a suitable symbolic logic.

logical flow chart—A detailed solution of the work order in terms of the logic, or built in operations and characteristics, of a specific machine. Concise symbolic notation is used to represent the information and describe the input, output, arithmetic, and logical operations involved. The chart indicates types of operations by use of a standard set of block symbols. A coding process normally follows the logical flow chart.

logical multiply—*Same as* and operator.

logical operation—(1)A logical or Boolean operation on N state variables which yields a single N state variable; e.g., a comparison on the 3-state variables A and B, each represented by –,), or +, which yields: – when A is less than B, 0 when A equals B, and + when A is greater than B. Specifically, operations such as AND, OR, and NOT on two-state variables which occur in the algebra of logic; i.e., Boolean algebra. (2) The operations of logical shifting, masking, and other non-arithmetic operations of a computer. *Contrasted with* arithmetic operation.

logical operator—*Same as* operator, 1.

logical shift—*Same as* cyclic shift.

logical sum—A result, similar to an arithmetic sum, obtained in the process of ordinary addition, except that the rules are such that a result of one is obtained when either one or both input variables is a one, and an output of zero is obtained when the input variables are both zero. The logical sum is the name given the result produced by the (inclusive or operator).

logical symbol—A sign used as an operator to denote the particular operation to be performed on the associated variables.

look up table—*Same as* table. Not to be confused with the verb form (table look up).

loop—(1) A self contained series of instructions in which the last instruction can modify and repeat itself until a terminal condition is reached. The productive instructions in the loop generally manipulate the operands, while bookkeeping instructions modify the productive instructions, and keep count of the number of repetitions. A loop may contain any number of conditions for termination. The equivalent of a loop can be achieved by the technique of straight line coding, whereby the repetition of productive and bookkeeping operations is accomplished by explicitly writing the instructions for each repetition. *Synonymous with* cycle (1). (2) A communications circuit between two private subscribers or between a subscriber and the local switching center.

low order—Pertaining to the weight or significance assigned to the digits of a number; e.g., in the number 123456, the low order digit is six. One may refer to the three low-order bits of a binary word, as another example. Clarified by (order, 3).

lpm—*L*ines *P*er *M*inute.

machine, accounting—*Same as* tabulator.

machine address—An absolute, direct, unindexed address expressed as such, or resulting after indexing and other processing has been completed.

machine check indicator—A protective device which will be turned on when certain conditions arise within the machine. The machine can be programmed to stop or run a separate correction routine or to ignore the condition.

machine error—A deviation from correctness in data resulting from an equipment failure.

machine language—*Same as* machine oriented language. *Related to* object language.

machine language code—*Same as* computer code (1). *Contrasted with* symbolic code.

machine operator—The person who manipulates the computer controls, places information media into the input devices, removes the output and performs other related functions.

machine oriented language—(1) A language designed for interpretation and use by a machine without translation. (2) A system for expressing information which is intelligible to a specific machine; e.g., a computer or class of computers. Such a language may include instructions which define and direct machine operations, and information to be recorded by or acted upon by these machine operations. (3) The set of instructions expressed in the number system basic to a computer, together with symbolic operation codes with absolute addresses, relative addresses, or symbolic addresses. *Synonymous with* machine language. *Clarified by* language. *Related to* object language. *Contrasted with* problem oriented language.

machine run—The execution of one or several machine routines which are linked to form one operating unit.

machine, self organizing—*See* self organizing machine.

machine sensible—Pertaining to information in a form which can be read by a specific machine.

machine translation—The automatic translation from one representation to another representation. The translation may involve codes, languages, or other systems of representation. *Related to* automatic dictionary.

machine, turing—*See* turing machine.

machine, universal turing—*See* universal turing machine.

machine word—A unit of information of a standard number of characters which a machine regularly handles in each transfer; e.g., a machine may regularly handle numbers or instruction in units of 36 binary digits; this is then the machine word. *Related to* information word.

macro instruction—(1) An instruction consisting of a sequence of micro instructions which are inserted into the object routine for performing a specific operation, (2) the more powerful instructions which combine several operations in one instruction.

magazine, input—*See* input magazine.

magazine, output—*See* output magazine.

magnetic core storage—A storage device in which binary data is represented by the direction of magnetization in each unit of an array of magnetic material, usually in the shape of toroidal rings, but also in other forms such as wraps on bobbins. *Synonymous with* core storage.

magnetic delay line—A delay line using magnetic material; e.g., a drum channel used as a delay line, or combinations of cores and other components used as a delay line. *Related to* delay line.

magnetic disk—A storage device on which information is recorded on the magnetizable surface of a rotating disk. A magnetic disk storage system is an array of such devices, with associated reading and writing heads which are mounted on movable arms. *Related to* disk storage.

magnetic disk storage—A storage device or system consisting of magnetically coated disks, on the surface of which information is stored in the form of magnetic spots arranged in a manner to represent binary data. These data are arranged in circular tracks around the disks and are accessible to reading and writing heads on an arm which can be moved mechanically to the desired disk and then to the desired track on that disk. Data from a given track are read or written sequentially as the disk rotates. *Related to* disk storage.

magnetic drum—A cylinder having a surface coating of magnetic material, which stores binary information by the orientation of magnetic dipoles near or on its surface. Since the drum is rotated at a uniform rate, the information stored is available periodically as a given portion of the surface moves past one or more flux detecting devices called heads located near the surface of the drum.

magnetic drum storage—The storage of data on the surface of magnetic drums. *Related to* magnetic drum.

magnetic shift register—A register which makes use of magnetic cores as binary storage elements, and in which the pattern of binary digital information can be shifted from one position to the next left or right position.

magnetic storage—A device or devices which utilize the magnetic properties of materials to store information.

magnetic tape—A tape or ribbon of any material impregnated or coated with magnetic or other material on which information may be placed in the form of magnetically polarized spots.

magnetic tape reader—A device capable of sensing information recorded on a magnetic tape in the form of a series of magnetized spots.

magnetic tape storage—A storage device in which data is stored in the form of magnetic spots on metal or coated plastic tape. Binary data are stored as small magnetized spots arranged in column form across the width of the tape. A read-write head is usually associated with each row of magnetized spots so that one column can be read or written at a time as the tape traverses the head.

magnetic tape unit—The mechanism, normally used with a computer, which handles magnetic tape and usually consists of a tape transport, reading or sensing and writing or recording heads, and associated electrical and electronic equipments. Most units may provide for tape to be wound and stored on reels; however, some units provide for the tape to be stored loosely in closed bins. *Clarified by* tape transport, paper tape unit.

magnetic wire—A wire made of or coated with a magnetic material and used for magnetic recording.

magnetostriction—A phenomenon wherein certain materials increase in length in the direction of the magnetic field when subjected to such a field, and restore to their original length when demagnetized.

magnetostrictive delay line—A delay line which utilizes the physical principle of magnetostriction. *Clarified by* magnetostriction.

main frame—(1) The central processor of the computer system. It contains the main storage, arithmetic unit and special register groups. *Synonymous* with CPU, central processing unit. (2) All that portion of a computer exclusive of the input, output, peripheral and in some instances, storage units.

main storage—Usually the fastest storage device of a computer and the one from which instructions are executed. *Contrasted with* auxiliary storage.

management information system—A communications process in which data are recorded and processed for operational purposes. The problems are isolated for higher level decision making and information is fed back to top management to reflect the progress or lack of progress made in achieving major objectives.

maintanence file—*See* file maintenance.

maintenance, preventive—*See* preventive maintenance.

maintenance, remedial—*See* remedial maintenance.

major cycle—(1) The maximum access time of a recirculating serial storage element, (2) the time for one rotation of a magnetic drum or of pulses in an acoustic delay line, (3) a number of minor cycles.

malfunction—A failure in the operation of the hardware of a computer.

malfunction routine—*Same as* diagnostic routine.

malfunction, program sensitive—*See* program sensitive malfunction.

manipulated variable—In a process that is desired to regulate some condition, a quantity or a condition that is altered by the computer in order to initiate a change in the value of the regulated condition.

manual control—The direction of a computer by means of manually operated switches.

map—To transform information from one form to another.

marginal check—A preventive maintenance procedure in which certain operating conditions are varied about their normal values in order to detect and locate incipient defective units; e.g., supply voltage or frequency may be varied. *Synonymous with* marginal test; high-low bias test. *Related to* check.

marginal test—*Same as* marginal check.

mark—A sign or symbol used to signify or indicate an event in time or space; e.g., end of word or message mark, a file mark, a drum mark, and end of tape mark.

mark sensing—A technique for detecting special pencil marks entered in special places on a punch card and automatically translating the marks into punched hole.

mask—*Same as* filter.

masking—(1) The process of extracting a nonword group or a field of characters from a word or a string of words, (2) the process of setting internal program controls to prevent transfers which otherwise would occur upon setting of internal machine latches.

master card—A card containing fixed or indicative information for a group of cards. It is usually the first card of that group.

master control—An application oriented routine usually applied to the highest level of a subroutine hierarchy.

master data—A set of data which is altered infrequently and supplies basic data for processing operations. The data content of a Master File. Examples include: names, badge numbers, or pay rates in personnel data; or stock numbers, stock descriptions, or units of measure in stock control data.

master file—A file containing relatively permanent information.

master instruction tape—A tape on which all the programs for a system of runs are recorded. *Synonymous with* MIT.

mathematical, logic—*Same as* symbolic logic, 2.

mathematical check—A check which uses mathematical identities or other properties, occasionally with some degree of discrepancy being acceptable: e.g., checking multiplication by verifying that $A \times B = B \times A$. *Synonymous with* arithmetic check.

mathematical model—The general characterization of a process, object, or concept, in terms of mathemetics, which enables the relatively simple manipulation of variables to be accomplished in order to determine how the process, object, or concept would behave in different situations.

matrix—(1) An array of quantitites in a prescribed form; in mathematics, usually capable of being subject to a mathematical operation by means of an operator or another matrix according to prescribed rules. (2) An array of coupled circuit elements; e.g., diodes, wires, magnetic cores, and relays, which are capable of performing a specific function; such as, the conversion from one numerical system to another. The elements are usually arranged in rows and columns. Thus a matrix is a particular type of encoder or decoder. *Clarified by* encoder; decoder.

matrix printer—*Same as* wire printer.

matrix, semantic—*See* semantic matrix.

mechanical differential analyzer—A form of analog computer using interconnected mechanical surfaces to solve differential equations; e.g., the Bush differential analyzer developed by Vannevar Bush at Massachusetts Institute of Technology which used differential gear boxes to perform addition and a combination of wheel disk spherical mechanisms to perform integration.

mechanical replacement—An action originated by the contractor and taken by him to substitute one machine for another that is installed at a customer's site. Such action usually is occasioned by the mechanical condition of the equipment being replaced.

mechanical translation—A generic term for language translation by computers or similar equipment.

medium—The physical substance upon which data is recorded; e.g., magnetic tape, punch cards and paper.

megabit—One million binary bits.

megacycle—A million cycles per second, 10^6 cycles per second.

memory—*Same as* storage.

memory register—*Same as* storage register.

mercury delay line—A sonic or acoustic delay line in which mercury is used as the medium of sound transmission, with transducers on each end to permit conversion to and from electrical energy. Related to (acoustic delay line).

mercury storage—The storage of data in a mercury delay line. *Related to* mercury delay line.

mercury tank—A container used to hold mercury.

merge—To combine items into one sequenced file from two or more similarly sequenced files without changing the order of the items.

message—(1) A group of words, variable in length, transported as a unit; (2) a transported item of information.

message exchange—A device, placed between a communication line and a computer, in order to take care of certain communication functions and thereby free the computer for other work.

message routing—The function performed at a central message processor of selecting the route, or alternate route if required, by which a message will proceed to the next point in reaching its destination.

method, Monte Carlo—*See* Monte Carlo method.

micro code—(1) A system of coding making use of suboperations not ordinarily accessible in programming; e.g., coding that makes use of parts of multiplication or division operations. (2) A list of small program steps. Combinations of these steps, performed automatically in a prescribed sequence form a macro operation like multiply, divide, and square root.

micro instruction—A small, single, short, add, shift or delete type of command.

micro programming—The technique of using a certain special set of instructions for an automatic computer, that consists only of basic elemental operations which the programmer may combine into higher level instructions, which he may then program using the higher level instructions only; e.g., if a computer has only basic instructions for adding, subtracting, and multiplying, the instruction for dividing would be defined by microprogramming.

microprogram—(1) A program of analytic instructions which the programmer intends to construct from the basic subcommands of a digital computer, (2) a sequence of pseudo commands which will be translated by hardware into machine subcommands, (3) a means of building various analytic instructions as needed from the subcommand structure of a computer, (4) a plan for obtaining maximum utilization of the abilities of a digital computer by efficient use of the subcommands of the machine.

microsecond—One millionth of a second, 10^{-6} seconds, abbreviated microsec.

millimicrosecond—*Same as* nanosecond.

millisecond—One thousandth of a second, 10^{-3} seconds, abbreviated msec. or ms.

minimum access code—A system of coding which minimizes the effect of delays for transfer of data or instructions between storage and other machine components. *Related to* optimum code; minimum latency code; minimum access coding.

minimum access programming—Programming in such a way that minimum waiting time is required to obtain information out of storage. *Synonymous with* minimul latency programming. *Contrasted with* random access programming.

minimum access routine—A routine so coded that by judicious arrangement of data and instructions in storage, the actual access time is less than the expected random access time. Such a routine is used with serial storage systems. *Synonymous with* minimum latency routine.

minimum latency code—*Same as* minimum access code.

minimum latency programming—*Same as* minimum access programming.

minimum latency routine—*Same as* minimum access routine.

minor cycle—The time interval between the appearance of corresponding parts of successive words in a storage device which provides serial access to storage positions.

minuend—The quantity from which another quantity is subtracted or is to be subtracted.

minus zone—The bit positions in a computer code which represent the algebraic minus sign.

mistake—A human failing; e.g., faulty arithmetic, use of incorrect formula, or incorrect instructions. Mistakes are sometimes called gross errors to distinguish from rounding and truncation errors. Thus, computers malfunction and humans make mistakes. Computers do not make mistakes and humans do not malfunction, in the strict sense of the word. *Contrasted with* error (2).

MIT—*M*aster *I*nstruction *T*ape. *Same as* master instruction tape.

mixed base notation—*Same as* mixed radix notation.

mixed base number—*Same as* mixed radix number.

mixed radix notation—A method of expressing a quantity, using two or more characters, where each character is of a different radix.

mixed radix number—A number consisting of two or more characters, representing a sum, in which the quantity represented by each character is based on a different radix. *Synonymous with* mixed base number.

mnemonic—Pertaining to the assisting, or intending to assist, human memory; thus a mnemonic term, usually an abbreviation, that is easy to remember; e.g., mpy for multiply and acc for accumulator.

mnemonic operation code—An operation code in which the names of operations are abbreviated and expressed mnemonically to facilitate remembering the operations they represent. A mnemonic code normally needs to be converted to an actual operation code by an assembler before execution by the computer. Examples of mnemonic codes are ADD for addition, CLR for clear storage and SQR for square root.

mode—(1) A computer system of data representation; e.g., the binary mode. (2) A selected mode of computer operation.

mode, noisy—*See* noisy mode.

model, mathematical—*See* mathematical model.

modifier—A quantity used to alter the normal interpretation and execution of an instruction; e.g., an index tag or indirect address tag.

modify—(1) To alter a portion of an instruction so its interpretation and execution will be other than normal. The modification may permanently change the instruction or leave it unchanged and affect only the current execution. The most frequent modification is that of the effective address through use of index registers. (2) To alter a subroutine according to a defined parameter.

modulation code—A code used to cause variations in a signal in accordance with a predetermined scheme; normally used to alter or modulate a carrier wave to transmit data. *Clarified by* modulator.

modulator—A device which varies a repetitive phenomenon in accordance with some predetermined scheme usually introduced as a signal. *Clarified by* modulation; demodulator code.

module—(1) An interchangeable plug-in item containing components, (2) an incremental block of storage or other building block for expanding the computer capacity.

modulo *n* check—(1) A check that makes use of a check number that is equal to the remainder of the desired number when divided by N; e.g., in a modulo 4 check, the check number will be 0, 1, 2, or 3 and the remainder of A when divided by 4 must equal the reported check number B; otherwise an equipment malfunction has occurred. (2) A method of verification by congruences; e.g., casting out nines. *Related to* self checking number.

monitor—To supervise and verify the correct operation of a program during its execution, usually by means of a diagnostic routine used from time to time to answer questions about the program.

monitor routine—*Same as* executive routine.

monitor system—*Same as* operating system.

Monte Carlo method—A trial and error method of repeated calculations to discover the best solution or a problem. Often used when a great number of variables are present, with inter relationships so extremely complex as to forestall straightforward analytical handling.

multi-address—*Same as* multiple address.

multi-precision arithmetic—A form of arithmetic similar to double precision arithmetic except that two or more words may be used to represent each number.

multi aspect—Pertaining to searches or systems which permit more than one aspect, or facet, of information to be used in combination, one with the other to effect identifying and selecting operations.

multiple address—A type of instruction which specifies the addresses of two or more items which may be the addresses of locations of inputs or outputs of the calculating unit or the addresses of locations of instructions for the control unit. The term multi-address is also used in characterizing computers; e.g., two, three, or four address machines. *Synonymous with* multi-address.

multiple address code—An instruction code in which an instruction word can specify more than one address to be used during the operation. In a typical instruction of a four address code the addresses specify the location of two operands, the location at which the results are to be stored and the location of the next instruction in the sequence. In a typical three address code, the fourth address specifying the location of the next instructions is dispensed with, the instructions are taken from storage in a preassigned order. In a typical two address code, the addresses may specify the locations of the operands. The results may be placed at one of the addresses or the destination of the results may be specified by another instruction.

multiple address instruction—An instruction consisting of an operation code and two or more addresses. Usually specified as a two address, three address, or four address instruction.

multiple length number—A number having two, three, or more times as many figures as are normally handled in a particular device.

multiple programming—The programming of a computer by allowing two or more arithmetical or logical operations to be executed simultaneously. *Contrasted with* serial programming.

multiple punching—(1) The reference to punch cards and more specifically to Hollerith cards; (2) the punching of two or more holes in a column.

multiplex—The process to transferring data from several storage devices operating at relatively low transfer rates to one storage device operating at a high transfer rate in such a manner that the high speed device is not obliged to wait for the low speed devices.

multiplexing—(1) The transmission of a number of different messages simultaneously over a single circuit. (2) Utilizing a single device for several similar purposes or using several devices for the same purpose; e.g., a duplexed communications channel carrying two messages simultaneously.

multiplication time—The time required to perform a multiplication. For a binary number it will be equal to the total of all the addition times and all the shift time involved in the multiplication.

multiply, logical—*Same as* and operator.

multiprocessor—A machine with multiple arithmetic and logic units for simultaneous use.

multiprogramming—A technique for handling numerous routines or programs simultaneously by means of an interweaving process.

nanosecond—One thousandth of a millionth of a second, 10^{-9} seconds. *Synonymous with* millimicrosecond.

nest—(1) To embed a subroutine or block of data into a larger routine or block of data, (2) to evaluate an nth degree polynomial by a particular algorithm which uses (n–1) multiply operations and (n–1) add operations in succession.

network, analog—*See* analog network.

network analyzer—An analog device designed primarily for simulating electrical networks. *Synonymous with* calculator network.

network calculator—*Same as* network analyzer.

neutral zone—An area in space or an interval of time in which a state of being other than the implementing state exists; e.g., a range of values in which no control' action occurs or a brief period between words when certain switching action takes place. Similar to (dead band).

ninety (90) column card—A punch card with 90 vertical columns representing 90 characters. The columns are divided in half horizontally, such that the vertical columns in the upper half of the card are numbered 1 through 45, and those in the lower half 46 through 90. Six punching positions may be used in each column; these are designated, from top to bottom, to represent the digits 0, 1, 3, 5, 7 and 9 by a single punch. The digits 2, 4, 6, and 8 and other characters may be represented by a combination of two or more punches. *Related to* punch card; eighty column card.

no address instruction—An instruction specifying an operation which the computer can perform without having to refer to its storage unit.

no charge machine fault time—The unproductive time due to computer fault such as the following: nonduplication, transcribing error, input-output malfunction and machine malfunction resulting in an incomplete run.

noise—The meaningless extra bits or words which must be ignored or removed from the data at the time the data is used. *Related to* false drops

noisy mode—A floating point arithmetic procedure associated with normalization in which ".1" bits, rather than "0" bits, are introduced in the low order bit position during the left shift.

non arithmethic shift—*Same as* cyclic shift.

non destructive read—A reading of the information in a register without changing that information.

non erasable storage—A storage device whose information cannot be erased during the course of computation; e.g., punched paper tape, and punched cards, magnetic slug, "missing core," and silvered or aluminized paper.

non scheduled maintenance time—The elapsed time during scheduled working hours between the determination of a machine failure and placement of the equipment back into operation.

non-volatile storage—A storage medium which retains information in the absence of power and which may be made available upon restoration of power; e.g., magnetic tapes, cores, drums, and discs. *Contrasted with* volatile storage.

no-op instruction—(1) An instruction which specifically instructs the computer to do nothing but process the next instruction in sequence. (2) A blank instruction. (3) A skip instruction. (4) A waste instruction. *Synonymous with* waste instruction and skip.

normal stage punching—A system of punching in which only eleven numbered rows of the card are used. *Contrasted with* punching, interstage.

normalize—(1) In programming to adjust the exponent and fraction of a floating point quantity so that the fraction lies in the prescribed normal standard, range. (2) In mathematical operations to reduce a set of symbols or numbers to a normal or standard form. *Synonymous with* standardize.

notation—(1) The act, process, or method of representing facts or quantities by a system or set of marks, signs, figures, or characters. (2) A system of such symbols or abbreviations used to express technical facts or quantities; as mathematical notation. (3) An annotation; note.

null—(1) An absence of information, as contrasted with zero or blank for the presence of no information; (2) zero; (3) pertaining to no deflection from a center or end position.

number—(1) The, or a total, aggregate, or amount of units. (2) A figure or word, or a group of figures or words, representing graphically an arithmetical sum; a numeral, as the number 45. *Clarified by* number systems. (3) A numeral by which a thing is designated in a series; as a pulse number. (4) A single member of a series designated by consecutive numerals; as, a part number. (5) A character, or a group of characters, uniquely identifying or describing an article, process, condition, document, or class; as, a 6SN7 tube. (6) To count; enumerate. (7) To distinguish by a number.

number systems—(1) A systemtic method for representing numerical quantities in which any quantity is represented as the sequence of coefficients of the suuccessive powers of a particular base with an appropriate point. Each succeeding coefficient from right to left is associated with and usually multiplies the next higher power of the base. The first coefficient to the left of the point is associated with the zero power of the base. For example, in decimal notation 371.426 represents $(3\times10^2) + (7\times10^1) + (1\times10^0) + (4\times10^{-1}) + (2\times10^{-2}) + (6\times10^{-3})$. (2) The following are names of the number systems with bases 2 through 20:2, Binary; 3, Ternary; 4, Quaternary; 5, Quinary; 6, Senary; 7, Septenary; 8, Octal, or Octonary; 8, Novenary; 10, Decimal; 11, Undecimal; 12, Duodecimal; 13, Terdenary; 14, Quaterdenary; 15, Quindenary; 16, Sexadecimal, or Hexadecimal; 17, Septendecimal; 18, Octodenary; 19, Novemdenary; 20, Vicenary. Also 32, Duosexadecimal, or duotricinary; and 60, Sexagenary. The binary, Octal, Decimal, and Sexadecimal systems are widely used in computers. *Synonymous with* duodecimal number; binary number system. *Related to* positional representation. *Clarified by* octal and binary digit.

numeral—A digit, or digits, normally used to represent a number.

numeric code—A system of numerical abbreviations used in the preparation of information for input into a machine; i.e., all information is reduced to numerical quantities. *Contrasted with* alphabetic code.

numerical analysis—The study of methods of obtaining useful quantitative solutions to mathematical problems, regardless of whether an analytic solution exists or not, and the study of the errors and bounds on errors in obtaining such solutions.

numerical control—Descriptive of systems in which digital computers are used for the control of operations, particularly of automatic machines; e.g., drilling or boring machines, wherein the operation control is applied at discrete points in the operation or process. *Contrasted with* process control.

n way switch—*Same as* variable connector (3).

object language—A language which is the output of an automatic coding routine. Usually object language and machine language are the same; however, a series of steps in an automatic coding system may involve the object language of one step serving as a source language for the next step and so forth.

object program—The program which is the output of an automatic coding system. Often the object program is a machine language program ready for execution, but it may well be in an intermediate language. *Synonymous with* target program; object routine. *Contrasted with* source program.

object routine—*Same as* object program.

octal—Pertaining to eight; usually describing a number system of base or radix eight; e.g., in octal notation, octal 214 is 2 times 64, plus 1 times 8, plus 4 times 1, and equals decimal 140. Octal 214 in binary coded octal is represented as 010, 001, 100; octal 214, as a straight binary number is written 100001100. Note that binary coded octal and straight binary differ only in the use of commas, in the example shown, the initial zero in the straight binary is dropped. *Clarified* by octal number.

octal digit—The symbol 0,1,2,3,4,5,6,7 used as a digit in the system of notation which uses 8 as the base or radix. *Clarified by* number systems.

octal number—A number of one or more figures, representing a sum in which the quantity represented by each figure is based on a radix of eight. The figures used are 0, 1, 2, 3, 4, 5, 6, and 7. *Clarified by* octal.

octonary signalling—A communications mode in which information is passed by the presence and absence or plus and minus variation of eight discrete levels of one parameter of the signalling medium.

odd-even check—*Same as* parity check.

off line—Descriptive of a system and of the peripheral equipment or devices in a system in which the operation of peripheral equipment is not under the control of the central processing unit. *Clarified by* off line equipment.

off line equipment—The peripheral equipment or devices not in direct communication with the central processing unit of a computer. *Synonymous with* auxiliary equipment.

off punch—A punch not properly positioned in a column of a card.

offset—The difference between the value or condition desired and that actually attained.

on-line—Descriptive of a system and of the peripheral equipment or devices in a system in which the operation of such equipment is under control of the central processing unit, and in which information reflecting current activity is introduced into the data processing system as soon as it occurs. Thus, directly in-line with the main flow of transaction processing. *Clarified by* on-line equipment. *Synonymous with* in line processing; on-line processing.

on-line processing—*Same as* on-line.

on-line data-reduction—The processing of information as rapidly as the information is received by the computing system or as rapidly as it is generated by the source.

on the fly printer—A high speed line printer using continuously rotating print wheels and fast acting hammers to print the successive letters contained in one line of text so rapidly that all of the characters in the printed line look as though they were all printed simultaneously.

one address—(1) A single address. (2) A system of machine instruction such that each complete instruction explicitly describes one operation and involves one storage location. *Synonymous with* single address. *Related to* one address instruction.

one address instruction—An instruction consisting of an operation and exactly one address. The instruction code of a signal address computer may include both zero and multi address instructions as special cases. *Related to* one address.

one level code—*Same as* absolute code.

one plus one address—An instruction system having the property that each complete instruction includes an operation and two addresses, one for the location of a register in the storage containing the item to be operated upon, and one for the location containing the next instruction.

one plus one address instruction—An instruction containing two or four addresses one of which specifies explicitly the location of the next instruction to be executed. It is usually used on computers whose storage has a latency factor; e.g., a drum computer.

open ended—The quality by which the addition of new terms, subject headings, or classifications does not disturb the pre-existing system.

open loop—Pertaining to a control system in which there is no self correcting action for misses of the desired operational condition, as there is in a closed loop system.

open routine—A routine which can be inserted directly into a larger routine without a linkage or calling sequence.

open shop—The operation of a computer facility where computer programming, coding and operating can be performed by any qualified employee of the organization, not necessarily by the personnel of the computing center itself and where the programmer may assist in, or oversee the running of his program on the computer. *Contrasted with* closed shop.

open subroutine—A subroutine inserted directly into the linear operational sequence, not entered by a jump. Such a subroutine must be recopied at each point that it is needed in a routine. *Synonymous with* direct insert subroutine.

operand—A quantity entering or arising in an instruction. An operand may be an argument, a result, a parameter, or an indication of the location of the next instruction, as opposed to the operation code or symbol itself. It may even be the address portion of an instruction.

operating ratio—The ratio of the number of hours of correct machine operation to the total hours of scheduled operation; e.g., on a 168 hour week scheduled operation, if 12 hours of preventive maintenance are required and 4.8 hours of unscheduled down time occurs, then the operating ratio is (168-16.8)/168, which is equivalent to a 90% operating ratio. *Synonymous with* computer efficiency.

operating system—An integrated collection of service routines for supervising the sequencing of programs by a computer. Operating systems may perform debugging, input-output, accounting, compilation, and storage assignment tasks. *Synonymous with* monitor system; executive system.

operation—A defined action. The action specified by a single computer instruction or pseudo instruction.

operation code—The part of a computer instruction word which specifies, in coded form, the operation to be performed.

operation number—(1) A number designating the position of an operation, or its equivalent subroutine in the sequence of operations comprising a routine; (2) a number identifying each step in a program stated in symbolic code.

operation register—A register in which an operation is stored and analyzed in order to set conditions for the execution cycle.

operation use time—In Federal Government ADP contracts the time during which the equipment is in operation, exclusive of idle time, standby time, maintenance time, or rerun time due to machine failure. Components not programmed for use in a specified computer run are not considered to be in use even though connected into the computer system.

operations research—The use of analytic methods adopted from mathematics for solving operational problems. The objective is to provide management with a more logical basis for making sound predictions and decisions. Among the common scientific techniques used in operations research are the following: linear programming, probability theory, information theory, game theory, Monte Carlo method, and queuing theory. *Synonymous with* O.R.

operator—(1) A mathematical symbol which represents a mathematical process to be performed on an associated operand, (2) the portion of an instruction which tells the machine what do do, (3) a machine operator.

optimize—To rearrange the instructions or data in storage so that a minimum number of time consuming jumps or transfers are required in the running of a program.

optimum code—A computer code which is particularly efficient with regard to a particular aspect; e.g., minimum time of execution, minimum or efficient use of storage space, and minimum coding time. *Related to* minimum access code.

optimum programming—Programming in order to maximize efficiency with respect to some criterion; e.g., least storage usage, least time share of peripheral equipment, or least use of time between operations.

O.R.—*O*perations *R*esearch. *Same as* operations research.

OR circuit—*Same as* or gate.

OR gate—An electrical gate or mechanical device which implements the logical OR operator. An output signal occurs whenever there are one or more inputs on a multi-channel input. An OR gate performs the function of the logical "inclusive OR Operator." *Synonymous with* or circuit. *Clarified by* disjunction.

OR operator—A logical operator which has the property such that if P or Q are two statements, then the statement P or Q is true or false varies according to the following table of possible combinations. *Clarified by* disjunction.

P	Q	P or Q
False	True	True
True	False	True
True	True	True
False	False	True

order—(1) A defined successive arrangement of elements or events. This term is losing favor as a synonym for instructions, due to ambiquity. (2) To sequence or arrange in a series. (3) The weight or significance assigned to a digit position in a number. *Clarified by* high order; low order.

origin—The absolute storage address in relative coding to which addresses in a region are referenced.

origination data—*See* data origination.

output—(1) The information transferred from the internal storage of a computer to secondary or external storage, or to any device outside of the computer; (2) the routines which direct 1; (3) the device or collective set of devices necessary for 1; (4) to transfer from internal storage on to external media.

output area—*Same as* output block (2).

output block—(1) A block of computer words considered as a unit and intended or destined to be transferred from an internal storage medium to an external destination. (2) A section of internal storage reserved for storing data which are to be transferred out of the computer. *Synonymous with* output area. (3) A block used as an output buffer.

output device—The part of a machine which translates the electrical impulses representing data processed by the machine into permanent results such as printed forms, punched cards, and magnetic writing on tape.

output equipment—The equipment used for transferring information out of a computer.

output magazine—A mechanism that accumulates cards after they have passed through a machine. *Synonymous with* output stacker.

output stacker—*Same as* output magazine.

overflow—(1) The condition which arises when the result of an arithmetic operation exceeds the capacity of the storage space alloted in a digital computer; (2) the digit arising from this condition if a mechanical or programmed indicator is included, otherwise the digit may be lost.

overflow check indicator—A device which is turned on by incorrect, or unplanned for, operations in the execution of an arithmetic instruction, particularly when an arithmetic operation produces a number too large for the system to handle.

overlay—A technique for bringing routines into high-speed storage from some other form of storage during processing, so that several routines will occupy the same storage locations at different times. Overlay is used when the total storage requirements for instructions exceed the available main storage.

overpunch—To add holes in a card column that already contains one or more holes. *Synonymous with* zone punch. ***Related to*** zone bits (1).

pack—To include several short items of information into one machine item or word by utilizing different sets of digits to specify each brief item.

packing density—The number of units of useful information contained within a given linear dimension, usually expressed in units per inch; e.g., the number of binary digit magnetic pulses or number of characters stored on tape or drum per linear inch on a single track by a single head.

padding—A technique used to fill out a block of information with dummy records.

panel, control—*See* control panel.

panel, graphic—*See* graphic panel.

paper tape—A strip of paper capable of storing or recording information. Storage may be in the form of punched holes, carbonization or chemical change of impregnated material, or by imprinting. Some paper tapes, such as punched paper tapes, are capable of being read by the input device of a computer or a transmitting device by sensing the pattern of holes which represent coded information.

paper tape readers—A device capable of sensing information punched on a paper tape in the form of a series of holes.

parallel—(1) To handle simultaneously in separate facilities. (2) To operate on two or more parts of a word or item simultaneously. *Contrasted with* serial.

parallel access—The process of obtaining information from or placing information into storage where the time required for such access is dependent on the simultaneous transfer of all elements of a word from a given storage location. *Synonymous with* simultaneous access.

parallel by character—The handling of all the characters of a machine word simultaneously in separate lines, channels or storage cells.

parallel computer—A computer in which the digits or data lines are handled concurrently by separate units of the computer. The units may be interconnected in different ways as determined by the computation to operate in parallel or serially. Mixed serial and parallel machines are frequently called serial or parallel according to the way arithmetic processes are performed. An example of a parallel computer is one which handles decimal digits in parallel although it might handle the bits which comprise a digit either serially or in parallel. *Contrasted with* serial computer.

parallel operation—The performance of several actions, usually of a similar nature, simultaneously through provision of individual similar or identical devices for each such action. Particularly flow or processing of information. Parallel operation is performed to save time over serial operation. Parallel operation usually requires more equipment. *Contrasted with* serial operation.

parallel processing—The operation of a computer so that programs for more than one run are stored simultaneously in its storage, and executed concurrently.

parallel running—(1) The running of a newly developed system in a data processing area in conjunction with the continued operation of the current system; (2) the final step in the debugging of a system, this step follows a system test.

parallel storage—The storage of data in which all bits, characters, or especially words are essentially equally available in space, without time being one of the factors. When words are in parallel, the storage is said to be parallel by words; when characters within words, or binary digits within words or characters, are dealt with simultaneously, not one after the other, the storage is parallel by characters, or parallel by bit respectively. *Contrasted with* serial storage.

parallel transfer—A method of data transfer in which the characters of an element of information are transferred simultaneously over a set of paths.

parameter—(1) A quantity in a subroutine, whose value specifies or partly specifies the process to be performed. It may be given different values when the subroutine is used in different main routines or in different parts of one main routine, but which usually remains unchanged throughout any one such use. *Related to* program parameter. (2) A quantity used in a generator to specify machine configuration, designate subroutines to be included, or otherwise to describe the desired routine to be generated. (3) A constant or a variable in mathematics, which remains constant during some calculation. (4) A definable characteristic of an item, device, or system.

parameter, preset—*See* preset parameter.

parameter, program—*See* program parameter.

partial carry—*Same as* carry (2).

parity bit—A check bit that indicates whether the total number of binary "1" digits in a character or word (excluding the parity bit) is odd or even. If a "1" parity bit indicates an odd number of "1" digits, then a "0" bit indicates an even number of them. If the total number of "1" bits, including the parity bit, is always even, the system is called an even parity system. In an odd parity system, the total number of "1" bits, including the parity bit, is always odd.

parity check—A summation check in which the binary digits, in a character or word, are added, modulo 2, and the sum checked against a single, previously computed parity digit; i.e., a check which tests whether the number of ones in a word is odd or even. *Synonymous with* odd-even check. *Related to* redundant check.

part address—The part of an instruction word that defines the address of a register or location.

part operation—The part in an instruction, that specifies the kind of arithmetical or logical operation to be performed, but not the address of the operands.

pass—A completed cycle of reading, processing and writing; i.e., a machine run.

patch—A section of coding inserted into a routine to correct a mistake or alter the routine. It is often not inserted into the actual sequence of the routine being corrected, but placed somewhere else, with an exit to the patch and a return to the routine provided. (2) To insert corrected coding.

pattern recognition—The recognition of shapes or other patterns by a machine system. Patterns may be such as physical shapes or speech patterns.

PCM—*P*unch *C*ard *M*achine. *Same as* electrical accounting machine.

peek-a-boo system—An information retrieval system which uses peek-a-boo cards; i.e., cards into which small holes are drilled at the intersections of coordinates (column and row designations) to represent document numbers. *Synonymous with* batten system; cordonnier system. *Related to* aspect card.

perforated tape—*Same as* punch tape.

perforation rate—The rate at which characters, rows or words are punched in a paper tape.

performance evaluation—The analysis in terms if initial objectives and estimates, and usually made on site, of accomplishments using an automatic data processing system, to provide information on operating experience and to identify corrective actions required if any.

performance period—A period of 30 consecutive calendar days during which a newly installed computer is being tested for acceptance by the U.S. Government. Such a period does not include equipment time used for data purification, file conversion, and similar preparatory operations or those hours of operation rescheduled as a result of equipment failure.

peripheral equipment—The auxiliary machines which may be placed under the control of the central computer. Examples of this are card readers, card punches, magnetic tape feeds and high speed printers.

Peripheral equipment may be used on line or off line depending upon computer design, job requirements and economics. *Clarified by* off line equipment.

permanent storage—A method or device used to retain intermediate or final results outside of the machine, usually in the form of punched cards or magnetic tape.

phase shift—The time difference between the input and output signal or between any two synchronized signals, of a control unit, system, or circuit.

phone data—*See* data phone.

photomicrography—The process of making a larger photograph of a much smaller original.

picosecond—One thousandth of a nanosecond, or 10^{-12} seconds; abbreviated psec.

piezoelectric—A term applied to the phenomenon whereby certain materials, commonly crystalline, develop useful electrical pressures (voltages) when the material is subjected to variable mechanical pressures, strains, or stresses; conversely, the materials develop mechanical strains or stresses when electrical voltages are applied.

pinboard—A type of control panel which uses pins rather than wires to control the operation of a computer. On certain small computers which use pinboards, a program is changed by the operator removing one pinboard and inserting another. *Related to* control panel (2).

ping-pong—The programming technique of using two magnetic tape units for multiple reel files and switching automatically between the two units until the complete file is processed.

plotter—A visual display or board in which a dependent variable is graphed by an automatically controlled pen or pencil as a function of one or more variables.

plotter, XY—*See* XY plotter.

plug, program patching—See program patching plug.

plugboard—*Same as* control panel (2).

plus zone—The bit positions in a computer code which represent the algebraic plus sign.

point—*Same as* radix point.

polyvalence—The property of being interrelated in several ways.

polyvalent notation—A method for describing salient characteristics, in condensed form, using two or more characters, where each character or group of characters represents one of the characteristics.

polyvalent number—A number, consisting of several figures, used for description, wherein each figure represents one of the characteristics being described.

positional notation—A method for expressing a quantity, using two or more figures, wherein the successive right to left figures are to be interpreted as coefficents of ascending integer powers of the radix. *Synonymous with* positional number.

positional number—*Same as* positional notation.

positional representation—A number representation or number system in which the significance or value of each digit depends upon its place or position with respect to a radix point.

positions, punching—*See* punching positions.

post—To enter an item on a record.

post edit—To edit the results of a previous computation.

post mortem dump—A listing of the contents of a storage device taken after a routine has been run in order that the final condition of sections of storage may be recorded for debugging purposes.

post mortem routine—A service routine useful in analyzing the cause of a failure, such as a routine that dumps out the content of a store after a failure. *Related to* post mortem.

posting terminal digit—The arranging and recording of serial numbers of documents on the basis of the final digit of each of the numbers.

power dump—The removal of all power accidentally or intentionally.

pre-edit—To edit the input data previous to the computation.

pre-store—To set an initial value for the address of an operand or of a cycle index, (2) to restore, (3) to store a quantity in an available or convenient location before it is required in a routine.

precision—(1) The degree of exactness with which a quantity is stated. (2) The degree of discrimination or amount of detail; e.g., a 3 decimal digit quantity discriminates among 1000 possible quantities. A result may have more precision than it has accuracy; e.g., the true value of pi to 6 significant digits is 3.14159; the value 3.14162 is precise to 6 figures, given to 6 figures, but is accurate only to about 5.

predicate—To affirm or deny, in mathematical logic, one or more subjects.

preliminary proposal review—An on site review to provide guidance to proponent agencies in the preparation of ADP system proposals.

preselection—A technique for saving time available in buffered computers (by which a block of data is read into computer storage from the next input tape to be called upon before the data are required in the computer. The selection of the next input tape is determined by instructions to the computer.

preset—(1) To set the contents of a storage location to an initial value, (2) to establish the initial control value for a loop.

presumptive address—*Same as* base address (1).

preventive maintenance—The maintenance of a computer system which attempts to keep equipment in top operating condition and to preclude failures during production runs.

primary storage—The main internal storage.

primitive—A primitive usually pertains to the lowest level of a machine instruction or lowest unit of language translation.

probability theory—A measure of likelihood of occurrence of a chance event, used to predict behavior of a group, not of a single item in the group.

problem definition—The art of compiling logic in the form of general flow charts and logic diagrams which clearly explain and present the problem to the programmer in such a way that all requirements involved in the run are presented.

problem oriented language—(1) A language designed for convenience of program specification in a general problem area rather than for easy conversion to machine instruction code. The components of such a language may bear little resemblance to machine instructions. (2) A machine independent language where one needs only to state the problem, not the how of solution. *Related to* program generators. *Contrasted with* procedure oriented language.

problem, trouble location—*See* trouble location problem.

procedure—A precise step-by-step method for effecting a solution to a problem.

procedure oriented language—A machine independent language which describes how the process of solving the problem is to be carried out; e.g., FORTRAN.

process—A general term covering such terms as assemble, compile, generate, interpret, and compute.

process chart—*Same as* flow chart.

process control—Descriptive of systems in which computers, most frequently analog computers, are used for the automatic regulation of operations or processes. Typical are operations in the production of chemicals wherein the operation control is applied continuously and adjustments to regulate the operation are directed by the computer to keep the value of a controlled variable constant.

processor—(1) A generic term which includes assembly, compiling, and generation; (2) a shorter term for automatic data processor or arithmetic unit.

program—(1) The complete plan for the solution of a problem, more specifically the complete sequence of machine instructions and routines necessary to solve a problem. (2) To plan the procedures for solving a problem. This may involve among other things the analysis of the problem, preparation of a flow diagram, preparing details, testing, and developing subroutines, allocation of storage locations, specification of input and output formats, and the incorporation of a computer run into a complete data processing system.

program address counter—*Same as* location counter (2).

program, assembly—*Same as* assembler.

program check—(1) A system of determining the correct program and machine functioning either by running a sample problem with similar programming and a known answer, or by using mathematical or logic checks such as comparing A times B with B times A. (2) A check system built into the program or computers that do not have automatic checking. This check system is normally concerned with programs run on computers which are not self-checking internally. *Synonymous with* routine check.

program counter—*Same as* control register.

program generator—A program which permits a computer to write other programs, automatically. Generators are of two types: (a) the character controlled generator, which operates like a compiler in that it takes entries from a library tape, but unlike a simple compiler in that it examines control characters associated with each entry, and alters instructions found in the library according to the directions contained in the control characters. (b) The pure generator which is a program that writes another program. When associated with an assembler a pure generator is usually a section of program which is called into storage by the assembler from a library tape and which then writes one or more entries in another program. Most assemblers are also compilers and generators. In this case the entire system is usually referred to as an assembly system. *Related to* problem oriented language.

program language—A language which is used by programmers to write computer routines.

program, object—*See* object program.

program parameter—A parameter incorporated into a subroutine during computation. A program parameter frequently comprises a word stored relative to either the subroutine or the entry point and dealt with by the subroutine during each reference. It may be altered by the routine and/or may vary from one point of entry to another.

program patching plug—A relatively small auxiliary plugboard patched with a specific variation of a portion of a program and designed to be plugged into a relatively larger plugboard patched with the main program.

program register—A register in which the current instruction of the program is stored. *Synonymous with* register instruction. *Contrasted with* register control.

program sensitive malfunction—A malfunction which occurs only when some unusual combination of program steps occur.

program, source—*See* source program.

program step—A phase of one instruction or command in a sequence of instructions. Thus, a single operation.

program stop—A stop instruction built into the program that will automatically stop the machine under certain conditions, or upon reaching the end of the processing, or completing the solution of a problem.

program storage—A portion of the internal storage reserved for the storage of programs, routines, and subroutines. In many systems protection devices are used to prevent inadvertent alteration of the contents of the program storage.

program, stored—*Same as* stored routine.

program, supervisory—*Same as* executive routine.

program tape—A tape which contains the sequence of instructions required for solving a problem and which is read into a computer prior to running a program.

program, target—*Same as* object program.

program test—A system of checking before running any problem in which a sample problem of the same type with a known answer is run.

program testing time—The machine time expended for program testing, debugging, and volume and compatibility testing.

propagated error—An error occurring in one operation which spreads through and influences later operations and results.

property sort—The selection of items from a group which satisfy a certain criterion.

proportional band—The range of values of a condition being regulated which will cause the controller to operate over its full range. Usually expressed by engineers in terms of percentage of instrument full scale range.

proportional control—A method of control in which the intensity of action varies linearly as the condition being regulated deviates from the condition prescribed.

pseudo instruction—(1) A symbolic representation in a compiler or interpreter. (2) A group of characters having the same general form as a computer instruction, but never executed by the computer as an actual instruction.

pseudo operation—An operation which is not part of the computer's operation repertoire as realized by hardware; hence an extension of the set of machine operations.

pseudo random—The property of satisfying one or more of the standard criteria for statistical randomness but being produced by a definite calculation process.

pseudo random number sequence—An order of numbers produced by a definite recursive rule but satisfying one or more of the standard tests for randomness. Such numbers may be uniform (any number in the set of possible numbers being equally likely), normal or Gaussian (having the property of normal or Gaussian distribution), or satisfy some other type of statistical distribution.

pulse—A significant, and sudden change of short duration in the level of some electric variable, usually voltage.

pulse code—(1) A code in which sets of pulses have been assigned particular meanings, (2) the binary representation of characters.

pulse repetition rate—The number of electric pulses per unit of time experienced by a point in a computer, usually the maximum normal or standard pulse rate.

punch—(1) To shear a hole by forcing a solid or hollow, sharp edged tool through a material into a die; (2) the hole resulting from (1) above.

punch card—A heavy stiff paper of constant size and shape, suitable for punching in a pattern that has meaning, and for being handled mechanically. The punched holes are sensed electrically by wire brushes, mechanically by metal finger, or photoelectrically by photocells.

punch card unit—*Same as* card punch.

punch position—The row position of a punched hole in a specific column of a punch card. In an 80 column punch card the rows are designated 0 to 9, X or Y; in a 90-column card the rows are designated 0, 1, 3, 5, 7, and 9.

punch tape—A tape, usually paper, upon which data may be stored in the form of punched holes. Hole locations are arranged in columns across the width of the tape. There are usually 5 to 8 positions, channels, per column, with data represented by a binary coded decimal system. All holes in a column are sensed simultaneously in a manner similar to that for punch cards.

punch tape code—A code used to represent data on punch tape.

punching positions—The specific areas; i.e., row-column intersects, on a punch card where holes may be punched.

punching rate—The number of cards, characters, blocks, fields or words of information placed in the form of holes distributed on cards, or paper tape per unit of time.

purification, data—*See* data purification.

push down list—A list of items where the last item entered is the first item of the list, and the relative position of the other items is pushed back one.

push up list—A list of items where each item is entered at the end of the list, and the other items maintain their same relative position in the list.

quadripuntal—Pertaining to four punches, specifically having four random punches on a punch card. This term is used in determinative documentation.

quantity—A positive or negative real number in the mathematical sense.

quantity, double precision—*See* double precision quantity.

quantize—*Same as* digitize.

quantizer—*Same as* digitizer.

quantum—The subranges resulting from quantization.

quasi instruction—*Same as* pseudo instruction.

quaternary signalling—An electrical communications mode in which information is passed by the presence and absence, or plus and minus variations of four discrete levels of one parameter of the signalling medium.

queing theory—A form of probability theory useful in studying delays or line-ups at servicing points.

question, encoded—*See* encoded question.

radix—The quantity of characters for use in each of the digital positions of a numbering system. In the more common numbering systems the characters are some or all of the Arabic numerals as follows:

System Name	Characters	Radix
BINARY	(0, 1)	2
OCTAL	(0,1,2,3,4,5,6,7)	8
DECIMAL	(0,1,2,3,4,5,6,7,8,9)	10

Unless otherwise indicated, the radix of any number is assumed to be 10. For positive identification of a radix 10 number, the radix is written in parentheses as a subscript to the expressed number; i.e., $126_{(10)}$. The radix of any nondecimal number is expressed in similar fashion; e.g., $11_{(2)}$ and $5_{(8)}$. *Synonymous with* base; base number; radix number.

radix complement—*Same as* complement (3).

radix minus 1 complement—*Same as* complement (2).

radix notation—(1) An annotation consisting of a decimal number, in parenthesis, written as a subscript suffix to a number, its decimal value indicating the radix of the number; e.g., $11_{(2)}$ indicates the number 11 is in the radix of two; $11_{(8)}$ indicates the number 11 is in the radix of eight. (2) A number written without its radix notation is assumed to be in the radix of ten.

radix number—*Same as* radix.

radix point—The dot that delineates the integer digits from the fractional digits of a number; specifically, the dot that delineates the digital position involving the zero exponent of the radix from the digital position involving the minus-one exponent of the radix. The radix point is often identified by the name of the system; e.g., binary point, octal point, or decimal point. In the writing of any number in any system, if no dot is included, the radix point is assumed to follow the rightmost digit.

RAM—*R*andom *A*ccess *M*emory. *Same as* random access storage.

random access—(1) Pertaining to the process of obtaining information from or placing information into storage where the time required for such access is independent of the location of the information most recently obtained or placed in storage; (2) pertaining to a device in which random access, as defined in definition 1, can be achieved without effective penalty in time.

random access memory—*Same as* random access storage.

random access programming—Programming without regard to the time required for access to the storage positions called for in the program.

random access storage—A storage technique in which the time required to obtain information is independent of the location of the information most recently obtained. This strict definition must be qualified by the observation that we usually mean relatively random. Thus, magnetic drums are relatively non random access when compared to magnetic cores for main storage, but are relatively random access when compared to magnetic tapes for file storage.

random number generator—A special machine routine or hardware designed to produce a random number or series of random numbers according to specified limitations.

random number sequence—An unpredictable array of numbers produced by change, and satisfying one or more of the tests for randomness.

range—(1) All the values which a function or word may have, (2) the difference between the highest and lowest of these values.

rapid access loop—A small section of storage, particularly in drum, tape or disk storage units, which has much faster access than the remainder of the storage.

rate action—A type of control action in which the rate of correction is made proportional to how fast the condition is going awry. This is also called derivative action.

raw data—Data which has not been processed. Such data may or may not be in machine-sensible form.

read—(1) To sense information contained in some source, (2) the sensing of information contained in some source.

read around number—The number of times a specific spot, digit, or location in electrostatic storage may be consulted before spill over will cause a loss of information stored in surrounding spots. The surrounding information must be restored before the loss occurs.

read-in—To sense information contained in some source and transmit this information to an internal storage.

read, non destructive—*See* non destructive read.

read out—To sense information contained in some internal storage and transmit this information to a storage external to the computer.

read punch unit—An input-output unit of a computing system which punches computed results into cards, reads input information into the system, and segregates output cards. The read-punch unit generally consists of a card feed, a read station, a punch station, another read station, and two output card stackers.

read time—*Same as* access time.

read while writing—The reading of a record or group of records into storage from tape at the same time another record or group of records is written from storage to tape.

read write check indicator—A device incorporated in certain computers to indicate upon interrogation whether or not an error was made in reading or writing. The machine can be made to stop, re-try the operation or follow a special subroutine depending upon the result of the interrogation.

read write head—A small electromagnet used for reading, recording, or erasing polarized spots, which represent information, on magnetic tape, disk or drum.

readiness review—An on site examination of the adequacy of preparations for effective utilization upon installation of a computer, and to identify any necessary corrective actions.

reading rate—The number of characters, words, fields, blocks or cards sensed by a sensing device per unit of time.

real time—*Same as* access time.

real time clock—A clock which indicates the passage of actual time, in contrast to a fictitious time set up by the computer program; such as elapsed time in the flight of a missile, wherein a 60 second trajectory is computed in 200 actual milliseconds, or a 0.1 second interval is integrated in 100 actual microseconds.

real time operation—The use of the computer as an element of a processing system in which the times of occurrence of data transmission are controlled by other portions of the system, or by physical events outside the system, and cannot be modified for convenience in computer programming. Such an operation either proceeds at the same speed as the events being simulated or at a sufficient speed to analyze or control external events happening concurrently.

real time processing—The processing of information or data in a sufficiently rapid manner so that the results of the processing are available in time to influence the process being monitored or controlled.

recognition, character—*See* character recognition.

recognition, pattern—*See* pattern recognition.

record—(1) A group of related facts or fields of information treated as a unit, thus a listing of information, usually in printed or printable form; (2) to put data into a storage device.

record, fixed length—*See* fixed length record.

record gap—An interval of space or time associated with a record to indicate or signal the end of the record.

record length—The number of characters necessary to contain all the information in a record.

record mark—A special character used in some computers either to limit the number of characters in a data transfer, or to separate blocked or grouped records in tape.

record, reference—*See* reference record.

record storage mark—A special character which appears only in the record storage unit of the card reader to limit the length of the record read into storage.

record, trailer—*See* trailer record.

record, unit—*See* unit record.

records, grouping of—*See* grouping of records.

recursive—Pertaining to a process which is inherently repetitive. The result of each repetition is usually dependent upon the result of the previous repetition.

red tape—*Same as* housekeeping

red tape operation—*Same as* bookkeeping operation.

redundant character—A character specifically added to a group of characters to insure conformity with certain rules which can be used to detect computer malfunction.

redundant check—A check which makes use of redundant characters.

reel—A spool of tape, generally magnetic tape.

reference address—*Same as* base address (1).

reference record—An output of a compiler that lists the operations and their positions in the final specific routine, and contains information describing the segmentation and storage allocation of the routine.

reference time—An instant near the beginning of switching chosen as an origin for time measurements. It is variously taken as the first instant at which the instantaneous value of the drive pulse, the voltage response of the magnetic cell, or the integrated voltage response reaches a specified fraction of its peak pulse amplitude.

regeneration—(1) The process of returning a part of the output signal of an amplifier to its input circuit in such a manner that it reinforces the excitation and thereby increases the total amplification, (2) periodic restoration of stored information.

register—A hardware device used to store a certain amount of bits or characters. A register is usually constructed of elements such as transistors or tubes and usually contains approximately one word of information. Common programming usage demands that a register have the ability to operte upon information and not merely store it; hardware usage does not make the distinction.

register length—The number of characters in a machine word. In a given computer, the number may be constant or variable.

registration—The accuracy of the positioning of punched holes in a card.

reimbursed time—The machine time which is loaned or rented to another office, agency or organization either on a reimbursable or reciprocal basis.

relative address—An address to which the base address must be added in order to find the machine address.

relative code—A code in which all addresses are specified or written with respect to an arbitrarily selected position, or in which all addresses are represented symbolically in a computable form.

reliability—(1) A measure of the ability to function without failure; (2) the amount of credence placed in a result.

relocate—To move a routine to another location.

remedial maintenance—The maintenance performed by the contractor following equipment failure; therefore, is performed as required, on an unscheduled basis.

reperforator—(1) The contraction of the words receiving perforator; (2) any tape punch which automatically converts coded electrical signals into perforations in tape.

repertory instruction—*See* instruction repertory.

replacement, mechanical—*See* mechanical replacement.

report generator—A technique for producing complete data processing reports giving only a description of the desired content and format of the output reports, and certain information concerning the input file.

representation, analog—*See* analog representation.

representation, positional—*See* positional representation.

representative calculating time—A method of evaluating the speed performance of a computer. One method is to use one-tenth of the time required to perform nine complete additions and one complete multiplication. A complete addition or a complete multiplication time includes the time required to procure two operands from high speed storage, perform the operation, and store the result and the time required to select and execute the required number of instructions to do this.

reproducer, card—*See* card reproducer.

requirements, information—*See* information requirements.

rerun—To repeat all or part of a program on a computer.

rerun point—The stage of a computer run at which all information pertinent to the running of the routine is available either to the routine itself, or to a rerun routine in order that a run may be rerun.

rerun routine—A routine designed to be used after a computer malfunction or a coding or operating mistake to reconstitute a routine from the last previous rerun point.

reset—To return a device to zero or to an initial or arbitrarily selected condition.

reset cycle—To return a cycle index to its initial value.

reset rate—The number of corrections per unit of time made by the control system.

residual error—The difference between an optimum result derived from experience or experiment and a supposedly exact result derived from theory.

residue check—(1) Any modulo N check, (2) a check of numerical data or arithmetic operations in which the number A is divided by N and the remainder B accompanies A as a check digit.

resolver—A device which separates or breaks up a quantity, particularly a vector, into constituent parts or elements; e.g., the mutually perpendicular components of a plane vector.

restart—To go back to a specific planned point in a routine, usually in the case of machine malfunction, for the purpose of rerunning the portion of the routine in which the error occurred. The length of time between restart points in a given routine should be a function of the mean free error time of the machine itself.

restore—To return an index register, a variable address, or other computer word to its initial preselected value.

retrieval, information—*See* information retrieval.

retrievals, false—*See* false retrievals.

return—The mechanism providing for a return in the usual sense. In particular a set of instructions at the end of a subroutine which permit control to return to the proper point in the main routine.

reverse code dictionary—An alphabetic or numeric alphabetic arrangement of codes, associated with their corresponding English words or terms.

review, preliminary proposal—*See* preliminary proposal review.

review, readiness—*See* readiness review.

revolver—*Same as* rapid access loop.

rewind—To return a film or magnetic tape to its beginning or passed location.

rewrite—The process in a storage device of restoring the information in the device to its state prior to reading.

ring counter—A loop of interconnected bistable elements such that one and only one is in a specified state at any given time and such that, as input signals are counted, the position of the element in the specified state moves in an ordered sequence around the loop.

ring shift—*Same as* cyclic shift.

rise time—The time required for the leading edge of a pulse to rise from one-tenth of its final value to nine-tenths of its final value. Rise time is proportional to the time constant of the circuit.

role indicator—A code assigned to a keyword to indicate the role of the keyword; e.g., a keyword may be a noun, verb, adjective, or adverb; therefore, an indicator is used to identify the specific role of the keyword.

rollback routine—*Same as* rerun routine.

roll-out—A process, often used in diagnostic routines, in which a register or counter is read out by the following process: Add 1 to the digits in each column simultaneously; do this n times, where n is the radix of the number in the register; when the result in each column changes from n–1 to 0, issue a signal.

round—Deletion of the least significant digit(s) with or without modifications to reduce bias.

rounding error—The error resulting from rounding off a quantity by deleting the less significant digits and applying some rule of correction to the part retained; e.g., 0.2751 can be rounded to 0.275 with a rounding error of .0001.

round off—*Same as* round.

round off error—*Same as* rounding error.

routine—A set of coded instructions arranged in proper sequence to direct the computer to perform a desired operation or sequence of operations. A subdivision of a program consisting of two or more instructions that are functionally related; therefore, a program.

routine library—A collection of standard, proven routines and subroutines by which problems and parts of problems may be solved.

row binary—A method of representing binary numbers on a card where successive bits are represented by the presence or absence of punches in a successive position in a row as opposed to a series of columns. Row binary is especially convenient is 40 bit word, or less, computers; wherein the card frequently is used to store 12 binary words on each half of the card.

row pitch—The distance measured along paper tape between the centers of the adjacent holes.

ruly English—A form of English in which every word has one and only one conceptual meaning and each concept has one and only one word to describe it. This is a hypothetical language based on English which compiles uniformly to a definite set of rules, without exceptions.

run—The performance of one program on a computer, thus the performance of one routine, or several routines linked so that they form an automatic operating unit, during which manual manipulations by the computer operator are zero, or at least minimal.

sampling rate—The rate at which measurements of physical quantities are made; e.g., if it is desired to calculate the velocity of a missile and its position is measured each millisecond, then the sampling rate is 1,000 measurements per second.

scale—A range of values frequently dictated by the computer word length or routine at hand.

scale factor—The coefficients used to multiply or divide quantities in a problem in order to convert them so as to have them lie in a given range of magnitude; plus one to minus one.

scan—To examine every reference or every entry in a file routinely as a part of a retrieval scheme; occasionally, to collate.

scanner—An instrument which automatically samples or interrogates the state of various processes, files, conditions, or physical states and initiates action in accordance with the information obtained.

scheduled operation—The periods of time during which the user plans to use specified equipment. Such a designation must be made a given number of hours in advance, provided however, that such scheduled hours of the operation may be modified after that time in the event of an emergency, or in the event that equipment failure creates a need for such rescheduling. Usually the foregoing is further modified in that during the performance period the hours rescheduled as a result of equipment failure usually are not considered as scheduled hours of operation in computing equipment effectiveness.

screen—(1) The surface in an electrostatic cathode ray storage tube where electrostatic charges are stored, and by means of which information is displayed or stored temporarily; (2) to make a preliminary selection from a set of entities, selection criteria being based on a given set of rules or conditions.

SDA—*S*ource *D*ata *A*utomation. The many methods of recording information in coded forms on paper tapes, punched cards, or tags that can be used over and over again to produce many other records without rewriting.

search—To examine a series of items for any that have a desired property or properties.

search time—The time required to locate a particular field of data in storage. Searching requires a comparison of each field with a predetermined standard until an identity is obtained. This is contrasted with access time which is based upon locating data by means of the address of its storage location.

second level address—*Same as* indirect address.

secondary storage—The storage facilities not an integral part of the computer but directly connected to and controlled by the computer; e.g., magnetic drum and magnetic tapes.

section, arithmetic—*Same as* arithmetic unit.

seek—To look for data according to information given regarding that data; occasionally used interchangeably and erroneously for (search), (scan) and (screen).

segment—(1) To divide a routine in parts, each consisting of an integral number of subroutines, and each part capable of being completed stored in the internal storage and containing the necessary instructions to jump to other segments. (2) That portion of a routine too long to fit into internal storage which is short enough to be stored entirely in the internal storage; such a segment contains the coding necessary to call in other segments automatically. Routines which exceed internal storage capacity may be automatically divided into segments by a compiler.

segment mark—A special character written on tape to separate one section of a tape file from another.

select—(1) To take the alternative A if the report on a condition is of one state, and alternative B if the report on the condition is of another state; (2) to choose a needed subroutine from a file of subroutines.

selection check—A check, usually automatic, to verify that the correct register or other device has been selected in the performance of an instruction.

selective trace—A tracing routine wherein only instructions satisfying certain specified criteria are subject to tracing. Typical criteria are: (a) Instruction type; e.g., arithmetic jump. (b) Instruction location; e.g., specific region. (c) Data location; e.g., specific region. For Case a, where tracing is performed on transfer, jump, instructions the term logical trace is sometimes used.

selector—A device which interrogates a condition and initiates one of several alternate operations.

self checking code—*Same as* error detecting code.

self checking number—A number with a suffix figure related to the figure(s) of the number, used to check the number after it has been transferred from one medium or device to another.

self demarking code—A code in which the symbols are so arranged and selected that the generation of false combinations by interaction of segments from two successive codes is prevented.

self organizing—Having the capability of classification or internal rearrangement, depending on the environment in accordance with given instructions or a set of rules.

self organizing machine—A class of machines which may be characterized loosely as containing a variable network in which the elements are organized by the machine itself, without external intervention, to meet criteria of successful operation.

semantic matrix—A graphical device for plotting in a standard conventional form whatever precise elements of meaning have been ascertained from the semantic analysis of a concept.

semiconductor—A solid with an electrical conductivity that lies between the high conductivity of metals and the low conductivity of insulators. Semiconductor circuit elements include crystal diodes and transistors.

sense—(1) To examine, particularly relative to a criterion; (2) to determine the present arrangement of some element of hardware, especially a manually set switch; (2) to read punched holes or other manually set switch; (3) to read punched holes or other marks.

sensitivity—The degree of response of an instrument or control unit to a change in the incoming signal.

sentinel—*Same as* flag (3).

septenary number—A number, usually of more than one figure representing a sum, in which the quantity represented by each figure is based on a radix of seven. The figures used are 0, 1, 2, 3, 4, 5, and 6.

sequence—(1) To put a set of symbols into an arbitrarily defined order;

i.e., to select A if A is greater than B. (2) An arbitrarily defined order of a set of symbols; i.e., an orderly progression of items of information or of operations in accordance with some rule.

sequence check—A data processing operation designed to check the sequence of the items in a file assumed to be already in sequence.

sequence checking routine—A routine which checks every instruction executed, and prints out certain data; e.g., to print out the coded instructions with addresses, and the contents of each of several registers, or it may be designed to print out only selected data, such as transfer instructions and the quantity actually transferred.

sequencer—*Same as* sorter.

sequential access storage—A storage technique in which the items of information stored become available only in a one after the other sequence, whether or not all the information or only some of it is desired; e.g., magnetic tape storage.

sequential control—A mode of computer operation in which instructions are executed in consecutive order by ascending or descending addresses of storage locations, unless otherwise specified by a jump.

sequential operation—The performance of actions one after the other in time. The actions referred to are of a large scale as opposed to the smaller scale operations referred to by the term serial operation. For an example of sequential operation consider $A \times (B \times C)$. The two multiplications indicated follow each other sequentially. However, the processing of the individual digits in each multiplication may be either parallel or serial.

serial—(1) The handling of one after the other in a single facility, such as transfer or store in a digit-by-digit time sequence, or to process a sequence of instructions one at a time; i.e., sequentially. (2) The time sequence transmission of, storage of, or logical operations on the parts of a word, with the same facilities for successive parts.

serial access—Pertaining to the process of obtaining information from or placing information into storage where the time required for such access is dependent on the necessity for waiting while nondesired storage locations are processed in turn.

serial computer—A computer in which digits or data lines are handled sequentially by separate units of the computer. Mixed serial and parallel machines are frequently called serial or parallel according to the way arithmetic processes are performed. An example of a serial computer is one which handles decimal digits serially although it might handle the bits which comprise a digit either serially or in parallel.

serial operation—The flow of information through a computer in time sequence using only one digit, word, line or channel at a time.

serial-parallel—(1) A combination of serial and parallel; e.g., serial by character, parallel by bits comprising the character. (2) Descriptive of a device which converts a serial input into a parallel output.

serial programming—The programming of a computer by which only one arithmetical or logical operation can be executed at one time; e.g., a sequential operation.

serial storage—A storage technique in which time is one of the factors used to locate any given bit, character, word, or groups of words appearing one after the other in time sequence, and in which access time includes a variable latency or waiting time of from zero to many word times. A storage is said to be serial by word when the individual bits comprising a word appear serially in time; or a storage is serial by character when the characters representing coded decimal or other non binary numbers appear serially in time; e.g., magnetic drums are usually serial by word but may be serial by bit, or parallel by bit, or serial by character and parallel by bit. *Related to* storage, sequential access.

serial transfer—A method of data transfer in which the characters of an element are transferred in sequence over a signal path in consecutive time positions.

serial transmission—To move data in sequence, one character at a time as contrasted with parallel transmission.

series, time—*See* time series.

service routine—A broad class of routines which are standardized at a particular installation for the purpose of assisting in maintenance and operation of the computer as well as the preparation of programs as opposed to routines for the actual solution of production problems. This class includes monitoring or supervisory routines, assemblers, compilers, diagnostics for computer malfunctions, simulation of peripheral equipment, general diagnostics and input data. The distinquishing quality of service routines is that they are generally standardized so as to meet the servicing needs at a particular installation, independent of any specific production type routine requiring such services.

servicing time—*Same as* engineering time.

servomechanism—A device to monitor an operation as it proceeds, and make necessary adjustments to keep the operation under control. A furnace thermostat is an example of a servomechanism.

set—(1) To place a storage device in a prescribed state. (2) To place a binary cell in the one state. (3) A collection of elements having some feature in common or which bear a certain relation to one another; e.g., all even numbers, geometrical figures, terms in a series, a group of irrational numbers, all positive even integers less than 100 may be a set or a sub-set.

set up time—The portion of the elapsed time between machine operations which is devoted to such tasks as changing reels of tape, and moving cards, tapes, and supplies to and from the equipment.

sexadecimal number—A number, usually of more than one figure, representing a sum in which the quantity represented by each figure is based on a ridix of sixteen. Also called Hexadecimal.

shift—To move the characters of a unit of information columnwise right or left. For a number, this is equivalent to multiplying or dividing by a power of the base of notation.

shift, circular—*Same as* cyclic shift.

shift, end around—*Same as* cyclic shift.

shift, logical—*Same as* cyclic shift.

shift, non arithmetic—*Same as* cyclic shift.

shift register—A register in which the characters may be shifted one or more positions to the right or left. In a right shift, the rightmost character(s) are lost. In a left shift, the leftmost character(s) are lost.

shift, ring—*Same as* cyclic shift.

short word—The fixed word of lesser length in computers capable of handling words of two different lengths. In many computers this is referred to as a half word because the length is exactly the half-length of the full word.

sign—(1) In arithmetic, a symbol which distinquishes negative quantities from positive ones. (2) An indication of whether a quantity is greater than zero, or less than zero. The signs often are the marks = and –, respectively; but other arbitrarily selected symbols may be used; such as a 0 and 1, or 0 and 9, then used as codes at a predetermined location, can be interpreted by a person or machine.

sign bit—A binary digit used as a sign draft.

sign check indicator—An error checking device, indicating no sign or improper signing of a field used for arithmetic processes. The machine can, upon interrogation be made to stop or enter into a correction routine.

sign digit—A character, frequently a single bit, used to designate the algebraic sign of the quantity.

signal—The event, phenomenon or electrical quantity which conveys information from one point to another.

signal attenuation—The reduction in the strength of electrical signals.

signal conditioning—To process the form or mode of a signal so as to make it intelligible to or compatible with a given device, including such manipulation as pulse b shaping, pulse clipping, digitizing, and linearizing.

signal to noise ratio—The ratio of the amount of signals conveying information to the amount of signals not conveying information.

signalling rate—The rate at which signals are transmitted.

signed field—A field which has a plus or minus character coding over the units position to designate the algebraic sign of the entire number.

significant digits—A set of digits, usually from consecutive columns beginning with the most significant digit different from zero and ending with the least significant digit whose value is known and assumed relevant; e.g., 2300.0 has five significant digits, whereas 2300 probably has two significant digits; however, 2301 has four significant digits and 0.0023 has two significant digits.

simulation—(1)The representation of physical systems and phenomena by computers, models or other equipment; e.g., an imitative type of data processing in which an automatic computer is used as a model of some entity; e.g., a chemical process. Information enters the computer to represent the factors entering the real process, the computer produces information that represents the results of the process, and the processing done by the computer programming, the technique of setting up a routine for one computer to make it operate as nearly as possible like some other computer.

simulator—(1) A computer or model which represents a system or phenomenon and which mirrors or maps the effects of various changes in the original, enabling the original to be studied, analyzed, and understood by means of the behavior of the model; (2) a program or routine corresponding to a mathematical model or representing a physical model; (3) a routine which is executed by one computer but which imitates the operations of another computer.

simultaneous access—*Same as* parallel access.

single address—*Same as* one address (2).

single step operation—A method of operating an automatic computer manually in which a single instruction or part of an instruction is performed in response to a single operation of a manual control. This method is generally used for detecting mistakes.

skeletal code—The framework of a routine which is completed by a generalized routine using input parameters.

skip—*Same as* skip instruction.

skip instruction—An instruction having no effect other than directing the processor to proceed to another instruction designated in the storage portion.

skip, tape—*See* tape skip.

snapshot dump—A dynamic partial print out during computing, at breakpoints and checkpoints, or selected items in storage.

software—The totality of programs and routines used to extend the capabilities of computers, such as compilers, assemblers, narrators, routines, and subroutines.

solid state—The electronic components that convey or control electrons within solid materials; e.g., transistors, germanium diodes, and magnetic cores. Thus, vacuum and gas tubes are not included.

solid state computer—A computer built primarily from solid state electronic circuit elements.

sonic delay line—*Same as* acoustic delay line.

sophisticated vocabulary—An advanced and elaborate set of instructions. Some computers can perform only the more common mathematical calculations such as addition, multiplication, and subtraction. A computer with a sophisticated vocabulary can go beyond this and perform operations such as linearize, extract square root, and select highest number.

sort—To arrange items of information according to rules dependent upon a key or field contained in the items or records; e.g., to digital sort is to sort first the keys on the least significant digit, and to resort on each higher order digit until the items are sorted on the most significant digit.

sort, four-tape—To four-tape sort is to merge sort in which input data are supplied on two tapes, and are sorted into incomplete sequences alter nately on two output tapes, the output tapes are used for input on the succeeding pass, resulting in longer and longer sequences after each pass until the data are all in one sequence on one output tape.

sort, merge—To produce a single sequence of items, ordered according to some rule, from two or more previously unordered sequences, without changing the items in size, structure, or total number, although more than one pass may be required for a complete sort, items are selected during each pass on the basis of the entire key.

sorter—A machine which puts items of information into a particular order; e.g., it will determine whether A is greater than, equal to or less than B and sort or order accordingly.

source data automation—The many methods of recording information in coded forms on paper tapes, punched cards, or tags that can be used over and over again to produce many other records without rewriting.

source document—A document from which basic data is extracted.

source language—The original form in which a program is prepared prior to processing by the machine.

source program—A computer program written in a language designed for ease of expression of a class of problems or procedures, by humans; e.g., symbolic or algebraic. A generator, assembler translator or compiler routine is used to perform the mechanics of translating the source program into an object program in machine language.

space—*Same as* blank (1).

space, dead—*Same as* dead band.

space, working—*Same as* working storage.

special purpose computer—A computer designed to solve a specific class or narrow range of problems.

specific address—*Same as* absolute address.

specific code—*Same as* absolute code.

specific program—A program for solving a specific problem only.

specific routine—A routine to solve a particular mathematical, logical, or data handling problem in which each address refers to explicitly stated registers and locations.

speed, transmission—*See* transmission speed.

spot punch—A hand operated device resembling a pair of pliers, for selectively punching holes in punch cards.

sprocket pulse—(1) A pulse generated by a magnetized spot which accompanies every character recorded on magnetic tape. This pulse is used during read operations to regulate the timing of the read circuits and also to provide a count on the number of characters read from tape. (2) A pulse generated by the sprocket or driving hole in paper tape which serves as the timing pulse for reading or punching the paper tape.

stacker, input—*Same as* input magazine.

stacker, output—*Same as* output magazine.

standard subroutine—A subroutine which is applicable to a class of problems.

standing-on-nines carry—A carry out of a digit position generated by a carry into the digit position and the normal adding circuit is bypassed.

standby application—An application in which two or more computers are tied together as a part of a single over-all system and which, as in the case of an inquiry application, stand ready for immediate activation and appropriate action.

underpunch—A punch in one of the lower rows, 1-9, of an 80 column 12 row punch card.

ultrasonics—The field of science devoted to frequencies of sound above the human audio range; i.e., above 20 kilocycles per second.

unconditional branch—*Same as* unconditional transfer.

unconditional jump—*Same as* unconditional transfer.

unconditional transfer—An instruction which switches the sequence of control to some specified location.

unconditional transfer of control—*Same as* transfer, unconditional.

underflow—(1) The condition which arises when a machine computation yields a result which is smaller than the smallest possible quantity which the machine is capable of storing, (2) a condition in which the exponent plus the excess becomes negative in a floating point arithmetic operation.

unit—A portion or subassembly of a computer which constitutes the means of accomplishing some inclusive operation or function.

unit, card punch—*Same as* card punch.

unit, card reader—*Same as* card reader (2).

unit, central processing—*Same as* main frame (1).

unit, paper tape—The mechanism which handles punched paper tape and usually consists of a paper tape transport, sensing and recording or perforating heads and associated electrical and electronic equipments.

unit record—(1) A separate record that is similar in form and content to other records; e.g., a summary of a particular employee's earnings to date. (2) Sometimes refers to a piece of non-tape auxiliary equipment; e.g., card reader, printer or console typewriter.

unit, tape—*See* tape unit.

uniterm—A word, symbol, or number used as a descriptor for retrieval of information from a collection; especially such a descriptor used in a coordinate indexing system.

uniterm indexing—A system of coordinate indexıng which utilizes single terms, called Uniterms, to define a document uniquely.

uniterm system—An information retrieval system which uses uniterm cards. Cards representing words of interest in a search are selected and compared visually. If identical numbers are found to appear on the uniterm card undergoing comparison these numbers represent documents to be examined in connection with the search.

uniterming—The selection of words, considered to be important and descriptive of the contents of a paper for later retrieval of the articles, reports, or other documents. The selcted words are then included in a uniterm index.

universal turing machine—A turing machine that can simulate any other turing machine.

unpack—To separate various sections of a tape record or computer word, and store them in separate locations. The sections usually correspond to format fields within the record or word.

unwind—To code explicitly, at length and in full all the operations of a cycle thus eliminating all redtape operations in the final problem coding. Unwinding may be performed automatically by the computer during assembly, generation, or compilation of a program.

update—(1) To put into a master file changes required by current information or transactions, (2) to modify an instruction so that the address numbers it contains are increased by a stated amount each time the instruction is performed.

up time—The time during which equipment is either producing work or is available for productive work.

utility program—*Same as* utility routine.

utility routine—A standard routine used to assıst in the operation of the computer; e.g., a conversion routine, a sorting routine, a printout routine, or a tracing routine.

validity—The correctness; especially the degree of the closeness by which iterated results approach the correct result.

validity check—A check based upon known limits or upon given information or computer results; e.g., a calendar month will not be numbered greater than 12, and a week does not have more than 168 hours.

variable—(1) A quantity which can assume any of the numbers of some set of numbers, (2) a condition, transaction or event which changes or may be changed as a result of processing additional data thru the system.

variable connector—(1) A flow chart symbol representing a sequence connection which is not fixed, but which can be varied by the flowcharted procedure itself. (2) The device which inserts instructions in a program corresponding to selection of paths appearing in a flow chart. (3) The computer instructions which cause a logical chain to take one of several alternative paths.

variable cycle operation—A computer action in which any cycle of action or operation may be of a different time length. Such action is characteristic of an asynchronous computer.

variable, two state—*Same as* two valued variable.

variable, two valued—*See* two valued variable.

variable word length—Having the property that a machine word may have a variable number of characters. It may be applied either to a single entry whose information content may be changed from time to time, or to a group of functionally similar entries whose corresponding components are of different lengths.

vector—A quantity having magnitude and direction, as contrasted with a scaler which has quantity only.

Venn diagram—A diagram in which each point represents an individual. Sets are represented by closed regions including all members of the set and excluding all nonmembers. The diagram is used to facilitate determination whether several sets include or exclude the same individuals.

verifier—A device on which a record can be compared or tested for identity character-by-character with a retranscription or copy as it is being prepared.

verify—To check a transcribing operation, by a compare operation. It usually applies to transcriptions which can be read mechanically or electrically.

vocabulary—A list of operating codes or instructions available to the programmer for writing the program for a given problem for a specific computer.

volatile storage—A storage medium in which information cannot be retained without continuous power dissipation.

volume test—The processing of a volume of actual data to check for program malfunctions.

Williams tube—A cathode ray tube used as an electrostatic storage device and of the type designed by F.C. Williams, University of Manchester, England.

wire printer—A high speed printer that prints character-like configurations of dots through the proper selection of wire ends from a matrix of wire ends, rather than conventional characters through the selection of type faces.

wired program computer—A computer in which the instructions that specify the operations to be performed are specified by the placement and interconnection of wires. The wires are usually held by a removable control panel, allowing flexibility of operation, but the term is also applied to permanently wired machines which are then called fixed program computers.

word—An ordered set of characters which occupies one storage location and is treated by the computer circuits as a unit and transferred as such. Ordinarily a word is treated by the control unit as an instruction, and by the arithmetic unit as a quantity. Word lengths may be fixed or variable depending on the particular computer.

word length—The number of characters in a machine word. In a given computer, the number may be constant or variable.

word mark—An indicator to signal the beginning or end of a word.

word time—(1) The amount of time required to move one word past a given point. The term is used especially in reference to words stored serially. (2) The time required to transport one word from one storage device to another.

working storage—A portion of the internal storage reserved for the data upon which operations are being performed.

write—(1) To transfer information, usually from main storage, to an output device; (2) to record data in a register, location, or other storage device or medium.

x punch—(1) A punch in the X or 11 row of an 80 column card. (2) A punch in position 11 of a column. The X punch is often used to control or select, or to indicate a negative number as if it were a minus sign.

xerographic printer—A device for printing an optical image on paper in which dark and light areas of the original are represented by electrostatically charged and uncharged areas on the paper. The paper is dusted with particles of finely powdered dry ink and the particles adhere only to the electrically charged areas. The paper with ink particles is then heated, causing the ink to melt and become permanently fixed to paper.

xerography—A dry copying process involving the photo electric discharge of an electrostatically charged plate. The copy is made bytumbling a resinous powder over the plate, the remaining electrostatic charge discharged and the resin transferred to paper or an offset printing master.

xy plotter—A device used in conjunction with a computer to plot coordinate points in the form of a graph.

y punch—(1) A punch in the Y or 12 row of an 80 column card; i.e., the top row of the card. (2) A punch in position 12 of a column. It is often used for additional control or selection, or to indicate a positive number as if it were a plus sign.

zero—A numeral normally denoting lack of magnitude. In many computers there are distinct representations for plus and minus zero.

zero access storage—The storage for which the latency (waiting time) is small. Though once widely used, this term is becoming less acceptable, since it constitutes a misnomer.

zero address instruction—An instruction consisting of an operation which does not require the designation of an address in the usual sense; e.g., the instruction, "shift left 0003", has in its normal address position the amount of the shift desired.

zero level address—*Same as* immediate address.

zero supression—The elimination of nonsignificant zeros to the left of significant digits usually before printing.

zone—(1) A portion of internal storage allocated for a particular function or purpose. (2) The three top positions of 12, 11 and 0 on certain punch cards, In these positions, a second punch can be inserted so that with punches in the remaining positions 1 to 9, alphabetic characters may be represented.

zone bit—(1) One of the two left most bits in a commonly used system in which six bits are used for each character. (2) Any bit in a group of bit positions that are used to indicate a specific class of items; e.g., numbers, letters, special signs, and commands.

zone punch—*Same as* overpunch.

Appendix A

Error Messages

The following shows the format of error messages:

Immediate-execution Statement	?XX ERROR
Deferred-execution Statement	?XX ERROR IN YY

In both of the statements, "XX" is the name of the error. "YY" is the line number of the statement that contains the error. No line number is printed for an immediate-execution statement. The following list contains the possible error codes and their descriptions.

?CAN'T CONTINUE ERROR

Attempt to continue a program when none existed, or after an error occurred, or after a line was deleted from or added to a program.

?DIVISION BY ZERO ERROR

Dividing by zero is an error.

?FORMULA TOO COMPLEX ERROR

More than two statements of the form IF "XX" THEN were executed.

?ILLEGAL DIRECT ERROR

You cannot use an INPUT, DEF FN, or DATA statement as an immediate-execution command.

?ILLEGAL QUANTITY ERROR

The parameter passed to a math or string function was out of range. ILLEGAL QUANTITY errors can occur due to:

a. a negative array SUBSCRIPT (e.g., A(−1) = 0)
b. using LOG with a negative or zero argument
c. using SQR with a negative argument
d. A↑B with A negative and B not an integer
e. use of MID$, LEFT$, RIGHT$, WAIT, PEEK, POKE, TAB, SPEC, ON . . . GOTO, or any of the graphics function with an improper argument.

?NEXT WITHOUT FOR ERROR

The variable in a NEXT statement did not correspond to the variable in a FOR statement which was still in effect, or a nameless NEXT did correspond to any FOR which was still in effect.

?OUT OF DATA ERROR

A READ statement was executed but all of the DATA statements in the program had already been read. The program tried to read too much data or insufficient data was included in the program.

?OUT OF MEMORY ERROR

Any of the following can cause this error; program too large, too many variables, FOR loops nested more than 10 levels deep, GOSUB's nested more than 24 levels deep, too complicated an expression, parentheses nested more than 36 levels deep, attempt to set LOMEM: too high, attempt to set LOMEM: lower than present value, attempt to set HIMEM: too low.

?OVERFLOW ERROR

The result of a calculation was too large to be represented in Applesoft BASIC's number format. If an underflow occurs, zero is given as the result and execution continues without any error message being printed.

?REDIM'D ARRAY ERROR

After an array was dimensioned, another dimension statement for the same array was encountered. This error often occurs if an array has been given the default dimension 10 because a statement like A(I) = 3 is followed later in the program by a DIM A(100). This error message can prove useful if you wish to discover on what program line a certain array was dimensioned: just insert a dimension statement for that array in the first line, RUN the program, and Applesoft will tell you where the original dimension statement is.

?RETURN WITHOUT GOSUB ERROR

A RETURN statement was encountered without a corresponding GOSUB statement being executed.

?STRING TOO LONG ERROR

Attempt was made by use of the concatenation operator to create a string more than 255 characters long.

?BAD SUBSCRIPT ERROR

An attempt was made to reference an array element which is outside the dimensions of the array. This error can occur if the wrong number of dimensions are used in an array reference; for instance, LET A(11) = Z when A has been dimensioned using DIM A(2).

?SYNTAX ERROR

Missing parenthesis in an expression, illegal character in a line, incorrect punctuation, etc.

?TYPE MISMATCH ERROR

The left-hand side of an assignment statement was a numeric variable and the right-hand side was a string, or vice versa; or a function which expected a string argument was given a numeric one or vice versa.

?UNDEF'D STATEMENT ERROR

An attempt was made to GOTO, GOSUB, or THEN to a statement line number which does not exist.

?UNDEF'D FUNCTION ERROR

Reference was made to a user-defined function which had never been defined.

Appendix B
Program Editing

It is expected that you will make a few mistakes when programming, especially if you are a beginner. To allow for corrections, there are many editing features in APPLESOFT BASIC. The following descriptions tell how to use them.

ESC

The escape key is always used with another key. First push and release ESC, and then push and release the other key. The four escape functions used for editing are:

escape A—moves cursor to the right
escape B—moves cursor to the left
escape C—moves cursor down
escape D—moves cursor up

Using these escape functions allows for movement of the cursor to any location on the screen without affecting anything that is already displayed there, or anything in memory.

RIGHT ARROW KEY

This key moves the cursor to the right. An important characteristic of this key is that it copies into memory all of the characters and symbols it moves across into memory. Using this key does not change the TV display.

LEFT-ARROW KEY

This key moves the cursor to the left. Each time that it is moved to the left, one character from the program line which you are currently typing will be erased. This occurs no matter what the cursor is moving over. The TV screen is not affected by the use of this key. Use escape B to move the cursor into the leftmost column; usually the left-arrow key won't work for this movement.

REPT

The REPT key causes a character to be rapidly repeated. To use this key, hold down the key that will type the character, then at the same time hold down the REPT key.

CTRL

Typing CTRL X will delete the line you are currently typing. This is useful if you realize that you have made a mistake before ending the line and pressing RETURN. Otherwise, you can simply type the line number you want to delete and press RETURN. Or, if you want to delete more than one line, you could use the delete command, as illustrated in the following example:

DEL 100, 200

all lines from 100 to 200 would then be deleted.

ESC @

To clear the screen, type ESC followed by an "at" sign. The cursor will appear at the top left-hand corner of the screen without the prompt. Once you press RETURN, the prompt character will appear.

EDITING EXAMPLES

1. Fixing Typos—If the computer prints SYNTAX ERR and then stops, use the following program as a model to correct the error.

    10 PRIMT "THIS IS A PREMGRAM"
    20 GOTO 10
    RUN
    ?SYNTAX ERR IN 10 appears

    Use ESC D, remembering to hit both keys each time, to move the cursor onto line #10. Then use ESC B to move it over the first character in the line (the 1 in 10). Now use the right arrow to move the cursor over the line until it is over the M in PRIMT. Type N to correct the word. Continue to use the arrow key to move the cursor over the E in PREMGRAM. Since there are numerous errors and too many letters here, it is easier to delete the rest of the line and retype the whole word, so type ESC E, and then type OGRAM" and hit RETURN

Inserting Text into an Existing Line—If you wanted to insert a TAB(10) command after the PRINT in line 10 of the previous example, first list the line to be changed:

LIST 10

Type ESC D's and an ESC B until the cursor is on the very first character of the line to be changed. Then use the right arrow and repeat keys to copy over to the first quotation mark. Now type another ESC D to move the cursor to the empty line just above the current line and the display will show the cursor over the quotation marks before THIS. Type the characters to be inserted. Type an ESC C to move the cursor in between IS and A. Now backspace to the first quotation mark using ESC B. From here, copy the rest of the line using the right arrow and repeat keys until the cursor is at the end of line 10. Depress the RETURN key and type LIST.

SUMMARY OF EDIT FEATURES

Enter edit mode—Press ESC
Exit edit mode—Press space bar
Move cursor—Press A, B, C, or D
Delete a character—Press
Retype a character—Press REPT
Clear from the cursor to the end of a line—Press ESC, then E
Clear from the cursor to the end of the screen—Press ESC, then F
Clear the entire screen—Press ESC, then CTRL and @
Stop listing—Press CTRL and S
Resume listing—Press CTRL and S

Appendix C

Reserved Words in Applesoft

&
ABS
AND
ASC
AT
ATN
CALL
CHR$
CLEAR
COLOR=
CONT
COS
DATA
DEF
DEL
DIM
DRAW
END
EXP
FLASH
FN
FOR
FRE
GET
GOSUB
GOTO
GR
HCOLOR=
HGR
HGR2
HIMEM:
HLIN
HOME
HPLOT
HTAB
IF
IN#
INPUT
INT
INVERSE
LEFT$
LEN
LET
LIST
LOAD
LOG
LOMEM:
MID$
NEW
NEXT
NORMAL
NOT
NOTRACE
ON
ONERR
OR
PDL
PEEK
PLOT
POKE
POP
POS
PRINT
PR#
READ
RECALL
REM
RESTORE
RESUME
RETURN
RIGHT$
RND
ROT=
RUN
SAVE
SCALE=
SCRN(
SGN
SHLOAD
SIN
SPC(
SPEED=
SQR
STEP
STOP
STORE
STR$
TAB(
TAN
TEXT
THEN
TO
TRACE
USR
VAL
VLIN
VTAB
WAIT
XPLOT
XDRAW

Appendix D

ASCII Character Codes

DEC	HEX	CHAR	WHAT TO TYPE
Ø	ØØ	NULL	ctrl @
1	Ø1	SOH	ctrl A
2	Ø2	STX	ctrl B
3	Ø3	ETX	ctrl C
4	Ø4	ET	ctrl D
5	Ø5	ENQ	ctrl E
6	Ø6	ACK	ctrl F
7	Ø7	BEL	ctrl G
8	Ø8	BS	ctrl H or ←
9	Ø9	HT	ctrl I
1Ø	ØA	LF	ctrl J
11	ØB	VT	ctrl K
12	ØC	FF	ctrl L
13	ØD	CR	ctrl M or RETURN
14	ØE	SO	ctrl N
15	ØF	SI	ctrl O
16	1Ø	DLE	ctrl P
17	11	DC1	ctrl Q
18	12	DC2	ctrl R
19	13	DC3	ctrl S
2Ø	14	DC4	ctrl T
21	15	NAK	ctrl U or →
22	16	SYN	ctrl V
23	17	ETB	ctrl W
24	18	CAN	ctrl X
25	19	EM	ctrl Y
26	1A	SUB	ctrl Z
27	1B	ESCAPE	ESC
28	1C	FS	
29	1D	GS	ctrl shift-M
3Ø	1E	RS	ctrl ▲
31	1F	US	
32	2Ø	SPACE	space
33	21	!	!
34	22	"	"
35	23	#	#
36	24	$	$
37	25	%	%
38	26	&	&
39	27	'	'
4Ø	28	(	(
41	29	)	)
42	2A	*	*
43	2B	+	°
44	2C	,	,
45	2D	-	-
46	2E	.	.
47	2F	/	/
48	3Ø	Ø	Ø
49	31	1	1
5Ø	32	2	2
51	33	3	3
52	34	4	4
53	35	5	5
54	36	6	6
55	37	7	7
56	38	8	8
57	39	9	9
58	3A	:	
59	3B	;	;
6Ø	3C	<	<
61	3D	=	=
62	3E	>	>
63	3F	?	?
64	4Ø	@	@
65	41	A	A
66	42	B	B
67	43	C	C
68	44	D	D
69	45	E	E
7Ø	46	F	F
71	47	G	G
72	48	H	H
73	49	I	I
74	4A	J	J
75	4B	K	K
76	4C	L	L
77	4D	M	M
78	4E	N	N
79	4F	O	O
8Ø	5Ø	P	P
81	51	Q	Q
82	52	R	R
83	53	S	S
84	54	T	T
85	55	U	U
86	56	V	V
87	57	W	W
88	58	X	X
89	59	Y	Y
9Ø	5A	Z	Z
91	5B	[	
92	5C	\	
93	5D	]	] (shift-M)
94	5E	▲	▲
95	5F	_	

Appendix E
Syntax

The following is an alphabetic list of the syntaxes used in this book. The definitions use metasymbols, keyed below, to show relationships. The metasymbols are not part of the APPLESOFT language.

Metasymbol Key:

| — used to separate alternatives

[] — used to enclose material which is optional

{ }— used to enclose material which may be repeated

/ - used to enclose material whose value is to be used

~ — indicates a required space

alphanumeric character

letter|digit

aop

arithmetic operator

+|−|*|/|↑

avar

arithmetic variable

name|name% (All simple variables occupy 7 bytes in memory, 2 bytes for the name and 5 bytes for the real or integer value.)

avar subscript (In arrays, reals occupy 5 bytes, integers 2 bytes.)

aexpr

arithmetic expression

avar|real|integer

avar subscript

(aexpr) (If parentheses are nested more than 36 levels deep, the ?OUT OF MEMORY ERROR occurs.)

[+|–|NOT] aexpr (Unary NOT appears here, along with unary + and –)
aexpr op aexpr
sexpr slop sexpr

character
letter|digit|special

ctrl
hold down the key marked CTRL while the following named key is pressed

def
deferred-execution mode

delimiter
~|(|)|=|–|+|*|↑|< |> |/|,|;|: (A name does not have to be separated from a preceding or following key word by any of these delimiters.)

digit
1|2|3|4|5|6|7|8|9|0

esc
a press of the Escape Key, marked ESC

expr
expression
aexpr|sexpr

imm
immediate-execution mode

integer
[+|–] {digit } (Integers must be in the range –32767 through 32767. When converting non-integers into integers, APPLESOFT may be considered to truncate the non-integer. However, this is not quite true in the limit as the non-integer approaches the next larger integer. An integer occupies 2 bytes in memory.)

integer variable name
name% (A real may be stored as an integer variable, but APPLESOFT first convert the real to an integer.)

letter
A|B|C|D|E|F|G|H|I|J|K|L|M|N|O|P|Q|R|S|T|U|V|W|X|Y|Z

line
linenum [{instruction: }] instruction return

lineum
line number

digit [{digit }] (Line numbers must be in the range 0 to 63999 or a ?SYNTAX ERROR message is displayed.)

literal

[{character }]

lower-case letter

a|b|c|d|e|f|g|h|i|j|k|l|m|n|o|p|q|r|s|t|u|v|w|x|y|z

metaname

{metasymbol }[digit]

metasymbol

Characters used in this book to indicate various structures or relationships in APPLESOFT, but which are not part of the language itself.

||[|]| {| }| / |~

lower-case letter

a single digit concatenated to a metaname

name

letter [{letter|digit }] (A name may be up to 238 characters in length. When distinguishing one name from another APPLESOFT ignores any alphanumeric characters after the first two. APPLESOFT does not distinguish between the names GOOD 4LITTLE and GOLDRUSH. However, even the ignored portion of a name must not contain a special or any of APPLESOFT's reserved words.)

name

real variable name

name%

integer variable name

name

string variable name

null string

""

op

operator

aop|alop

prompt character

] (The right bracket is displayed when APPLESOFT is ready to accept a command.)

real

[+|-] [{digit }.] [{digit }] [E[+|-] digit [digit]]

(The letter E, as used in|real number notation, stands for "exponent." It is shorthand for *10 . Ten is raised to the power of the number on E's right, and number on E's left is multiplied by the result. A real occupies 5 bytes in memory.)

real variable name

name

reserved word

certain groups of characters used by APPLESOFT to specify instructions or portions of instructions. A name must not include a reserved word. Refer to Appendix C for a list of APPLESOFT's reserved words.

reset

a press of the key marked RESET

return

a press of the key marked RETURN

sexpr

string expression

svar|string

sexpr sop sexpr

slop

string logical operator

= |> |> = | => < |< = | =< |<> |><

sop

string operator

+

special

special symbol used by APPLESOFT

!|#|$|%|&|'|"|(|)|*|/|↑|< |> |=|+|−|:|;|,|.|@|?|]

(Control characters and the null character are also specials. The right bracket (]) can be typed on the on the APPLE keyboard, but APPLESOFT uses it for the prompt character only. In this book it is used as a metasymbol.)

subscript

(aexpr[{,aexpr }]) (The maximum number of dimensions is 89, although in practice this is limited by the extent of memory available. Aexpr must be positive, and in use it is converted to an integer.)

string

"[{character }]" (A string occupies 2 bytes in memory for its location pointer, plus 1 byte for each character in the string.)

"[{character }] return (This form of the string can appear only at the end of a line. Closing quote not needed.)

string variable name

name$

svar

string variable

name$|name$ subscript (The location pointer and variable name each occupy 2 bytes in memory. The length and each string character occupy one byte.)

var

variable

avar|svar

Appendix F
The 6502 Instruction Set

Mini-Assembler	Formats
Mode	Format
Accumulator	None
Immediate	# ${value}
Absolute	${address}
Zero Page	${address}
Indexed Zero Page	${address},X
	${address},Y
Indexed Absolute	${address},X
	${address},Y
Implied	None
Relative	${address}
Indexed Indirect	(${address},X)
Indirect Indexed	(${address}),Y
Absolute Indirect	(${address})

A	Accumulator
X, Y	Index Registers
M	Memory
$\bar{C}$	Borrow
P	Processor Status Register
S	Stack Pointer
✓	Change
−	No Change
+	Add
·	Logical AND
−	Subtract
⊻	Logical Exclusive Or
↑	Transfer From Stack
↓	Transfer To Stack
→	Transfer To
←	Transfer To
V	Logical OR
PC	Program Counter
PCH	Program Counter High
PCL	Program Counter Low
OPER	Operand
#	Immediate Addressing Mode

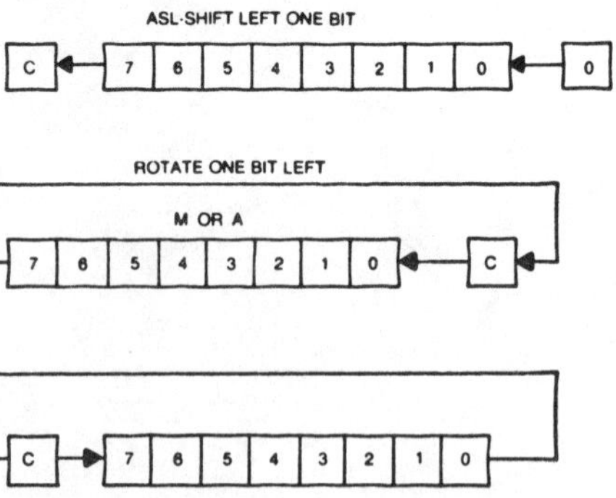

NOTE 1 BIT — TEST BITS

Bit 6 and 7 are transferred to the status register. If the result of A ∧ M is zero then Z = 1, otherwise Z= 0.

6502 MICROPROCESSOR INSTRUCTIONS

ADC	Add Memory to Accumulator with Carry
AND	"AND" Memory with Accumulator
ASL	Shift Left One Bit (Memory or Accumulator)
BCC	Branch on Carry Clear
BCS	Branch on Carry Set
BEQ	Branch on Result Zero
BIT	Test Bits in Memory with Accumulator
BMI	Branch on Result Minus
BNE	Branch on Result not Zero
BPL	Branch on Result Plus
BRK	Force Break
BVC	Branch on Overflow Clear
BVS	Branch on Overflow Set
CLC	Clear Carry Flag
CLD	Clear Decimal Mode
CLI	Clear Interrupt Disable Bit
CLV	Clear Overflow Flag
CMP	Compare Memory and Accumulator
CPX	Compare Memory and Index X
CPY	Compare Memory and Index Y
DEC	Decrement Memory by One
DEX	Decrement Index X by One
DEY	Decrement Index Y by One
EOR	"Exclusive-Or" Memory with Accumulator
INC	Increment Memory by One
INX	Increment Index X by One
INY	Increment Index Y by One
JMP	Jump to New Location
JSR	Jump to New Location Saving Return Address
LDA	Load Accumulator with Memory
LDX	Load Index X with Memory
LDY	Load Index Y with Memory
LSR	Shift Right One Bit (Memory or Accumulator)
NOP	No Operation
ORA	"OR" Memory with Accumulator
PHA	Push Accumulator on Stack
PHP	Push Processor Status on Stack
PLA	Pull Accumulator from Stack
PLP	Pull Processor Status from Stack
ROL	Rotate One Bit Left (Memory or Accumulator)
ROR	Rotate One Bit Right (Memory or Accumulator)
RTI	Return from Interrupt
RTS	Return from Subroutine
SBC	Subtract Memory from Accumulator with Borrow
SEC	Set Carry Flag
SED	Set Decimal Mode
SEI	Set Interrupt Disable Status
STA	Store Accumulator in Memory
STX	Store Index X in Memory
STY	Store Index Y in Memory
TAX	Transfer Accumulator to Index X
TAY	Transfer Accumulator to Index Y
TSX	Transfer Stack Pointer to Index X
TXA	Transfer Index X to Accumulator
TXS	Transfer Index X to Stack Pointer
TYA	Transfer Index Y to Accumulator

PROGRAMMING MODEL

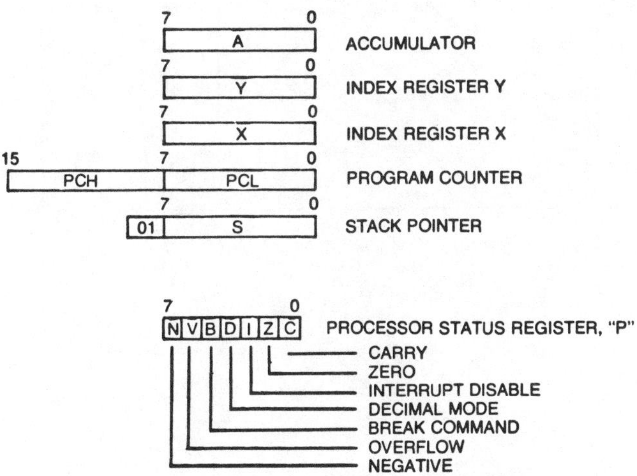

INSTRUCTION CODES

Name Description	Operation	Addressing Mode	Assembly Language Form	HEX OP Code	"P" Status Bytes	Reg. N Z C I D V
ADC Add memory to accumulator with carry	A-M-C→A C	Immediate	ADC #Oper	69	2	√√√--√
		Zero Page	ADC Oper	65	2	
		Zero Page.X	ADC Oper.X	75	2	
		Absolute	ADC Oper	6D	3	
		Absolute X	ADC Oper.X	7D	3	
		Absolute Y	ADC Oper.Y	79	3	
		(indirect.X)	ADC (Oper.X)	61	2	
		(Indirect).Y	ADC (Oper).Y	71	2	
AND "AND"memory with accumulator	A ∧ M→A	Immediate	AND #Oper	29	2	√√----
		Zero Page	AND Oper	25	2	
		Zero Page.X	AND Oper.X	35	2	
		Absolute	AND Oper	2D	3	
		Absolute.X	AND Oper.X	3D	3	
		Absolute.Y	AND Oper.Y	39	3	
		(Indirect.X)	AND (Oper.X)	21	2	
		(Indirect).Y	AND (Oper).Y	31	2	
ASL Shift left one bit (Memory or Accumulator)	See Page One	Accumulator	ASL A	0A	1	√√√---
		Zero Page	ASL Oper	06	2	
		Zero Page X	ASL Oper.X	16	2	
		Absolute	ASL Oper	0E	3	
		Absolute.X	ASL Oper.X	1E	3	
BCC Branch on carry clear	Branch on C=0	Relative	BCC Oper	90	2	------
BCS Branch on carry set	Branch on C=1	Relative	BCS Oper	B0	2	------
BEQ Branch on result zero	Branch on Z=1	Relative	BEQ Oper	F0	2	------
BIT Test bits in memory with accumulator	A ∧ M. M_7→N M_6→V	Zero Page	BIT Oper	24	2	M_7 √ ---M_6
		Absolute	BIT Oper	2C	3	
BMI Branch on result minus	Branch on N=1	Relative	BMI Oper	30	2	------
BNE Branch on result not zero	Branch on Z=0	Relative	BNE Oper	D0	2	------
BPL Branch on result plus	Branch on N=0	Relative	BPL Oper	10	2	------
BRK Force Break	Forced Interrupt PC+2 ↓ P↓	Implied	BRK	00	1	---1--
BVC Branch on overflow clear	Branch on V=0	Relative	BVC Oper	50	2	------

INSTRUCTION CODES

Name Description	Operation	Addressing Mode	Assembly Language Form	HEX OP Code	No. Bytes	"P" Status Reg. N Z C I D V
BVS Branch on overflow set	Branch on V=1	Relative	BVS Oper	70	2	------
CLC Clear carry flag	0→C	Implied	CLC	18	1	---0--
CLD Clear decimal mode	0→D	Implied	CLD	D8	1	-0----
CLI	0→1	Implied	CLI	58	1	---0--
CLV Clear overflow flag	0→V	Implied	CLV	B8	1	0-----
CMP Compare memory and accumulator	A − M	Imediate	CMP #Oper	C9	2	√√√---
		Zero Page	CMP Oper	C5	2	
		Zero Page,X	CMP Oper,X	D5	2	
		Absolute	CMP Oper	CD	3	
		Absolute,X	CMP Oper,X	DD	3	
		Absolute,Y	CMP Oper,Y	D9	3	
		(Indirect,X)	CMP (Oper,X)	C1	2	
		(Indirect),Y	CMP (Oper),Y	D1	2	
CPX Compare memory and index X	X − M	Immediate	CPX #Oper	E0	2	√√√---
		Zero Page	CPX Oper	E4	2	
		Absolute	CPX Oper	EC	3	
CPY Compare memory and index Y	Y − M	Immediate	CPY #Oper	C0	2	√√√---
		Zero Page	CPY Oper	C4	2	
		Absolute	CPY Oper	CC	3	
DEC Decrement memory by one	M − 1→M	Zero Page	DEC Oper	C6	2	√√----
		Zero Page,X	DEC Oper,X	D6	2	
		Absolute	DEC Oper	CE	3	
		Absolute,X	DEC Oper,X	DE	3	
DEX Decrement index X by one	X − 1→X	Implied	DEX	CA	1	√√----
DEY Decrement index Y by one	Y − 1→Y	Implied	DEY	88	1	√√----

INSTRUCTION CODES

Name Description	Operation	Addressing Mode	Assembly Language Form	HEX OP Code	No. Bytes	"P" Status Reg. N Z C I D V
EOR "Exclusive-Or" memory with accumulator	A V M → A	Immediate	EOR #Oper	49	2	√ √ ----
		Zero Page	EOR Oper	45	2	
		Zero Page, X	EOR Oper, X	55	2	
		Absolute	EOR Oper	4D	3	
		Absolute, X	EOR Oper, X	5D	3	
		Absolute, Y	EOR Oper, Y	59	3	
		(Indirect, X)	EOR (Oper, X)	41	2	
		(Indirect), Y	EOR (Oper), Y	51	2	
INC Increment memory by one	M + 1 → M	Zero Page	INC Oper	E6	2	√ √ ----
		Zero Page, X	INC Oper, X	F6	2	
		Absolute	INC Oper	EE	3	
		Absolute, X	INC Oper, X	FE	3	
INX Increment index X by one	X + 1 → X	Implied	INX	E8	1	√ √ ----
INY Increment index Y by one	Y + 1 → Y	Implied	INY	C8	1	√ √ ----
JMP Jump to new location	(PC+1) → PCL (PC+2) → PCH	Absolute	JMP Oper	4C	3	------
		Indirect	JMP (Oper)	6C	3	
JSR Jump to new location saving return address	PC+2 ↓ (C+1) → PCL (PC+2) → PCH	Absolute	JSR Oper	20	3	------
LDA Load accumulator with memory	M → A	Immediate	LDA #Oper	A9	2	√ √ ----
		Zero Page	LDA Oper	A5	2	
		Zero Page, X	LDA Oper, X	B5	2	
		Absolute	LDA Oper	AD	3	
		Absolute, X	LDA Oper, X	BD	3	
		Absolute, Y	LDA Oper, Y	B9	3	
		(Indirect, X)	LDA (Oper, X)	A1	2	
		(Indirect), Y	LDA (Oper), Y	B1	2	
LDX Load index X with memory	M → X	Immediate	LDX #Oper	A2	2	√ √ ----
		Zero Page	LDX Oper	A6	2	
		Zero Page, Y	LDX Oper, Y	B6	2	
		Absolute	LDX Oper	AE	3	
		Absolute, Y	LDX Oper, Y	BE	3	
LDY Load index Y with memory	M Y	Immediate	LDY #Oper	A0	2	
		Zero Page	LDY Oper	A4	2	√ √ ----
		Zero Page, X	LDY Oper, X	B4	2	
		Absolute	LDY Oper	AC	3	
		Absolute, X	LDY Oper, X	BC	3	

INSTRUCTION CODES

Name Description	Operation	Addressing Mode	Assembly Language Form	HEX OP Code	No. Bytes	"P" Status Reg. N Z C I D V
LSR Shift right one bit (memory or accumulator)	See Page One	Accumulator	LSR A	4A	1	Ø√√---
		Zero Page	LSR Oper	46	2	
		Zero Page,X	LSR Oper,X	56	2	
		Absolute	LSR Oper	4E	3	
		Aboslute,X	LSR Oper,X	5E	3	
NOP No operation	No Operation	Implied	NOP	EA	1	------
ORA "OR" memory with accumulator	A∨M → A	Immediate	ORA #Oper	09	2	√√----
		Zero Page	ORA Oper	05	2	
		Zero Page,X	ORA Oper,X	15	2	
		Absolute	ORA Oper	0D	3	
		Absolute,X	ORA Oper,X	1D	3	
		Absolute,Y	ORA Oper,Y	19	3	
		(Indirect,X)	ORA (Oper,X)	01	2	
		(Indirect),Y	ORA (Oper),Y	11	2	
PHA Push accumulator on stack	A↓	Implied	PHA	48	1	------
PHA Push processor status	P↓	Implied	PHP	08	1	------
PLA Pull accumulator from stack	A↑	Implied	PLA	68	1	√√----
PLP Pull processor status from stack	P↑	Implied	PLP	28	1	From Stack
ROL Rotate one bit left (memory or accumulator)	See Page One	Accumulator	ROL A	2A	1	√√√---
		Zero Page	ROL Oper	26	2	
		Zero Page,X	ROL Oper,X	36	2	
		Absolute	ROL Oper	2E	3	
		Absolute,X	ROL Oper,X	3E	3	
ROR Rotate one bit right (memory or accumulator)	See Page One	Accumulator	ROR A	6A	1	√√√---
		Zero Page	ROR Oper	66	2	
		Zero Page,X	ROR Oper,X	76	2	
		Absolute	ROR Oper	6E	3	
		Absolute,X	ROR Oper,X	7E	3	

INSTRUCTION CODES

Name Description	Operation	Addressing Mode	Assembly Language Form	HEX OP Code	No. Bytes	"P" Status Reg. N Z C I D V
RTI Return from interrupt	P↑ PC↑	Implied	RTI	40	1	From Stack
RTS Return from subroutine	PC↑ PC→1→PC	Implied	RTS	60	1	------
SBC Subtract memory from accumulator with borrow	A − M − C̄→A	Immediate	SBC # Oper	E9	2	√√√--√
		Zero Page	SBC Oper	E5	2	
		Zero Page,X	SBC Oper,X	F5	2	
		Absolute	SBC Oper	ED	3	
		Absolute,X	SBC Oper,X	FD	3	
		Absolute,Y	SBC Oper,Y	F9	3	
		(Indirect,X)	SBC(Oper,X)	E1	2	
		(Indirect),Y	SBC (Oper),Y	F1	2	
SEC Set carry flag	1→C	Implied	SEC	38	1	--1---
SED Set decimal mode	1→D	Implied	SED	F8	1	----1-
SEI Set interrupt disable status	1→I	Implied	SEI	78	1	---1--
STA Store accumulator in memory	A→M	Zero Page	STA Oper	85	2	------
		Zero Page,X	STA Oper,X	95	2	
		Absolute	STA Oper	8D	3	
		Absolute,X	STA Oper,X	9D	3	
		Absolute,Y	STA,Oper,Y	99	3	
		(Indirect,X)	STA (Oper,X)	81	2	
		(indirect),Y	STA (Oper),Y	91	2	
STX Store index X in memory	X→M	Zero Page	STX Oper	86	2	------
		Zero Page,Y	STX Oper,Y	96	2	
		Absolute	STX Oper	8E	3	
STY Store index Y in memory	Y→M	Zero Page	STY Oper	84	2	------
		Zero Page,X	STY Oper,X	94	2	
		Absolute	STY Oper	8C	3	
TAX Transfer accumulator to index X	A→X	Implied	TAX	AA	1	√√----
TAY Transfer accumulator to index Y	A→Y	Implied	TAY	A8	1	√√----
TSX Transfer stack pointer to index X	S→X	Implied	TSX	BA	1	√√----
TXA Transfer index X to accumulator	X→A	Implied	TXA	8A	1	√√----
TXS Transfer index X to stack pointer	X→S	Implied	TXS	9A	1	------
TYA Transfer index Y to accumulator	Y→A	Implied	TYA	98	1	√√----

Hex Code Cross Reference Table.

ØØ — BRK
Ø1 — ORA — (Indirect,X)
Ø2 — NOP
Ø3 — NOP
Ø4 — NOP
Ø5 — ORA — Zero Page
Ø6 — ASL — Zero Page
Ø7 — NOP
Ø8 — PHP
Ø9 — ORA — Immediate
ØA — ASL — Accumulator
ØB — NOP
ØC — NOP
ØF — ORA — Absolute
ØE — ASL — Absolute
ØF — NOP
1Ø — BPL
11 — ORA (Indirect),Y
12 — NOP
13 — NOP
14 — NOP
15 — ORA — Zero Page,X
16 — ASL — Zero Page,X
17 — NOP
18 — CLC
19 — ORA — Absolute,Y
1A — NOP
1B — NOP
1C — NOP
1D — ORA — Absolute,X
1E — ASL — Absolute,X
1F — NOP
2Ø — JSR
21 — AND — (Indirect,X)
22 — NOP
23 — NOP
24 — BIT — Zero Page
25 — AND — Zero Page
26 — ROL — Zero Page
27 — NOP
28 — PLP
29 — AND — Immediate
2A — ROL — Accumulator
2B — NOP
2C — BIT — Absolute
2D — AND — Absolute
2E — ROL — Absolute
2F — NOP
3Ø — BMI
31 — AND — (Indirect),Y
32 — NOP
33 — NOP
34 — NOP
35 — AND — Zero Page,X
36 — ROL — Zero Page,X
37 — NOP
38 — SEC
39 — AND — Absolute,Y
3A — NOP
3B — NOP
3C — NOP
3D — AND — Absolute,X
3E — ROL — Absolute,X
3F — NOP
4Ø — RTI
41 — EOR — (Indirect,X)
42 — NOP
43 — NOP
44 — NOP
45 — EOR — Zero Page
46 — LSR — Zero Page
47 — NOP
48 — PHA
49 — EOR — Immediate
4A — LSR — Accumulator
4B — NOP
4C — JMP — Absolute
4D — EOR — Absolute
4E — LSR — Absolute
4F — NOP
5Ø — BVC
51 — EOR (Indirect),Y
52 — NOP
53 — NOP
54 — NOP
55 — EOR — Zero Page,X
56 — LSR — Zero Page,X
57 — NOP
58 — CLI
59 — EOR — Absolute,Y
5A — NOP
5B — NOP
5C — NOP
5D — EOR — Absolute,X
5E — LSR — Absolute,X
5F — NOP
6Ø — RTS
61 — ADC — (Indirect,X)
62 — NOP
63 — NOP
64 — NOP
65 — ADC — Zero Page
66 — ROR — Zero Page
67 — NOP
68 — PLA
69 — ADC — Immediate
6A — ROR — Accumulator
6B — NOP
6C — JMP — Indirect
6D — ADC — Absolute
6E — ROR — Absolute
6F — NOP
7Ø — BVS
71 — ADC — (Indirect),Y
72 — NOP
73 — NOP
74 — NOP
75 — ADC — Zero Page,X
76 — ROR — Zero Page,X
77 — NOP
78 — SEI
79 — ADC — Absolutely,Y
7A — NOP
7B — NOP
7C — NOP
7D — ADC — Absolute,X NOP
7E — ROR — Absolute,X NOP
7F — NOP
8Ø — NOP
81 — STA — (Indirect,X)
82 — NOP
83 — NOP
84 — STY — Zero Page
85 — STA — Zero Page
86 — STX — Zero Page
87 — NOP
88 — DEY
89 — NOP
8A — TXA
8B — NOP
8C — STY — Absolute
8D — STA — Absolute
8E — STX — Absolute
8F — NOP
9Ø — BCC
91 — STA — (Indirect),Y
92 — NOP
93 — NOP
94 — STY — Zero Page, X
95 — STA — Zero Page, X
96 — STX — Zero Page, Y
97 — NOP
98 — TYA
99 — STA — Absolute,Y
9A — TXS
9B — NOP
9C — NOP
9D — STA — Absolute, X
9E — NOP
9F — NOP
AØ — LDY — Immediate
A1 — LDA — (Indirect, X)
A2 — LDX — Immediate
A3 — NOP
A4 — LDY — Zero Page
A5 — LDA — Zero Page
A6 — LDX — Zero Page
A7 — NOP
A8 — TAY
A9 — LDA — Immediate
AA — TAX
AB — NOP
AC — LDY — Absolute
AD — Absolute
AE — LDX — Absolute
AF — NOP
BØ — BCS
B1 — LDA — (Indirect),Y
B2 — NOP
B3 — NOP
B4 — LDY — Zero Page, X
B5 — LDA — Zero Page, X
B6 — LDX — Zero Page, Y
B7 — NOP
B8 — CLV
B9 — LDA — Absolute,Y

Hex Code Cross Reference Table.

BA — TSX
BB — NOP
BC — LDY — Absolute, X
BD — LAD — Absolute, X
BE — LDX — Absolute, Y
BF — NOP
CØ — CPY — Immediate
C1 — CMP — (Indirect, X)
C2 — NOP
C3 — NOP
C4 — CPY — Zero Page
C5 — CMP — Zero Page
C6 — DEC — Zero Page
C7 — NOP
C8 — INY
C9 — CMP — Immediate
CA — DEX
CB — NOP
CC — CPY — Absolute
CD — CMP — Absolute
CE — DEC — Absolute
CF — NOP
DØ — BNE
D1 — CMP — (Indirectly),Y
D2 — NOP
D3 — NOP
D4 — NOP
D5 — CMP — Zero Page, X
D6 — DEC — Zero Page, X
D7 — NOP
D8 — CLD
D9 — CMP — Absolute,Y
DA — NOP
DB — NOP
DC — NOP
DD — CMP — Absolute, X
DE — DEC — Absolute, X
DF — NOP
EØ — CPX — Immediate
E1 — SBC — (Indirect, X)
E2 — NOP
E3 — NOP
E4 — CPX — Zero Page
E5 — SBC — Zero Page
E6 — INC — Zero Page
E7 — NOP
E8 — INX
E9 — SBC — Immediate
EA — NOP
EB — NOP
EC — CPX — Absolute
ED — SBC — Absolute
EE — INC — Absolute
EF — NOP
FØ — BEQ
F1 — SBC — (Indirect),Y
F2 — NOP
F3 — NOP
F4 — NOP
F5 — SBC — Zero Page,X
F6 — INC — Zero Page, X
F7 — NOP
F8 — SED
F9 — SBC — Absolute, Y
FA — NOP
FB — NOP
FC — NOP
FD — SBC — Absolute, X
FE — INC — Absolute, X
FF — NOP

Appendix G
Subroutine Entry Points

$FDED **Output a character**
The character to be output should be in the accumulator. Calls $FDF0 from $36 and 37.

$FDFO **Output to screen**
$FOF0 displays at the current output cursor position and advances the cursor. It places the character using the setting of the Normal/Inverse location, handles the control characters RETURN, linefeed, and bell, and returns with all registers intact.

$FE80 **Set Inverse mode**
Sets Inverse video mode.

$FE84 **Set Normal mode**
Sets Normal video mode.

$FD8E **Generate a RETURN**
Sends a RETURN character to the current output device.

$FD8B **RETURN with clear**
$FD8B clears the screen from the current cursor position to the edge of the text window, then calls CROUT.

$FDDA **Print a hexadecimal byte**
This subroutine outputs the contents of the accumulator in hexadecimal on the current output device.

$FDE3 **Print a hexadecimal digit**

This subroutine outputs the lower nybble of the accumulator as a single hexadecimal digit.

$F941 **Print A and X in hexadecimal**

This outputs the contents of the A and X registers as a four-digit hexadecimal value. The accumulator contains the first byte output, the X register contains the second.

$F948 **Print 3 spaces**

Upon exit, the accumulator usually contains $A0, the X register contains 0.

$F94A **Print many blank spaces**

This subroutine outputs from 1 to 256 blanks. Upon entry, the X register should contain the number of blanks to be output. 1FX=0 the number equals 256.

$FF3A **Output a bell character**

This subroutine sends a CTRL G to the current output device.

$FBDD **Beep the Apple's speaker**

This subroutine beeps the Apple's speaker for .1 second at 1KHz.

$FD0C **Get an input character**

This is the standard character input subroutine. Calls $FD1B from $38 and 39.

$FD35 **Get an input character or ESC code**

$FD35 is an alternate input subroutine which gets characters from the standard input, but also interprets the eleven escape codes.

$FD1B **Read the Apple's keyboard**

This is the keyboard input subroutine. It reads the Apple's keyboard, waits for a keypress, and randomizes the random number seed. When it gets a keypress it returns with the keycode in the accumulator.

$FD6A **Get an input line with prompt**

$FD6A is the subroutine which gathers input lines. Your programs can call it with the proper prompt character in location $33 and it will return with the input line in the input buffer (beginning at location $200) and the X register holding the length of the input line.

$FD67 **Get an input line**

$FD67 is an alternate entry point for $FD6A which issues a carriage return to the standard output before falling into $FD6A.

$FD6F **Get an input line, no prompt**

$FD6F is an alternate entry point for $FD6A which does not issue a prompt before it gathers the input line.

$FCA8 **Delay**

This subroutine delays for a specific amount of time, then returns to the program which called it. The amount of delay is specified by the contents of the accumulator. The delay is $\frac{1}{2}(26+27A+5A^2)$ μseconds.

$F864 **Set Low-Res Graphics color**

This subroutine sets the color for the Low-Res screen to the color in the accumulator.

$F85F **Increment color by 3**

This adds 3 to the current color used for Low-Res Graphics.

$F800 **Plot a block on the Low-Res screen**

This subroutine plots a single block on the Low-Res screen. The block's vertical position is passed in the accumulator, its horizontal position in the Y register.

$F819 **Draw a horizontal line of blocks**

This subroutine draws a horizontal line of blocks on the Low-Res screen. The vertical coordinate of the line is in the accumulator, the leftmost horizontal coordinate in the Y register, and the rightmost horizontal coordinate in location $2C.

$F828 **Draw a vertical line of blocks**

This subroutine draws a vertical line of blocks of the predetermined color on the Low-Res screen. The horizontal coordinate of the line is in the Y register, the top vertical coordinate in the accumulator, and the bottom vertical coordinate in location $2D.

$F832 **Clear the entire Low-Res screen**

$F832 clears the entire Low-resolution Graphics screen.

$F836 **Clear the top of the Low-Res screen**

$F836 is the same as $F832 except that it clears only the top 40 rows of the screen.

$F871 **Read the Low-Res screen**

This subroutine returns the color of a single block on the Low-Res screen. Call it as you would call $F800. The color of the block will be returned in the accumulator.

$FB1E **Read a Game Controller**

$FB1E will return a number which represents the position of a game controller. The number of the game controller (0 to 3) is in the X register. $FB1E returns with a number from $00 to $FF in the Y register.

$FF2D **Print "ERR"**

Sends "ERR", followed by a bell, to the screen.

$FF4A **Save all registers**

The contents of the 6502's internal registers are saved in locations $45 through $49 in the order A-X-Y-P-S.

$FF3F **Restore all registers**

The contents of the 6502's internal registers are loaded from locations $45 through $49.

Index

Index

Edited by Dennis Thurlow